IRISH SOCIAL SE

John Curry recently retired from an active career, mainly in the public service. He was Director of the National Social Service Board through most of the 1980s and during that time also served as Secretary of the National Council for the Aged (1981–4). He was Chairman of the influential Commission on Social Welfare (1983–6), a member of the National Economic and Social Council (1984–9) and Chairman of the Review Group on the Treatment of Households in the Social Welfare Code (1989–91). He was also Chief Executive of the People in Need Trust, and he served in different senior positions in the Health Service Executive in the years prior to his retirement. He has lectured on social policy at NUI Maynooth, and continues to lecture on social policy at the Institute of Public Administration.

IRISH SOCIAL SERVICES

JOHN CURRY

FIFTH EDITION

IPA
INSTITUTE OF PUBLIC
ADMINISTRATION

First published 1980
Second edition 1993
Reprinted 1994
Reprinted 1997
Third edition 1998
Reprinted 2003
Fourth edition 2003
Reprinted 2005
Reprinted 2010
Fifth edition 2011

Institute of Public Administration
57–61 Lansdowne Road
Dublin 4
Ireland

ISBN   978-1-904541-95-0
(ISBN   0 902173 97 9   first edition)
(ISBN   1 872002 07 2   second edition)
(ISBN   1 902448 01 4   third edition)
(ISBN   1 904541 00 3   fourth edition)

British Library Cataloguing-in-Publication Data

A catalogue record for this book is available from the British Library.

Cover design by Alice Campbell, Dublin
Typeset by Computertype, Dublin
Printed by Turner's Printing Company Ltd, Longford

Contents

Tables

Acronyms

CORI	Conference of Religious of Ireland
CPA	Combat Poverty Agency
EC	European Community
EEA	Employment Equality Authority
EEC	European Economic Community
ESRI	Economic and Social Research Institute
EU	European Union
GHDP	*General Hospital Development Plan*
GMS	General Medical Service
HEA	Higher Education Authority
HETAC	Higher Education and Training Awards Council
HIQA	Health Information and Quality Authority
HSE	Health Service Executive
ICSH	Irish Council for Social Housing
IHRC	Irish Human Rights Commission
IYJS	Irish Youth Justice Service
NAPS	*National Anti-Poverty Strategy*
NCEA	National Council for Educational Awards
NCSE	National Council for Special Education
NESC	National Economic and Social Council
NESF	National Economic and Social Forum
NEWB	National Educational Welfare Board
NHO	National Hospitals Office
NTACC	National Traveller Accommodation Consultative Committee
NTPF	National Treatment Purchase Fund
OECD	Organisation for Economic Cooperation and Development
OMCYA	Office of the Minister for Children and Youth Affairs
PCCC	Primary, Community and Continuing Care
PRSI	pay-related social insurance
PRTB	Private Residential Tenancies Board

USC	universal social charge
VEC	vocational education committee
VHI	Voluntary Health Insurance Board

Preface to Fifth Edition

Since the first edition of *Irish Social Services* was published just over three decades ago in 1980, much has changed. There has been continuing evolutionary development in each of the main areas of social provision – housing, income maintenance, health services and education. In all cases, the services now provided are considerably superior to those in place three decades ago.

Since the publication of the fourth edition in 2003, change has been even more dramatic. Unprecedented levels of economic growth during the period of the Celtic Tiger and a more favourable demographic structure augured well for the future funding of the social services at the beginning of the new millennium. This was in marked contrast to the situation in the late 1980s when high unemployment and emigration were features of the Irish economy. However, the Celtic Tiger period came to an abrupt end as a downturn in the economy in 2008, exacerbated by a crash in the property market and a banking crisis, put a halt to over a decade of sustained growth in the economy and increased investment in social provision. The rapid deterioration in the state of the public finances meant that reductions in public expenditure across all areas became inevitable. In this context, areas of high public expenditure such as the social welfare system became a particular focus for attention. The prospect for restoring social expenditure levels to those experienced during the boom years of the Celtic Tiger remains highly uncertain.

The purpose of this book is to provide the reader with a broad, informed overview of the evolution, nature and scope of the key social services in Ireland. Because of the scope of the areas covered, it has not been possible to treat each of them in depth. Many issues may be pursued further with the aid of the bibliography. Statistics throughout the book are the latest available at the time of writing and are provided mainly to display a snapshot in time or to indicate trends.

These statistics may be readily updated, in most instances, by reference to the sources.

The past few decades have been characterised by a wide range of social policy developments, often underpinned by legislation. There is now a rich source of information and analysis on social policy in the form of a variety of reports. While it is not possible to document in depth the wide variety of developments and discussion arising from these, it is hoped that this edition captures the essential elements of a constantly evolving situation in relation to social provision in Ireland.

From the IPA's Publications Division, I would like to thank Hannah Ryan, Production Executive, and especially John Paul Owens, Editor, for his invaluable input.

John Curry
26 April 2011

1

Introduction

The social services are the main instruments of social policy. They are provided by the state and other agencies to improve individual and community welfare. The main social services are income maintenance, housing, education, health and welfare or personal social services. Before considering the general relevance of these services in Irish society it is useful to examine the background against which social services developed and the broad objectives behind the services.

What is social policy?

Donnison, in a report in the mid 1970s for the National Economic and Social Council (NESC), defined social policy as:

> Those actions of government which deliberately or accidentally affect the distribution of resources, status, opportunities and life chances among social groups and categories of people within the country and thus help to shape the general character and equity of its social relations.[1]

By this definition it could be argued that virtually all government policies or programmes have some implications for the well-being of the population. Consequently, all government programmes could be assessed in terms of their contribution to the achievement of national social objectives. Certain public programmes, specifically those of income maintenance, housing, education and health, have been traditionally regarded as the main constituent elements of social policy since they are the most visible instruments of achieving the distributive aims of government. In addition to these public programmes there are others, such as fiscal (e.g. taxation) and occupational (e.g. benefits relating to a particular employment) measures, that could also be included since they too provide benefits for individuals and the community at large. The primary focus of this book, however, is on the four main social service areas outlined – income maintenance, housing, education and health. Other areas such as the welfare of certain groups, poverty and equality issues are also considered.

The NESC has indicated that government intervention by means of social policy is a response to four factors.[2]

i.   A socially acceptable distribution of income and other resources could not be guaranteed by a market economy, i.e. one in which the state does not intervene. A market economy would not, for example, guarantee an income to those unable to earn a living in the labour market. In any case, the distribution of incomes guaranteed in the market may be the result of many factors, some of which are accidental and have little to do with equity.

ii.   A socially desirable level of provision of some particular goods and services and their consumption by different groups will not necessarily be achieved through the market. For example, the attainment of certain levels of education and the utilisation of health care services confer benefits not only on the individual but also on the community in general. If left to market forces alone, the utilisation of certain services would be less than optimal since many would not be in a position to afford them.

iii. The states of dependency in which people may find themselves, such as unemployment or illness, are social risks that are a hazard for the entire community and are not necessarily due to individual shortcomings. Governments can ensure, through appropriate social policy measures, that the community as a whole shares the burden of dependency.

iv.   The concept of citizenship has evolved from a purely legal status of belonging to a particular country to one that confers rights to participation in the well-being of the community, including social services provided as an expression of social solidarity.

Over several decades, intervention by governments in developed countries has, in general, increased in relation to social policy.

Aims of social policy

If the above are the main factors accounting for government intervention in the social services area, the precise objectives of such intervention are not always clarified. This is certainly true of Ireland. In the absence of explicit objectives, Kennedy examined various official sources to determine what the aims of social policy were in post-war Ireland.[3] She concluded that three main aims were discernible:

i.   the relief of poverty and the provision of a minimum standard of living for all;
ii. equalisation of opportunity;
iii. increased productivity and economic growth.

These, according to Kennedy, could be described as the humanitarian, egalitarian and economic aims of social policy, respectively.

In 1981 the NESC outlined what it considered to be the aims of social policy.[4] These were as follows:

- the reduction in inequalities of income and wealth by transferring resources to those in need and by equitably distributing the burden of such support;
- the elimination of inequalities of opportunity that arise from inherited social and economic differences;
- the provision of employment for those seeking work;
- the provision of access for all, irrespective of income, to certain specified services;
- the development of services that make provision for particular disadvantaged groups in the community;
- the development of responsible citizenship based on an explicit recognition of the network of mutual obligations in the community.

Interestingly, these aims were referred to, though not necessarily endorsed, by the Fine Gael/Labour Coalition Government of 1982–7 in its national plan, *Building on Reality*.[5]

The aims as outlined by the NESC are being met to a greater or lesser degree. The extent to which they are being achieved will be referred to, as appropriate, in the following chapters.

Importance and relevance of social services

There are several reasons why the social services are an integral part of Irish society. These include the extent of utilisation of the services and the level of public expenditure on them.

Practically everyone in Irish society avails of the social services. Two-fifths of the population are in receipt of weekly income maintenance payments, and at some stage the members of practically every household avail themselves of a scheme or schemes administered by the

Department of Social Protection. Just over one-fifth of the population are engaged in full-time education. Most of the housing stock has been either provided directly or subsidised by the state. In addition, about one-third of the population are eligible for the full range of health services free of charge, and approximately one-fifth attend hospital emergency departments annually.

Over a period of years the amount of government expenditure on social services has increased. In 2010 public current expenditure on social services (income maintenance, health services, education and housing) accounted for 80 per cent of total government current expenditure, with income maintenance alone accounting for about one-third of the total.[6]

Therefore, the social services can be vitally important for the general public, with some people dependent on them for their very livelihood. For government, the social services are a commitment to society, accounting for a considerable proportion of public expenditure.

Factors influencing social service provision

In most countries social service provision has evolved over a period of time. Coughlan has summarised the situation as follows:

> Most people are aware of the ad hoc and fragmentary way in which the social services came into being; they were largely a piecemeal growth, introduced at different times to cover different categories of need and in response to different pressures, the result of a wide variety of motives – humanitarianism, social idealism, political expediency, the desire to damp down social discontent, the response to the spread of democracy and universal suffrage, the need to provide an environment conducive to industrial development. Seldom were they the expression of a coherent philosophical outlook.[7]

While broadly similar social services exist in most developed countries, there are considerable differences based on entitlement, the type of services provided and the priorities given to certain services. In relation to health services, for example, the extent to which free services are available to all or part of the population can vary greatly.

In Ireland the development of the social services has also been piecemeal, as the following chapters will illustrate. Developments normally occur for a variety of reasons in response to various needs and demands, with the government having regard to cost considerations.

Once governments commit to providing social services, various factors come into play to influence the shape, the nature and the future development of these services. A number of key factors have been identified that determine the type and level of services provided in any country.[8] These include socio-demographic, economic and ideological factors. In the following examination of the development of Irish social policy a number of factors are briefly considered. It should be stressed, however, that the interplay of all these factors is important rather than the primacy of any one in particular.

Socio-demographic factors

It is axiomatic that changes in the total population and changes in the composition of the population will determine or influence certain priorities. Thus, very simply, whether the population is increasing or declining will have implications for social services in general but for education and housing in particular. In the 1950s, when net outward migration was running at an annual average of 40,000, it was deemed that housing demand had been virtually met, and consequently housing output declined (see Chapter 3). Within a decade, however, the situation had been reversed: the population increased for the first time since the 1840s, emigration declined steadily, the demand for housing increased and housing output rose.

Apart from trends in the total population, provision of services is also influenced by changes in the birth rate and life expectancy. Increases or decreases in the birth rate have obvious implications for childcare services, educational facilities and income supports for children. One of the notable features of the Irish demographic situation over the past few decades has been the change in the number of births. The number of births fell from 74,000 in 1980 to 48,000 in 1994 (a decline of 35 per cent). Since 1994 there has been a steady increase, with a more rapid increase in recent years, and in 2008 there were 75,000 births. The fall in the birth rate after 1980 had an impact on first- and second-level education, where numbers enrolled declined after reaching peaks in 1985 and 1990, respectively.

An increase in life expectancy has implications for the provision of pensions as well as for health and welfare services for older persons (see Chapter 6). In the mid 1920s life expectancy was 57.4 years for males and 57.9 years for females. Life expectancy increased throughout the twentieth century with the result that in 2007 the figures were 76.8 years for males and 81.6 years for females. The number of older persons (persons aged 65 or over) in the population increased from 271,700 in 1926 to 467,900 in 2006 (an increase of 72 per cent), and is projected to increase further.

Over the last few decades there have been considerable changes in the age structure of the population (Table 1.1). One of the features has been the relative decline in the young population (under 14 years) while all other age groups have recorded increases. The young population share of the total population has fallen from almost one-third to one-fifth. By contrast, the position has been reversed for those in the prime working-age group (25–44 years), whose numbers more than doubled (115 per cent) between 1971 and 2006. Over the same period the number in the 45–64-year age group increased by just over half (52 per cent), and the number of older persons (65 years and over) increased by 42 per cent. The age-dependency ratio (the ratio between the working-age groups – age 15–64 – and the groups aged under 15 and over 65) has fallen, from 100:74 in 1971 to 100:54 in 1996, to 100:42 in 2006. This ratio indicates the relative burden of providing services that benefit the young and old. Those in the working-age group have to bear the burden, through direct or indirect taxation, of providing services for the dependent groups. The real burden of dependency (i.e. the ratio between those actually at work and others) is much greater (see later in this chapter).

Table 1.1: *Age structure of population, selected years, 1971–2006*

	0–14	15–24	25–44	45–64	65+	Total
1971						
Number (000s)	931	483	626	608	330	2,978
Percentage	31.3	16.2	21.0	20.4	11.1	100.0
1981						
Number (000s)	1,044	602	838	591	369	3,444
Percentage	30.3	17.5	24.3	17.2	10.7	100.0
1991						
Number (000s)	963	598	949	618	395	3,523
Percentage	27.3	17.0	26.9	17.6	11.2	100.0
1996						
Number (000s)	859	633	1,016	704	414	3,626
Percentage	23.7	17.5	28.0	19.4	11.4	100.0
2006						
Number (000s)	864	633	1,346	929	468	4,240
Percentage	20.4	14.9	31.7	21.9	11.1	100.0

Source: Census of population (Central Statistics Office).

The distribution of population between urban and rural areas and the density of population also have important implications for the social services. It is less costly per unit, for example, to provide certain services such as water supply in high-density urban areas than in sparsely populated rural areas. Also, specialised services such as hospitals are usually located in the larger urban areas, making access difficult for those living in remote rural areas. Approximately three-fifths of the population in Ireland live in urban areas (towns with 1,500 persons or more). Many rural areas contain disproportionate numbers of older people, a legacy mainly of persistent and selective outmigration over a period of time. This has implications for the provision of services for older people.

In a study commissioned by the Combat Poverty Agency (CPA) and published in 1997, the Economic and Social Research Institute (ESRI) considered the welfare implications of demographic change into the early part of the present century. The study, *Welfare Implications of Demographic Trends*, pointed out that concerns about the rising burden of welfare in the context of a falling population were unfounded. In support of this it claimed that the real burden of dependency would fall to 100 workers per 133 dependants by the year 2010 (from 100:220 in the mid 1980s), that the number of people at work would continue to rise and the unemployment rate would be halved by 2010, and that the savings in unemployment payments would make up for any increase in the cost of pensions. The study, having traced the impact of population decline up to the 1960s and the demographic features of recent decades, concluded:

> For the first time in the modern era, it is possible for Ireland to look forward with some confidence to a period of well-balanced population performance combined with economic progress … The policy challenge in Ireland as far as population trends and their effects on welfare and support is not so much to prepare for imminent threat as to make the best use of the unprecedented opportunities which are now developing.[9]

Within a few years of the publication of the report, the demographic situation had changed even more markedly than the authors had predicted. In 1991 the worker/dependency ratio was 100:214; this had been exacerbated by the steady rise in unemployment throughout the 1970s and 1980s. By 2001, however, the ratio had dropped to 100:123 (ten years in advance of and less than that forecast), unemployment had been more than halved and state revenue continued to grow due to a combination of an increased workforce and unprecedented growth in the economy.

Economic factors

The financial resources available influence the level of state involvement in social service provision. In a period of economic growth it is likely that developments and expansion of social services will occur. By contrast, when there is little or no economic growth the aim may well be to simply retain, if not reduce, the existing level of services. Kennedy outlined different social policy phases, both expansionary and regressive, in Ireland between the end of World War II and the 1970s.[10] While the 1950s was a period of relative economic stagnation with few developments in the social service area, the period from the mid 1960s to the early 1970s was one of economic growth accompanied by a series of developments across the social services.

For several decades one of the features of the Irish economy was the rise in unemployment. The average annual number on the live register of unemployment rose steadily from 70,300 in 1974 to 109,000 in 1977, to 254,000 in 1991 and to 294,300 in 1993. The rise in unemployment resulted not only in a drop in revenue to the state through taxes but also in an increase in state expenditure on income-support schemes for the unemployed and their families. The NESC identified the creation of employment and the consequent reduction of unemployment and involuntary emigration as primary objectives in the strategic issues for the 1990s.[11]

From the mid 1990s, there was a sharp upturn in the Irish economy with unprecedented levels of economic growth and job creation, now referred to as the Celtic Tiger period. Because of this economic growth, the numbers at work increased steadily from 1.16 million in 1990 to 2.11 million in 2007, and the average annual number on the live register of unemployment fell from a peak of 294,300 in 1993 to 142,300 in 2001. By 2001 the unemployment rate had fallen below 4.0 per cent, a level generally regarded as the equivalent of full employment.

By 2008, however, the economic situation had changed due to a combination of a global slowdown and an international banking crisis, which was exacerbated by a rapid contraction in the construction sector and a banking crisis in Ireland. The crash in the property market had serious consequences for the economy in general. Within less than a year Ireland had moved from high rates of economic growth to a major recession. The net result was a rapid deterioration in the public finances and a sharp increase in unemployment. The standardised rate of unemployment increased from 4.6 per cent in 2007 to 11.8 per cent in 2009.

The need to rein in public expenditure, where social services accounted for such a high proportion of the total, became a pressing issue from mid 2008 onwards. Beginning with Budget 2008, corrective action was taken to reduce public expenditure across a range of services, and areas of possible reduction were reviewed as a matter of urgency. In 2009 the *Report of the Special Group on Public Service Numbers and Expenditure Programmes*, usually referred to as the McCarthy report (after the chairman of the review group), made wide-ranging recommendations for cost savings amounting to almost €6 billion affecting all parts of the public service. Some of these recommendations were adopted in amended form, and the report remains a framework for further reductions in public expenditure. Throughout 2010 the state of the public finances deteriorated and the banking crisis intensified further. By the end of the year the government was compelled to avail of financial aid from the EU and the International Monetary Fund (IMF), to be provided over a four-year period, in order to restore the banking sector to viability and to put the public finances in order. The parameters of revenue raising and public-expenditure reduction were set out by government in the *National Recovery Plan 2011–2014* (2010) and were underpinned by the conditions of the EU–IMF deal, which involves regular monitoring to ensure that targets are met.

All of the above factors combined to set the scene for further expenditure reductions in the areas of social welfare, health and education. While reductions in weekly social welfare payments have been the most high profile of the public-expenditure cutbacks, many other areas of social provision have also been affected, and they include the virtual stalling of progress in certain areas, postponement of developments in others and a lowering of the priority status in some others. The implications or impact of recent measures are referred to, as appropriate, in various chapters of this book.

Party political influences

While party political ideology may have influenced the shape of social service provision in other countries, its impact in Ireland has not been as significant. In general, there are no fundamental differences between the Irish political parties on matters of social policy. This is not to deny that a different emphasis or priority may have been given to some developments depending on the party or parties in government. What is clear, however, is that there has been a broad continuity in relation to social policy irrespective of the parties or combination of parties in power. There has not been any major social policy development that opposition parties may have criticised but that on gaining power themselves they have been prepared to undo. All too frequently, however, opposition to social policy developments has been largely of a political opportunist nature, involving point scoring, rather than principled objection. A classic case in point is afforded by the family planning legislation introduced in 1978 by the Fianna Fáil government to allow for the availability of contraceptives, hitherto banned. In 1985 the Fine Gael/Labour Coalition Government amended the 1978 act in order to make contraceptives more readily available. Fianna Fáil, the then main opposition party, opposed this yet, ironically, in 1991–2 Fianna Fáil, by then in government in coalition with the Progressive Democrats, were in a position to liberalise the law further (albeit against a background of an increase in AIDS) in order to make contraceptives even more widely available.

It would be difficult to describe any of the Irish political parties as having strong ideologies in relation to social policy. Most tend to be pragmatic and to reflect the attitudes of the population towards social service provision in general and towards specific developments required. Furthermore, there is broad support among the population at large for services provided either directly by the state or by other agencies with state support.

While the differences in ideology between parties on social policy issues may be negligible, individual politicians have made significant contributions to the development of social services. One such politician was Donogh O'Malley, who, as Minister for Education, was responsible for introducing free post-primary education in 1967, several years before its introduction was planned for and without having sufficient regard to the cost implications from the viewpoint of the Department of Finance. Without his unorthodox initiative, it has been contended, it is unlikely that free post-primary education in its present form would ever have been introduced.[12] In this way, O'Malley made a far greater impact during his short term as Minister for Education than some of his predecessors or successors.

The role of the Catholic Church

Until relatively recently, one of the more notable features of Irish society has been the pre-eminence of Catholic social teaching. In the past this emphasised the principle of subsidiarity, i.e. that the state should not undertake functions that could be fulfilled by individuals, the family or the local community, and that the state's role should be to supplement, not to supplant. The debate over the proposed Mother and Child Scheme in the late 1940s illustrated the importance of this issue (see Chapter 5). Since Vatican Council II (1962–5), the Catholic Church has increasingly concerned itself with inadequacies in social provision. It has urged the introduction of measures designed not simply to ameliorate the effects of disadvantage and poverty in society but also to remove the cause of these problems. This renewed emphasis on social issues by the Catholic Church was exemplified by the sentiments expressed in the hierarchy's pastoral *The Work of Justice* (1977) and several reports by the Council for Social Welfare (a subcommittee of the Catholic hierarchy). The Conference of Religious of Ireland (CORI), formerly the Conference of Major Religious Superiors, has also been to the forefront not only in highlighting issues of social concern but also in proposing alternative policies.

Partnership and lobby groups

The influence of vocational and lobby groups in the development of social service provision in Ireland should not be ignored. In some countries the trade union movement has had a formative influence on social service developments. In Ireland this role has probably been more limited, but significant nonetheless. While the primary concern of trade unions has been the remuneration and general working conditions of their members, as one of the main social partners they have been to the forefront in pressing for social reforms. The National Understandings between government, employers and trade unions in the early 1980s followed a period of national wage agreements and contained a number of commitments related to social policy. Since the late 1980s the trade unions have had a significant input in various national partnership agreements – the *Plan for National Recovery* (1987), the *Programme for Economic and Social Progress* (1991), the *Programme for Competitiveness and Work* (1993), *Partnership 2000* (1996), the *Programme for Prosperity and Fairness* (2000), *Sustaining Progress* (2003) and *Towards 2016* (2006). These documents, agreed between government and the social partners (employers, trade unions and farmers), contain extensive and detailed commitments to social policy developments. The inclusion of these commitments is attributable largely to the influence of the trade union movement. The discussions prior to the agreement on *Partnership 2000* marked a new departure, with the involvement of representatives of community and voluntary groups, such as the Irish National Organisation of the Unemployed, CORI and the Society of St Vincent de Paul, in the consultative process. This process was continued in subsequent national partnership agreements.

The concept of consultation and partnership involving the four different 'pillars' (employers, trade unions, farmers, voluntary/ community sector) had become such an integral part of policymaking since the late 1980s that it was difficult to imagine developments outside this framework in the future. Increasingly, however, a body of opinion emerged which argued that the partnership model had begun to outlive its usefulness. With the economic downturn in 2008 and the consequent reductions in public expenditure, including public service pay, reaching consensus among the partners on a range of issues became far more difficult, and, following a period of twenty-three years, the social partnership process was effectively stalled at the end of 2009. This has meant that the review and monitoring processes normally associated with agreements, especially in relation to social policy commitments in *Towards 2016*, have been virtually abandoned.

Many voluntary bodies involved in providing services also have a lobby role and frequently press for changes in areas under their remit. Some of these have representative umbrella organisations that perform this particular function on behalf of their members. Lobbying usually takes place in advance of proposed legislation and, more commonly, in the form of pre-budget submissions.

Colonial and external influences

The foundations of many existing social services in Ireland were laid by British governments before independence was achieved in the 1920s.[13] Many of the key landmark developments in areas such as education, health and income maintenance were put in place while Ireland was ruled by Britain. These are outlined more fully in the following chapters, and a brief overview is given here.

The Poor Law, introduced in Ireland in 1838, had a profound effect on the development of social services. It was out of the Poor Law, for example, that the public hospital system developed. The initial central feature of the Poor Law was the workhouse, which was designed for the very destitute. The philosophy of the Poor Law was based on the concept of less eligibility, i.e. the conditions of persons within the workhouse should be less eligible than those of the lowest-paid worker outside. While many of the workhouses, the visible signs and reminders of the mid-nineteenth-century Poor Law, were demolished and remodelled for other purposes such as county homes after independence in the early 1920s, some have survived as integral features of the structures of some hospitals. Other Poor Law services survived until the 1970s, including the dispensary system, replaced by the choice-of-doctor scheme in 1972, and outdoor relief/home assistance, replaced by the supplementary welfare allowance scheme in 1977.

The education system at first, second and third level was also developed during the nineteenth century. The national system of primary education commenced in 1831 with the establishment of the National Board of Education, the national secondary school system was established in 1878, while much of the future university system was also established during that century.

The two decades prior to independence marked an important stage in the development of social services as Ireland benefited from the Liberal reforms in Britain. This period witnessed the introduction of the first state income maintenance schemes, such as the means-tested old-age pension (1908) and unemployment and sickness insurance-based schemes (1911), and the resolution of a decades-long controversy on the university question (1908).

The British influence continued long after independence: the contiguity of Britain and the free flow of labour between the countries (mostly to Britain) inevitably meant that comparisons would be made between the social services in each country. Consequently, there had been a general tendency to look to Britain as the first reference point when a new scheme or development was being considered. Not infrequently, modified versions of schemes already in existence in Britain have been introduced in Ireland.

Ireland's entry to the European Economic Community (EEC) in 1973 also had an impact on social service provision. If nothing else, it served to heighten comparisons between Ireland and other member states and to provide wider reference points than heretofore. The influence of membership of the EU has been of a direct and indirect nature. The direct influence has been exemplified by EU directives, such as the directive in 1978 on the equal treatment of men and women in matters of social security. Ireland has also benefited directly in other ways such as funding for training programmes under the European Social Fund and funding of anti-poverty programmes.[14] The indirect influence is more difficult to determine but it is nonetheless important. While it was never the intention of the EU to secure uniformity in social service provision, obvious gaps – for example, in income maintenance (social security) coverage – became apparent from the time Ireland became a member. The publication of a Green Paper (a discussion document) by the Department of Social Welfare on *Social Insurance for the Self-Employed* (1978) was undoubtedly influenced by the fact that Ireland was the only EU country at the time that did not extend social insurance cover to the self-employed.

Social policy analysis

Over the past few decades there has been increased interest in social policy and more extensive analysis of social policy issues in Ireland. This is reflected in the output of publications dealing with social services and social issues in general. Several of these have helped not only to shape policy but also to create and increase public awareness of social issues. Reference must first be made, however, to an early pioneering work – a paper on *Social Security* read by Dr Dignan, Bishop of Clonfert and Chairman of the National Health Insurance Society, to the management committee of the society in 1944. In his paper Dr Dignan outlined what at the time appeared to be radical proposals for reform of the Irish social welfare system.

It is only since the mid 1960s that publications containing analysis of the various social services began to emerge in Ireland. These works include Coughlan's *Aims of Social Policy* (1966); the publications of Kaim-Caudle in the 1960s and early 1970s, especially *Social Policy in the Irish Republic* (1967); and O'Cinneide's *A Law for the Poor* (1970) and *The Extent of Poverty in Ireland* (1972).

The publications of several agencies have also contributed to the debate on social services. At one level, governments have initiated or commissioned reports on various aspects of the social services, e.g. *Investment in Education* (1965), *Report of the Commission on Inquiry into Mental Illness* (1966), *Report on the Industrial and Reformatory School System* (1970), *Report of the Commission on the Status of Women* (1972), *Report of the Commission on Social Welfare* (1986), *Report of the Commission on Health Funding* (1989) and *A Strategy for Equality: Report of the Commission on the Status of People with Disabilities* (1996). At another level, various advisory and research agencies have been established and through their publications have contributed to the growing debate on social issues.

In 1973 the NESC was established and, in accordance with its constitution and terms of reference, its main task was to provide a forum for discussion on the principles relating to the efficient development of the national economy and the achievement of social justice. The reports of the NESC, as well as being invaluable sources of information, have raised important social policy issues, influenced policymaking and contributed to a continuing debate on social problems and policies. The NESC report *The Developmental Welfare State* (2005) was the first major review of the Irish welfare state and provided a life cycle approach to social policy development that was adopted in the partnership agreement *Towards 2016*.

In 1992 the government established the National Economic and Social Forum (NESF), with a broader base of representation than that in the NESC. Apart from the traditional social partners (employers, trade unions, farmers and the community/voluntary sector) the membership also included representatives from political parties. The NESF, charged with developing economic and social policy initiatives, especially initiatives to combat unemployment, has also published a number of reports that have helped to contribute to the formation of a national consensus on social and economic matters. In 2010, as part of a rationalisation of state-sponsored agencies, the NESF was dissolved and its functions were absorbed into the NESC.

The ESRI also continues to perform an important policymaking function with its focus on research on economic and social change. ESRI reports that have made a significant contribution to national debate on social policy issues include those by Tussing on *Irish Educational Expenditures – Past, Present and Future* (1978) and by Rottman et al. on *The Population Structure and Living Circumstances of Irish Travellers* (1986), as well as several publications on poverty.

The work of the CPA, a statutory body established in 1986 that succeeded the non-statutory National Committee on Pilot Schemes to Combat Poverty (1974–80), has highlighted the extent and nature of poverty in Irish society. In 2009 the CPA and its functions were integrated into the Office for Social Inclusion in the Department of Social and Family Affairs (see Chapter 8).

CORI became an increasingly influential body in the social policy area from the mid 1980s. Apart from its regular commentary on government social and economic policy measures as they arise, important publications include *Pathways to a Basic Income* (1997) and *Social Policy in Ireland: Principles, Practices and Problems* (1998). In 2009 the leading figures behind CORI, Fr Sean Healy and Sr Brigid Reynolds, founded a new advocacy and social analysis organisation, Social Justice Ireland, which took over the programmes and advocacy projects formerly run by CORI.

The above developments serve to illustrate the growing interest in and concern with social policy issues in Ireland, and the need to assess the impact of social policy measures. This is in marked contrast to the situation several decades ago when the same services were rarely subjected to any serious debate or analysis.

Notes

1. National Economic and Social Council, *Report No. 8, An Approach to Social Policy* (Stationery Office, Dublin, 1975), p. 30.

2. National Economic and Social Council, *Report No. 61, Irish Social Policies: Priorities for Future Development* (Stationery Office, Dublin, 1981), pp.12–30.

3. F. Kennedy, *Public Social Expenditure in Ireland* (Economic and Social Research Institute, Dublin, 1975), pp. 54–8.

4. National Economic and Social Council, *Report No. 61*, op. cit., pp.15–20.

5. Government of Ireland, *Building on Reality* (Stationery Office, Dublin, 1984), pp. 87–8.

6. Department of Finance, *2010 Revised Estimates for the Public Service* (Stationery Office, Dublin, 2010), Table 5A.

7. A. Coughlan, *Aims of Social Policy* (Tuairim Pamphlet, No. 14, Dublin, 1966), p. 4.

8. See J. Higgins, *States of Welfare: Comparative Analysis in Social Policy* (Basil Blackwell and Martin Robertson, Oxford, 1981), Chapter 4.

9. T. Fahey and J. Fitzgerald, *Welfare Implications of Demographic Trends* (Combat Poverty Agency, Dublin, 1997), pp. 116–17.

10. F. Kennedy, op. cit., pp. 11–20.

11. National Economic and Social Council, *Report No. 89, A Strategy for the Nineties: Economic Stability and Structural Change* (Stationery Office, Dublin, 1990), p. 6.

12. S. O'Connor, *A Troubled Sky: Reflections on the Irish Educational Scene, 1957–1968* (Educational Research Centre, St Patrick's College, Dublin, 1986), pp. 152–3.

13. See H. Burke, 'Foundation stones of Irish social policy, 1831–1951', in G. Kiely et al., *Irish Social Policy in Context* (University College Dublin Press, Dublin, 1999).

14. See I. Mangan, 'The influence of EC membership on Irish social policy and social services', in S. O'Cinneide (ed.), *Social Europe: EC Social Policy and Ireland* (Institute of European Affairs, Dublin, 1993); S. Langford, 'The impact of the European Union on Irish social policy development in relation to social exclusion', in G. Kiely et al., op. cit.

2

Income Maintenance

Introduction

In this chapter the term 'income maintenance' is used to describe the system of cash payments made to people who experience certain contingencies, such as unemployment and sickness. This system is more popularly referred to in Ireland as 'social welfare', and that terminology is derived from the fact that for fifty years, from 1947 to 1997, the Department of Social Welfare was responsible for the administration of the vast majority of the cash payments (and some benefits in kind); in 1997 the department was renamed the Department of Social, Community and Family Affairs, in 2002 it was renamed the Department of Social and Family Affairs, and in 2010 it was renamed the Department of Social Protection. The term 'social welfare', however, may have a much broader meaning in other countries. It should also be noted that in many other countries the term 'social security' is used to describe the system of cash payments and, additionally, in some, eligibility for health services.

The basic purpose of an income maintenance system is to provide income support for people who, for whatever reason, experience a loss of income or whose existing income is regarded as being insufficient. In this context it is useful to make a broad distinction between those in the labour market and those outside it. Examples of those in the labour market that experience an income loss are the unemployed and the short-term ill, while the retired and chronically ill are examples of those outside the labour market.

Over several decades the types of income contingencies catered for have become accepted in most developed countries. They include unemployment, retirement, widowhood and invalidity. It is not unusual, however, for countries to have special measures for other categories. This is true of Ireland, where a special scheme was introduced for deserted wives in the 1970s.

Types of income maintenance schemes

There are three main types of income maintenance schemes: social insurance, social assistance (means-tested) and universal.

The distinguishing feature of social insurance schemes is that eligibility is determined on the basis of social insurance contributions paid. They are financed by compulsory contributions from employers, employees and the self-employed. Once the contribution conditions are satisfied, there is an intrinsic entitlement to benefit irrespective of any other income the person may have.

In the case of social assistance or means-tested schemes, eligibility is determined by an assessment of means. The claimant is entitled to a payment only if the means are below the threshold set for the particular scheme. Partial rather than maximum payment will be paid where the means are greater than the minimum floor set. In general, claimants of social assistance will have either no social insurance contribution record or a broken social insurance record, which effectively disqualifies them from social insurance payments. Means-tested schemes are financed from general taxation.

Under a universal scheme there are neither social insurance contribution conditions nor means tests, and a payment is made without respect to income. The most important universal scheme in Ireland is that of child benefit, payable in respect of all children up to a specified age.

The Irish income maintenance system embraces the three types of schemes referred to above. For some time the trend has been to extend the social insurance base, but the social assistance schemes are likely to be an important element of the system for many decades to come.

Social insurance and social assistance schemes are often referred to as contributory and non-contributory schemes, respectively. This is because of the way in which they are funded. In many instances there are complementary social insurance and social assistance schemes. For example, there are widow's and state (contributory) pensions for those who satisfy the contribution conditions, while on the social assistance side there are widow's and state (non-contributory) pensions for those who do not satisfy the contribution conditions and who qualify on the basis of a means test. With the exception of jobseeker's payments, social insurance payments are usually higher than those for social assistance, although the percentage difference is not consistent across schemes.

Evolution of income maintenance system

The income maintenance system evolved over several decades. Schemes were introduced at different times in response either to an increased emphasis on the needs of particular groups or to newly emerging needs. An outline of the chronological development of the main income maintenance schemes is given in Table 2.1. This is not meant to be comprehensive but is simply indicative of the piecemeal nature of the development of the system. Since the background to the development of the income maintenance schemes is given elsewhere, only a broad outline is presented here.[1]

Under the Irish Poor Law system that originated in 1838, workhouses were established throughout the country. The Poor Law was never intended by its founders to be a system of income support, but due to various circumstances involvement in this area was grudgingly and reluctantly conceded. The central philosophy of the Poor Law was that destitution could only be relieved in the workhouses and that no help whatsoever was to be made available outside of the workhouse. The circumstances of the great famine in the 1840s, which led to overcrowding of the workhouses and widespread destitution, forced the Poor Law Commissioners to concede the granting of help (in the form of outdoor relief) outside of the workhouses. While this was only a temporary measure, it eventually became an established part of the Poor Law system. By the beginning of the twentieth century, the only resort of those on low incomes was the outdoor relief of the Poor Law. In the 1920s the system of outdoor relief was renamed home assistance.[2] Reliance on the Poor Law was gradually lessened as separate schemes were introduced for different categories of claimants.

The first categorical scheme of income maintenance was the old-age (non-contributory) pension that came into effect in 1909 following the passing of the Old Age Pension Act the previous year. This was a landmark development, achieved after twenty years of campaigning by social reformers and several unsuccessful attempts to introduce the necessary legislation.[3] The 1908 act has been described as 'arguably the most radical and far-reaching piece of welfare legislation enacted in Ireland in the twentieth century'.[4] Since then various schemes for other categories have been introduced, as Table 2.1 illustrates. It is interesting to note that the complementary old-age (contributory) pension was not introduced until over half a century later, in 1961.

Table 2.1: *Chronological development of main social welfare schemes*

Year	Insurance schemes	Assistance schemes	Other schemes
1838			Poor Law
1909		Old-age pension	
1911	Unemployment benefit Sickness benefit		
1920		Blind pension	
1923			Home assistance
1933		Unemployment benefit	
1935	Widow's and orphan's pensions	Widow's and orphan's pensions	
1942			Cheap fuel scheme
1944			Children's allowance Cheap footwear
1947	Department of Social Welfare established		
1961	Old-age pension		
1966		Smallholder's assistance	
1967	Occupational injuries		Free travel Electricity allowance
1968			Free TV licence
1970	Retirement pension Invalidity pension	Deserted wife's allowance	
1973	Deserted wife's benefit	Unmarried mother's allowance	
1974	Payment-related benefit	Single woman's allowance Prisoner's wife's allowance	
1977		Supplementary welfare allowance	
1980			National fuel scheme
1984		Family income supplement	
1989		Lone parent's allowance	
1990		Carer's allowance Back to education scheme	
1993		Back to work scheme	
1994	Widower's pension		
1997		Widower's pension One-parent family payment	
2000	Carer's benefit		

There is no particular pattern to the way in which the various schemes were introduced. Particular circumstances frequently surrounded the introduction of each scheme. From Table 2.1, it is obvious that the development of the system was not planned in a coherent manner. At best it can be said that schemes were introduced at different times to meet different needs.

The widow's and orphan's pensions (contributory and non-contributory) were introduced in 1935 following a report of the Poor Law Commission in 1927. The unemployment benefits scheme based on social insurance (1911) provided benefit only for short-term unemployment, whereas the widespread and prolonged unemployment of the early 1930s inevitably led to the introduction of a means-tested assistance scheme to enable the unemployed who had exhausted their unemployment benefit to continue to receive a payment (albeit at a reduced rate subject to a means test). The introduction of schemes for women in the early 1970s must be considered against the background of the burgeoning women's movement in Ireland and elsewhere at the time and the recommendations of the report of the Commission on the Status of Women (1972).

With the introduction of the various schemes, the home assistance scheme (derived from the Poor Law) became more and more marginal. Its highly discretionary nature was due to the fact that local authorities administered it without formal guidelines from central level.[5] It was a scheme of last resort, and one to cater for emergencies. Home assistance, the last link with the nineteenth-century Poor Law, was finally replaced in 1977 by supplementary welfare allowance, administered by health boards subject to the control of the Minister for Social Welfare.

In Table 2.1 a number of schemes that are neither social assistance nor social insurance may be noted. Two of these, children's allowance (renamed child benefit in 1986) and free travel, are universal schemes. The former, as already indicated, is a scheme whereby monthly payments are made in respect of each child up to age sixteen, or age eighteen if in full-time education (see later section on child income support). Under the free travel scheme all persons of state-pension qualifying age (sixty-six years) and certain other categories are entitled to use public transport facilities and some private transport facilities free of charge. The household benefits package consists of three allowances – electricity or gas allowance, telephone allowance and free television licence – and is normally available to persons aged over seventy years. The cheap fuel scheme was introduced during World War II when fuel was scarce, and its application was confined to recipients of certain social welfare payments in urban areas mainly along the eastern seaboard. The scheme remained in existence long after the war, and eventually the demand for a similar scheme for the rest of the country was met in 1980 with the introduction of a national fuel scheme. Two separate fuel schemes existed until 1988, when a unified scheme was introduced for the entire country. It is now in the form of weekly cash payments between September and April for persons on long-term social welfare payments who are unable to provide for their own heating needs.

Modifications have been made to schemes since their introduction. This has mainly related to the easing of eligibility conditions. For example, the old-age (non-contributory) pension (later renamed the state (non-contributory) pension), introduced in 1909, was described, with some justification, as 'a pension too low at an age too high after a means test which was too severe'.[6] The present situation is quite different; the qualifying age has been reduced from seventy years to sixty-six years (between 1973 and 1977), and the means test has been eased considerably. Apart from increases in the rates of payment, the eligibility criteria for all schemes have been modified since their inception.

Changes in terminology

From September 2006 the names of some social welfare schemes were changed as part of a modernisation of the system:

Old names	New names
old-age (contributory) pension	state pension (contributory)
old-age (non-contributory) pension	state pension (non-contributory)
retirement pension	state pension (transition)
unemployment benefit	jobseeker's benefit
unemployment assistance	jobseeker's allowance
unemployment supplement	incapacity supplement
disability benefit	illness benefit
orphan's (contributory) allowance	guardian's payment (contributory)
orphan's (non-contributory) pension	guardian's payment (non-contributory)

Main features of social insurance schemes

As already indicated, eligibility for the social insurance schemes is based on social insurance contributions. Up to 1974 the social insurance contribution was in the form of a 'stamp' at a flat rate irrespective of income. In that year a partial pay-related social insurance (PRSI) system was introduced, and in 1979 a more comprehensive system was introduced. Contributions are based on a percentage of earnings up to a certain ceiling. Since 2001 the standard rate of contribution for employees has been 4.0 per cent, and until recently this amount was paid up to an income ceiling, which was usually adjusted upwards on an annual basis. In 2009 the ceiling was €75,036, and in 2011 the ceiling was abolished, which meant that a contribution became liable on all income. In a year of uninterrupted employment an insured person will have 52 contributions paid. The maximum rate of contribution for employers since 2002 is 10.75 per cent of employee income with no ceiling (the ceiling was abolished in 2001).

The qualifying conditions vary from scheme to scheme. In general, however, a contribution record over a relatively long period is required for the long-term payments, such as the state pension (contributory). This is usually in the form of an average number of contributions paid or credited (see later in this chapter) over a number of years. For example, in order to qualify for the maximum rate of state pension (contributory), an average number of 48 weeks' PRSI paid or credited from 1953 or from the time insurable employment commenced to the end of the tax year before reaching pensionable age is required.

Qualification for short-term benefits, such as jobseeker's and illness, is based on a contribution record of a shorter duration than that for the long-term benefits. For example, jobseeker's benefit is payable if the claimant has at least 104 weeks' PRSI paid and at least 39 weeks' PRSI paid or credited in the relevant tax year (the second last complete tax year prior to the year the claim is made); jobseeker's benefit rates are also graduated according to earnings in the relevant tax year.

Apart from contributions that have been paid, provision is also made for credited contributions that apply in certain circumstances. These credited contributions, or credits, are an important part of the social insurance system. They are awarded when persons normally active in the labour force face circumstances where they may not be in a position to make paid social insurance contributions. A person on jobseeker's benefit, for example, may continue to receive credited contributions that, in effect, are the equivalent of paid contributions. Credits help to maintain a social insurance record over a period of unemployment or illness and are an important means of securing entitlement to long-term benefits.

There are a number of different social insurance classes that determine the rate of contribution. Persons in Class A account for the majority of contributors who pay the standard rate of 4.0 per cent, and are entitled to the full range of social insurance benefits. There are special social insurance categories for others who are not entitled to the same range of benefits. For example, permanent and pensionable civil servants who were employed in the civil service prior to October 1995 pay a contribution of 0.9 per cent and, in return, are entitled to a limited number of benefits. The rationale behind the classification of the population into different social insurance classes is related to work status. In the case of civil servants employed prior to 1995, the rationale for not paying the full contribution would appear to be that, having secure employment and consequently being most unlikely to become unemployed, as well as having adequate occupational pensions, it was unnecessary for them to contribute towards such benefits. The end result is a rather complex system of social insurance classes.

The insured population has increased steadily from the late 1990s, reflecting the growth in employment. The numbers increased from 2.2 million in 1998 to 3.1 million in 2007; over three-quarters (77.1 per cent) of the total were in Class A with entitlement to the full range of benefits.

Main features of social assistance schemes

Eligibility for all social assistance schemes is determined on the basis of a means test carried out by officers of the Department of Social Protection. The assessment process has traditionally been unduly complex and very difficult for applicants to understand.

In the assessment of means a number of items are taken into account. These include cash income less certain allowances and the value of investments. While a number of modifications to the means test took place in the early 1970s, it was not until 1997 that further substantial amendments were made, especially to the formulae for the assessment of savings. Up to 2001, different methods were used for calculating interest from investments (such as bank deposits, stocks and shares) for various social assistance schemes. Since 2002, however, the assessment has been simplified and the same formula applies to all schemes. Under this formula a certain amount of savings (€20,000 in 2011) is disregarded and a value is applied to the balance on a sliding scale. The amount of savings and other means will determine whether a person is entitled to the maximum assistance or partial assistance, or is ineligible for assistance.

Details of the contribution conditions attached to the various social insurance schemes and of the means requirements for social assistance schemes are given on the Department of Social Protection's website (www.welfare.ie).

Other social welfare schemes

Apart from the social insurance and social assistance schemes, reference has already been made to a number of miscellaneous schemes administered by the Department of Social Protection. The most notable of these is child benefit, formerly known as children's allowance (see later section on child income support). Others include the various 'free' schemes such as electricity allowance and telephone rental for certain categories of recipients.

Beneficiaries of social welfare

An important feature of the Irish income maintenance system is that, once a claimant has established entitlement, payments include an additional amount in respect of any qualified adult and child dependants. This has been a traditional feature of the system and was only modified following the implementation of a European Community (EC) directive in 1986 on the equal treatment of men and women. Up to then spouses (married women mostly) were regarded as being financially dependent. With the greater participation by married women in the labour force, however, this situation had changed over a period of time, but this change was not reflected in the income maintenance system. For example, if a man became unemployed and qualified for unemployment benefit, he received a personal rate of payment together with an adult dependant rate even if his wife was employed and earning a relatively high income. In compliance with the directive, this situation was changed amid considerable controversy at the end of 1986.

A full additional increase for a qualified adult may now be paid where a spouse's or partner's income or earnings are less than a specified amount (€100 per week in 2011) and they are not receiving a social welfare payment in their own right. A reduced allowance may be paid where the spouse's or partner's income or earnings are more than the specified amount (between €100 and €280 per week in 2011), and no allowance is paid where the spouse's or partner's income or earnings exceed a specified amount (€280 per week in 2011). With regard to payment for qualified children, if a full personal rate and full qualified adult allowance are payable, then the full child dependant allowance is payable. If, however, the spouse or partner has an income or earnings over a specified amount, then only half the qualified child allowance is paid for each child. Therefore, in effect, there are either full, reduced or no weekly payments for dependants depending on the income circumstances of each household.

The above brief description of the situation in relation to dependants in the income maintenance system is a necessary prelude to understanding trends in the number of beneficiaries. Recipients are those who apply for a payment. Recipients together with their adult and child dependants constitute the beneficiaries. In 2009 there were 1,379,206 recipients of weekly social welfare payments, but the total number of beneficiaries was 2,076,256.

Over the past forty years or so the number of beneficiaries has quadrupled (Table 2.2); recipients of child benefit are not included in these figures. In 1966 the 566,400 beneficiaries accounted for about 20 per cent of the total population. Over the next forty years the number of beneficiaries increased gradually to reach 1,580,000 in 2007. The economic downturn in 2007 led to an upsurge in beneficiaries of unemployment and some other income-support schemes, bringing the total to over 2 million in 2009, or approximately 46.0 per cent of the total population.

Table 2.2: *Beneficiaries of weekly social welfare payments, selected years, 1966–2009**

Year	Beneficiaries	% of total population
1966	566,400	19.6
1982	1,110,900	32.3
1996	1,485,500	41.0
2001	1,460,000	38.0
2008	1,799,875	40.7
2009	2,076,256	46.4

* Recipients, adult dependants and child dependants. The figures do not include recipients of child benefit.

Source: Annual *Statistical Information on Social Welfare Services* (Department of Social Protection).

The apparently high figure of beneficiaries does not imply that about two-fifths of the population are solely dependent on social welfare payments. Some recipients of social insurance payments, such as state contributory pensions, may well have other sources of income that do not affect their entitlement to their insurance payment. It is only those on the maximum rates of social assistance payments who are likely to rely most heavily on social welfare payments for their livelihood. Over half (54.6 per cent) of beneficiaries in 2009 were in receipt of social assistance payments.

The growth in the number of beneficiaries over the past forty years is accounted for by a number of factors. The most significant of these was the introduction of new schemes over this period (see Table 2.1), such as lone parent's allowance, carer's allowance, family income supplement and widower's pension. In themselves these new schemes would have contributed to the increase in the number of beneficiaries. Another important factor has been the modification of eligibility conditions for various schemes. Examples include the lowering of the qualifying age for old-age pensions in the 1970s, changes to contribution conditions for social insurance schemes and easing of the means test for social assistance schemes. Not only were changes made to the eligibility criteria for the family income supplement scheme over time, but it was also the subject of a media advertising campaign to encourage higher take-up. A further factor is the increase in life expectancy, leading to persons drawing down pensions over a longer period. These and other factors have had the combined effect of ensuring that more people qualify for payments.

Apart from changes in the total number of beneficiaries, there have been important changes in the composition of the social welfare population. The most important variable here has been the rise or fall in the numbers unemployed. The increase in beneficiaries of unemployment payments accounted for half of the growth between 1966 and 1996. However, as unemployment declined from the mid 1990s up to 2007, increases in the number of beneficiaries of other schemes more than offset this decline. The result was that the social welfare population did not decline significantly during a period of economic growth and low unemployment as might have been expected.

Table 2.3: *Main categories of social welfare population by year, selected years, 1966–2009*

Category	1966 (%)	1993 (%)	1999 (%)	2007 (%)	2009 (%)
Unemployed	25	43	20	13	28
Older persons	33	21	22	26	21
Widowed/lone parents	16	16	23	23	18

Source: Annual *Statistical Information on Social Welfare Services* (Department of Social Protection).

Changes in unemployment are reflected in the composition of the
social welfare population (Table 2.3). In 1966 the unemployed and their
dependants accounted for one-quarter of the total, but by 1993 this had
increased to two-fifths. By 2007, reflecting the improved employment
situation in the economy, the figure had fallen to about one-eighth, but
with rising unemployment it increased to over one-quarter in 2009.
Beneficiaries of state pensions accounted for one-fifth of the total in
2009 as compared with one-third in 1966. Beneficiaries of widowed and
lone parent payments increased from less than one-sixth in 1966
to almost one-quarter in 1999, and fell to slightly less than one-fifth in
2009.

Financing and expenditure

As already indicated, a distinction can be made between the financing
of the social insurance schemes and the financing of the social assistance
schemes.

Social insurance schemes are financed from PRSI contributions from
employers and employees, with the state making good any deficit on
outgoings from general taxation. Financing of social assistance schemes
comes from general taxation. Employer and employee PRSI contributions, as well as those from the self-employed, go into the Social
Insurance Fund (see Table 2.4).

Table 2.4: *Sources of income for Social Insurance Fund, selected years, 1967–2009**

	1967 (€44m) (%)	1980 (€636m) (%)	1996 (€2,399m) (%)	2001 (€4,306m) (%)	2009 (€9,777m)** (%)
Employer	30.5	53.2	64.5	75.0	54.1
Employee	29.1	22.1	25.2	19.5	16.0
Self-employed	–	–	5.0	4.4	3.2
State	38.1	24.5	5.3	–	25.4
Investment and other receipts	2.3	0.2	0.0	1.1	1.3
Total	100.0	100.0	100.0	100.0	100.0

* Up to 1990 the occupational injuries insurance was not included in the above
figures. It was funded solely by employers from a separate fund. In 1990 this
fund was amalgamated with the Social Insurance Fund and this accounts for the
increase in the employers' share and the drop in the state's share.
** Provisional.

Source: Annual *Statistical Information on Social Welfare Services* (Department of Social
Protection).

The tripartite system of funding (employers/workers/state) is not based on any set formula. In practice, the shares have fluctuated over time. The *White Paper on Social Security* (1949) argued that the fund should be financed equally by employers, employees and the state.[7] This recommendation was not acted upon. In 1975 Richie Ryan, TD, Minister for Finance, stated:

> The Government have decided in principle to transfer the exchequer contribution towards the cost of social insurance to the other contributors to the social insurance fund over a period of six years or so.[8]

This was not acted upon either. The employer share is now considerably higher than it was four decades ago, while the employee share has declined over that period.

In 1998, due to the substantial increase in employment and the consequent increase in the flow of contributions from employers, employees and self-employed, the Social Insurance Fund was in surplus for the first time. In 2001 there was an estimated surplus of €630 million. The surplus situation continued for the next few years until 2008 when there was a shortfall due to the sharp rise in unemployment. This shortfall was made up by the state from general taxation.

The increase in contributions to the Social Insurance Fund during the years of economic growth allowed for a reduction in the standard rate of the PRSI contribution paid by employees, from 5.5 per cent of reckonable income in 1998 to 4.0 per cent by 2001.

When the financing of the social assistance schemes is allied to that of the social insurance schemes, the state's contribution amounts to more than half of the total expenditure on the social welfare system (Table 2.5).

Administration

Prior to the National Insurance Act, 1911, a number of friendly societies provided schemes for sickness benefit. Following the act, sickness and unemployment schemes continued to be operated mainly by the existing societies under the general supervision of the Irish Insurance Commissioners. A statutory condition of a society's admittance to the scheme was that the society be non-profit-making. Commercial insurance companies, which formed separate non-profit-making branches, also became involved in the scheme. By 1933 the number of insured persons in the state was about 474,000, and these were catered for by 65 approved societies with membership ranging from 55 in a small

Table 2.5: *Sources of income for all expenditure on social welfare, selected years,*
1967/8–2009*

	1967/8 (€86m) (%)	1980 (€1,108m) (%)	1996 (€5,771m) (%)	2001 (€7,842m) (%)	2009** (€20,529m) (%)
Employer	18.4	31.8	27.8	–	–
Employee	14.5	12.4	10.9	46.8***	47.6***
Self-employed	–	–	2.1	–	–
State	65.3	55.4	59.1	52.7	52.4
Other receipts	1.8	0.4	0.1	0.5	–
Total	100.0	100.0	100.0	100.0	100.0

* The occupational injuries insurance was not included in these figures until 1990.
** Provisional.
*** Social Insurance Fund.

Source: Annual *Statistical Information on Social Welfare Services* (Department of Social Protection).

mutual benefit society to over 100,000 in a central society covering the whole country.[9] These societies had considerable freedom in selecting workers to be admitted to membership, with the result that some societies were relatively more prosperous than others. The latter, by accumulating reserves, were able to increase the statutory cash benefits, but at the other end of the scale some small societies had difficulty even in meeting the statutory benefits. Apart from these differences between societies, the administrative costs of the scheme were also relatively high.

The National Health Insurance Act, 1933, made provision for the amalgamation of all societies into a single agency – the National Health Insurance Society. In 1947 the Department of Social Welfare was established, and all social insurance and assistance functions previously performed by the Department of Local Government and Public Health (e.g. old-age pensions, widow's and orphan's pensions) and the Department of Industry and Commerce (e.g. unemployment assistance, children's allowance) were transferred to the new department. The National Health Insurance Society was dissolved in 1950 and its functions were taken over by the Minister for Social Welfare. The Social Welfare Act, 1952, established a unified social insurance scheme, replacing the separate schemes for unemployment, national health, and widow's and orphan's pensions. The net effect of these changes was not only to simplify administrative procedures and reduce costs but also to ensure that one government minister was responsible for the direction of all social insurance and assistance schemes.

While the Department of Social Protection has overall responsibility, the cooperation of other government agencies is essential to the administration of the income maintenance system. An Post, through its extensive network of post offices, provides outlets for payments such as child benefit and state pensions. The Office of the Revenue Commissioners collects the PRSI contributions from employers, employees and the self-employed. Between 1926 and 2004 the Garda Síochána certified evidence of unemployment for claimants living more than six miles from a social welfare office.

Appeals system

An important element of the administration of the income maintenance system is the right to appeal. This is designed to safeguard the rights of claimants who feel they have been unfairly refused payment or awarded less than the maximum payment. Appeals are dealt with by appeals officers and may be decided summarily (especially those dealing with contribution records) or orally.

The number of appeals constitutes a relatively small proportion of the total number of annual claims (Table 2.6). The 12,353 appeals in 1995 accounted for 0.8 per cent of total claims (1,516,801). Official statistics on the total number of annual claims have not been published in recent years, but it is estimated that there are approximately 1.7 million per annum, in which case the number of appeals still represents a small proportion of the total claims. Within a short time of the establishment of the Appeals Office in 1990 there was a downward trend in the number of appeals – from 19,314 in 1991 to 12,353 in 1995. Much of this could be attributed to the improved claim procedures as recommended by the Appeals Office. In 2008, however, there was a sharp increase to 17,833, a 27 per cent increase on the 2007 number of 14,070, and the highest number received since 1993. By 2009 the number had soared to 25,963, the highest number registered since the Appeals Office was established. As might be expected, much of the increase in 2008 and 2009 related to appeals concerning unemployment, reflecting the sharp rise in unemployment in the economy.

It had not been the practice of the Department of Social Welfare to publish statistics on the outcome of appeals, but this changed with the establishment of the Appeals Office, in line with the recommendations of the Commission on Social Welfare. The 2009 report of the Appeals Office indicated that of the 17,787 appeals finalised 48 per cent had a favourable outcome, 36 per cent were disallowed and 16 per cent were withdrawn.[10] The favourable outcomes were comprised of three categories: appeal fully allowed (17.9 per cent of total), appeal partly

Table 2.6: *Number of social welfare claims and appeals, selected years, 1985–2009**

	Claims	Appeals
1985	1,174,050	17,288
1990	1,080,873	15,871
1995	1,516,801	12,353
2001	n/a	15,961
2008	n/a	17,833
2009	n/a	25,963

* Excluding claims for 'free schemes', such as free travel, electricity allowance and free phone rental.

Sources: Annual *Statistical Information on Social Welfare Services* (Department of Social Protection); *Report of Social Welfare Appeals Office* (Social Welfare Appeals Office).

allowed (2.9 per cent of total) and decision revised by a deciding officer (27.4 per cent of total). These annual outcomes were broadly consistent with those over the previous decade or so.

Of the appeals received in 2009, the two largest categories concerned the various illness schemes (41.2 per cent of total) and those related to jobseeker's payments (31.4 per cent of total).

Commission on Social Welfare

Despite the central role of the income maintenance schemes in the lives of so many people, the considerable public expenditure involved and the piecemeal development of the system, it is surprising that no fundamental review had taken place before the establishment of the Commission on Social Welfare in 1983. This is in marked contrast to other areas such as health and education. Admittedly, three official reports on the system were published – *White Paper on Social Security* (1949); and two Green Papers, *A National Income-Related Pension Scheme* (1976) and *Social Insurance for Self Employed* (1978). In addition, a special committee was established to examine the system of workmen's compensation arising from occupational injuries, and its report was published in 1962. Otherwise, the system was not subject to the periodic review that has been characteristic of other areas; nor was there any popular demand for reform. The main areas of concern to particular groups were the rates of payment, and these would normally be the subjects of pre-budget submissions. In 1982 the National Social Service Board, in its pre-budget submission, called for the establishment of a commission to carry out a fundamental review of the system.[11] A commitment to establish such a commission was part of the programme of the Fine Gael/Labour Coalition Government, which came into office in 1982. The Commission on Social Welfare was established in 1983.

The commission's report, published in 1986, opted for an evolutionary rather than a radical change to the system. It envisaged reforms within the framework of the existing system rather than replacing that system. At no stage had any guiding principles been laid down for the income maintenance system. The commission therefore considered that the principles that should guide the development of the system were adequacy, redistribution, comprehensiveness, consistency and simplicity. The reformed system, as proposed by the commission, reflected a mix of these principles but with a special emphasis on the principle of adequacy.

The four key elements of the reformed system proposed by the commission concerned the payment structure, social insurance, social assistance and financing.

The payment structure

The most fundamental issue facing the commission was the adequacy of payments. There had never been any official attempt to establish what a minimally adequate income for a person dependent on income maintenance should be. The payment structure had simply evolved without any explicit reference to particular indicators, such as wage levels. Since the early 1970s, however, there has been a conscious attempt to ensure that increases in payments are in line with inflation.

By using a number of indicators, the commission estimated that a minimally adequate income for a single person in 1985 was in the range of £50 to £60 per week (€63.50 to €78.20), the top point being equivalent to approximately half the net average industrial earnings. The commission recognised that its calculation of a minimally adequate income could be open to criticism but stated:

> in the absence of any explicit official criteria and because of the limitations of available data we had no option but to attempt to establish a minimally adequate income. Not to have done so would, in our view, have been a serious omission. Furthermore, if our approach is considered to be deficient then an acceptable alternative should be provided.[12]

Some of the existing payments were well below the estimated minimally adequate income, while others were at or near the top part of the range. The commission was faced with a variety of payment levels for different categories and contingencies for which there was no apparent rationale.

The lowest payment in the system for a single person (unemployment assistance) was 60 per cent of the highest payment (old-age (contributory) pension). Inevitably, incongruous situations arose where, for example, a person long-term unemployed with a dependent spouse and two children received considerably less than a couple receiving the old-age pension.

The variation in rates of payment for different categories mainly arose from piecemeal changes over time rather than any systematic evaluation of the income needs of particular categories. The result was a payment structure that was not only complex but also discriminatory against individuals and families with similar financial needs. A hierarchical system existed, with the highest payments going to older people, followed by widows, and with the unemployed at the bottom. Insofar as there was any rationale for the different rates of payment it may have had more to do with popular notions of need in Irish society and with attitudes towards groups that were regarded as 'deserving' and 'undeserving' poor. The commission recommended that, in general, the same basic payment should apply to all recipients with the main difference being a differential of the order of 10 per cent between insurance and assistance payments.

A number of other issues arose in the context of the payment structure. The commission made recommendations on each of these, designed to bring a greater degree of consistency into the system. Thus, for example, there were no less than thirty-six different rates of child dependant payments, depending on the birth order of the child and the recipient category of the parent. The lowest child dependant payment was 42 per cent of the highest, and children of widows attracted the highest amounts. In the commission's view, the range was unjustified and it recommended a rationalisation of child dependant payments. Similarly, the commission argued that the existing limited pay-related element (associated with some payments only) should be phased out and that the priority should be the attainment of a minimally adequate income for all recipients.

Social insurance

The commission favoured the retention of the social insurance system. The *raison d'être* of social insurance had never been sufficiently articulated in Ireland. For this reason the commission emphasised that social insurance was an expression of social solidarity and citizenship in which the risks, costs and benefits are spread as widely as possible in the community. Furthermore, in the commission's view, social insurance contributions create a sense of entitlement to benefit and generate support among the community for these benefits. The commission recommended that all income earners should therefore contribute to and benefit from social insurance, where appropriate. The main group outside the social insurance system when the report was published was the self-employed, including farmers, who accounted for about 20 per cent of the labour force.

Apart from the self-employed, there were other smaller groups not liable for social insurance contributions, such as members of religious orders and certain ministers of religion. Furthermore, public servants were liable only for a modified rate of contribution on grounds that their conditions of employment did not warrant coverage for all benefits. The commission recommended that all public servants be liable for the full rate of contribution.

Social assistance

The widening of coverage for social insurance as proposed by the commission would lead to a decline in the need for means-tested social assistance payments. Social assistance would then be a residual element in the income maintenance system.

The commission recommended that there should be a comprehensive social assistance scheme for those who, for whatever reason, do not qualify for social insurance. The main condition would be the establishment of an income need irrespective of the cause of that need. This would lead to the elimination of the unnecessary categorical social assistance schemes that existed (e.g. lone parent's allowance, widow's pension, prisoner's wife's allowance). The income need would be established by reference to a means test. The commission recommended that the means test be rationalised and simplified, and that the main constituents be better publicised.

Financing

It has already been noted that the social insurance system in Ireland is funded on a tripartite basis by employers, workers and the state, and that social assistance is funded entirely out of general taxation. There is no set formula that determines the apportionment of costs between the three partners to the Social Insurance Fund, and the commission did not support the notion of pre-stated shares.

While the commission recognised that social insurance is not directly comparable with private commercial insurance, it nevertheless has a significant insurance dimension that is not outweighed by the absence of an actuarial link between benefits and contributions. The commission also considered the question of the employment effects of employers' social insurance contributions, a subject of debate on a number of occasions in the recent past. In the commission's view, the evidence concerning the effects on employment was inconclusive. Nor did it justify a departure from the payroll base of contributions that the commission concluded was the broadest, most clearly identifiable and predictable base available.

On grounds of redistribution the commission concluded that the income ceiling on contributions should be gradually abolished; this move would need to be coordinated with the evolution of earnings and income tax. (This process was completed in 2011.)

Developments post commission's report

Following decades of piecemeal development, the *Report of the Commission on Social Welfare* had provided a blueprint for the rational development of the income maintenance system. Many of the developments that subsequently occurred resulted from the report's recommendations.

While the commission had estimated that additional revenue could be generated from broadening the social insurance base, there would be a net cost to the exchequer from implementing its recommendations. Partly, though not exclusively for cost reasons, the commission recommended that the development of the reformed system be undertaken on a gradual basis, and it listed areas requiring priority attention. These included improvement in the basic rate of payment for those on the lowest social welfare rates and a broadening of the social insurance base.

The government statement issued on publication of the commission's report in August 1986 noted that, due to the existing economic circumstances, it would not be possible to fully implement the commission's proposals.

Subsequently, Gemma Hussey, TD, Minister for Social Welfare, stated in the Dáil that:

> there is no question of the report being dismissed or ignored. There is absolutely no doubt that radical changes will be necessary over the next few years in the social welfare system. While we must be selective in bringing forward proposals for additional expenditure, there is considerable scope for reform of the system in line with the general approach which the commission has adopted.[13]

While the government's initial reaction to the commission's report appeared to be hostile, there was a general welcome for the thrust of its recommendations from a variety of organisations. The apparent rejection of the report by the government led to the formation of a coalition of over twenty voluntary groups – Campaign for Welfare Reform – to lobby for the implementation of its recommendations. The notion of the minimally adequate income was highlighted in the debate that ensued, and the figure proposed by the commission was not challenged.

From the late 1980s onwards some progress began to be made in implementing the recommendations. The budgets of 1989 to 1992 provided for higher increases for those on the lowest payment levels, and this had the effect of significantly narrowing the gap between the highest and lowest payment (see Table 2.7). In the mid 1980s the lowest payment (jobseeker's allowance) was 60 per cent of the highest payment (state pension (contributory) for those aged over eighty years). Over a period there has been a gradual narrowing of the difference between these two payments. Furthermore, while jobseeker's allowance was the lowest payment in the mid 1980s, there has been a rationalisation of payments for different schemes, with the result that the maximum weekly payment is now the same for a number of schemes, including jobseeker's allowance, jobseeker's benefit, illness benefit, widow/widower's (non-contributory) pension, carer's allowance and supplementary welfare

Table 2.7: *Trends in highest and lowest weekly payments, selected years, 1985–2011*

	1985 (€)	1988 (€)	1990 (€)	2002 (€)	2009 (€)	2011 (€)
A: Highest payment (state pension (contributory) over 80 years)	69.70	77.00	83.30	153.70	240.30	240.30
B. Lowest payment (see note 2)	41.60	49.50	57.15	118.80	204.30	188.00
B as percentage of A	60%	64%	69%	77%	85%	78%

Notes: 1. Up to 1989 there was a distinction in the personal and married rates for jobseeker's assistance between urban and rural areas. In 1985 the rural personal rate was €40.30. The distinction was abolished in 1989 and the rural rate increased to the same level as the urban.
2. For several years the lowest payment was unemployment assistance and supplementary allowance. When some payment rates were equalised, several schemes had a similar maximum rate, such as jobseeker's benefit, illness benefit, widow/widower's (non-contributory) pension, carer's allowance and supplementary welfare allowance. In 2010 lower payments were introduced for those under twenty-five years of age on jobseeker's allowance or jobseeker's benefit, but these are not referred to in this table.

allowance. In the budgets of 1997 to 2002, higher increases were given to recipients of state pensions, with the result that the narrowing of the gap was halted temporarily. The budgets of 2005 to 2007 provided for higher increases for the lowest rate, resulting in the gap narrowing further. By 2009 the lowest weekly personal payment was 85 percent of the highest weekly personal payment. However, a reduction in all weekly social welfare payments, with the exception of state pensions, in 2010 and 2011 has resulted in the differential between the lowest and highest payments being widened once more.

The number of different rates of payment for dependent children was rationalised considerably: from thirty-six rates in 1988 to three rates by 1991, and then to a single rate in 2007. In 1988 the self-employed, members of religious orders and all ministers of religion became liable for social insurance contributions. The largest category within the self-employed at the time was farmers. The widening of the social insurance base was perhaps the most significant development in the income maintenance system in decades as it had seemed, for some time, that the political will to bring the self-employed into the system had been lacking. It meant that significant sections of the population became entitled to certain benefits as of right without having to undergo a means test. This development is especially reflected in the increased numbers in receipt of contributory state pensions and the corresponding decline in numbers of recipients of the non-contributory state pension (see Chapter 6).

Other developments, though not recommended by the commission, included the introduction of a lone parent social assistance scheme in 1989 and a carer's allowance scheme in 1990. The lone parent scheme represented a move towards a more rational system of income support for lone parents, including male lone parents, with dependent children. The introduction of the carer's allowance was the culmination of a campaign to ensure that the role of a growing number of carers, mainly females, in society and their need for an independent income were recognised. Since the introduction of carer's allowance the number of recipients has increased substantially, from 3,355 in 1991 to 11,416 in 1998, and to 48,223 in 2009.

As mentioned previously, the Social Welfare Act, 1990, provided for the establishment of a separate Appeals Office, headed by a director and chief appeals officer, as an executive office of the Department of Social Welfare. The establishment of the Appeals Office was designed to emphasise the independence of the appeals system and to ensure that it was perceived to be impartial and independent. In accordance with the commission's recommendations, the Appeals Office is obliged to publish an annual report on its activities with comment, where necessary, on the workings of the social welfare system and the implications of its decisions for policymaking. The annual reports contain informative case studies, which outline the process of appeals and the reasons for decisions taken.

The Director of the Appeals Office has raised the issue of legislative independence for the office, indicating that while the independence of the appeals officers is not in doubt, there is no legal recognition of the Social Welfare Appeals Office as a statutory entity in its own right.[14]

In the decade or so following publication, various groups used the *Report of the Commission on Social Welfare* in their pre-budget submissions and as a yardstick to evaluate reforms in the system. Of greatest significance perhaps was the commitment made in the *Programme for Economic and Social Progress* (1991), agreed between government and the social partners, to implement the priority recommendations of the report over a three-year period. This was the first commitment at official level to implement the commission's recommendations on a minimally adequate income, and came five years after the report's publication. This was followed by further commitments in the *Programme for Competitiveness and Work* (1993) and *Partnership 2000* (1996). These commitments were largely due to the influence of the trade union movement. By Budget 1998, Charlie McCreevy, TD, Minister for Finance, could state that the rates of payment for all but two categories (unemployment assistance and supplementary welfare allowance) were above the minimum rates recommended by the commission.

Income adequacy

One of the central features of the commission's report was the emphasis on a minimally adequate income. This was the first time that the adequacy of social welfare payments had been subjected to any critical scrutiny. It was to remain an important issue in the following years. As already indicated, based on a variety of indicators, the commission recommended a minimum adequate income weekly rate of between €63.50 and €78.20 (£50 to £60) with an immediate priority rate of €57 per week.

Within a decade of the commission's report, the Department of Social Welfare commissioned the ESRI to undertake a study of the commission's minimum adequate income. The fact that the department had commissioned the review was in itself significant: it represented an acknowledgement that the commission's emphasis on adequacy had been justified. The report, *A Review of the Commission on Social Welfare's Minimum Adequate Income*, published in 1996, indicated that no method of measuring adequacy could 'allow one to derive in an unproblematic, objective and scientific way, estimates of adequacy which would be universally acceptable and convincing'.[15] Nevertheless, the authors provided a new estimate of a minimum adequate income ranging from €86.30 to €121.90 per week. The review also pointed out that social welfare payments in Ireland were generally above those in the UK relative to average earnings but below the average for EU countries as a whole.

The *National Anti-Poverty Strategy* (NAPS) was published by government in 1997 (see Chapter 8). One of the five key areas selected for attention over the ten-year life span of the strategy was income adequacy. The objective was to ensure that all policies in relation to income support (e.g. unemployment, tax, social welfare, pensions) provided sufficient income for a person to move out of poverty and live in a manner compatible with human dignity.[16]

The National Pensions Board also considered the issue of adequacy of payments, admittedly only in relation to the state pension, in its report *Securing Retirement Income: National Pensions Policy Initiative* (1998). Here, the focus was on providing a 'reasonable' level of income. The board chose the upper limit of the ESRI's minimum rate, and this rate was expressed as a percentage (34 per cent) of average industrial earnings.[17]

The *Programme for Prosperity and Fairness* (PPF; 2000) contained commitments over the three-year term of that programme to increase all social welfare payments in real terms and to ensure that substantial progress would be made towards a target of €127 per week for the lowest rate of social welfare. The PPF also stated:

> Recognising the complex issues involved in developing a benchmark for adequacy of adult and child social welfare payments including the implications of adopting a specific approach to the ongoing up-rating or indexation of payments, a Working Group will be established with an independent chairperson to examine the issues … and to report by April 2001.[18]

Composed of representatives of the social partners and of some government departments, and known as the Social Welfare Benchmarking and Indexation Group, the working group completed its report in September 2001. The majority of the group proposed a formal linkage between adult social welfare rates and average earnings in order to ensure that the income of social welfare recipients kept pace with those of the wider population. While recognising that the exact rate was a matter for government, the group proposed that a target of 27 per cent of gross average industrial earnings (on a current year basis) should be established and that this target should be met by 2007. A minority of the group felt it was inappropriate to establish a formal benchmark. Instead, they argued that existing arrangements should continue to apply, i.e. that having regard to the demands on the exchequer 'it would be left to the discretion of the government to determine the level of social welfare increases from year to year'.[19]

The revised NAPS of 2002 (under the PPF) contained a commitment by government to increase the lowest rates of social welfare to €150 per week in 2002 terms by 2007, but it did not refer to any formal link with gross average industrial earnings.[20]

The partnership agreement *Towards 2016* reiterated the commitment of achieving the NAPS target of €150 per week in 2002 terms for the lowest social welfare rates by 2007. It also recommended 'the value of the rates to be maintained at this level over the course of the agreement, subject to available resources'.[21]

As a result of increases in the budgets of 2005 to 2007, the target set in 2002 was achieved by 2007, when the lowest payment rate amounted to €185.80. CORI maintained that this was equivalent to 30 per cent of gross average earnings in 2002 terms and that the achievement of the benchmark 'marked a fundamental turning point in Irish public policy'.[22] In establishing target rates, government policy had, in practice, moved towards an acceptance of a formal link with average earnings. The first formal acknowledgement of that link was made in 2010 when the government indicated that it would 'seek to sustain the value of the state pension at 35 per cent of average weekly earnings'.[23]

The Commission on Social Welfare was first to raise in a fundamental manner the adequacy of social welfare payments. By establishing a target for a minimally adequate income for social welfare recipients in the mid 1980s it had ensured that this important aspect of the social welfare system would be the subject of scrutiny and debate. In subsequent years the issue of adequacy was a feature of the wider social policy agenda and led to a growing consensus among various groups that social welfare payment rates should be related to gross average industrial earnings.

Basic income

For some time it has been suggested that the income tax and social welfare systems should be integrated so as to eliminate the need for the latter. This would involve the payment of a basic income to be granted, unconditionally, to everyone on an individual basis, and this would be paid irrespective of income from other sources. This new system, it is argued, would eliminate the poverty and unemployment traps inherent in the present systems. Because it would be neutral as to the work status of the individual, it would facilitate the free movement of persons between employment and unemployment without creating any disincentives.

Variants of this basic income have been proposed in various reports.[24] The NESC, for example, published a consultant's report on this subject in 1979 but did not recommend its adoption. The Commission on Social Welfare also examined the feasibility of its introduction but opted for reform of the existing social welfare system rather than the more radical reform inherent in the basic income proposal.

Arising from a commitment in the *Programme for Partnership Government* between the Fianna Fáil and Labour Parties in 1992 to examine the integration of the tax and social welfare codes, an expert working group was established. In their report, *Integrating Tax and Social Welfare* (1996), the expert group assessed a number of options ranging from full integration of the tax and social welfare systems in the form of a basic income to options that provided for better coordination of the systems. The expert group did not recommend the introduction of a basic income, mainly because the rate of income tax required to fund it, 68 per cent, was considered too high; this, in turn, was considered likely to have a negative impact on employment. Having examined a range of associated issues, the expert group did, however, recommend a simplification and coordination of the tax and social welfare systems.

In 1997 CORI published a study, *Pathways to a Basic Income*, in which it argued that its proposals for a basic income could be funded by a tax rate of between 44 per cent and 49 per cent. *The Irish Times* commented that:

> On the face of it, the kind of payments favoured by CORI would appear to require substantial tax increases – especially for the top 30 per cent of earners on a scale which no political party has the courage to propose at this time.[25]

Partnership 2000, agreed between government and the social partners, contained a commitment that 'a further independent appraisal of the concept of, and the full implications of, introducing a basic income payment for all citizens will be undertaken'.[26]

In keeping with this commitment a Green Paper, *Basic Income*, was published in 2002. The Green Paper outlined the essential elements of a basic income:

- It would be an unconditional amount paid by government to each individual in the state.
- The payment would be tax-free.
- All other income – for example, from a job – would be taxed.

- It would involve replacing the existing social welfare and income tax systems with a universal payment to all adults and a lesser amount to children.
- A flat rate of income tax would apply.
- A social solidarity fund would be established to compensate persons on low incomes who would lose out from the abolition of social welfare payments.

The Green Paper indicated that 'there is a considerable element of uncertainty in predicting the likely dynamic effects of the introduction of a Basic Income system'.[27]

In announcing the publication of the Green Paper, the Taoiseach, Bertie Ahern, TD, indicated that it honoured the commitment to inform and widen future public consideration of the concept. The overriding impression, however, was that publication of the Green Paper had more to do with honouring a commitment than with any intention of introducing a basic income in the future. It did not become the subject of any public debate in subsequent years. However, CORI continued to make the case for a basic income, and recommended that government should support a debate on the Green Paper and that further research should also be supported.[28]

If a basic income were to be introduced, it would be reasonable to expect that a period of economic growth, such as that which Ireland experienced for over a decade up to 2007, would present the most opportune time to do so. With the downturn in the economy, however, the prospects of even further considering the introduction of a basic income would appear to have receded.

Child income support

Child income support is an important yet complex aspect of the Irish income maintenance system. Part of the complexity stems from the fact that there are now three forms of child income support:

i.   the universal child benefit (formerly children's allowance);
ii. child dependant allowances paid to recipients of weekly social welfare payments;
iii. family income supplement.

Child benefit

Children's allowance was introduced in 1944, with the monthly allowance being paid in respect of the third and subsequent children. In introducing the legislation in the Dáil, Sean Lemass, TD, Minister for Industry and Commerce, gave the following as the rationale for the scheme:

> The basis of the argument in favour of the establishment of a children's allowance scheme is that among the many causes of want, apart from unemployment, ill-health ... there is the fact that in an economic system such as ours, where wages are related to standards of productivity, or determined by supply and demand, the amount the wage earner can obtain is frequently inadequate to provide for the reasonable requirements of a large family ... it is, I think, necessary to emphasise that the basis of the whole case for the establishment of a children's allowance service is the need of large families.[29]

Subsequently, various changes were made to the scheme and it became payable to the second child in 1952 and to the first child in 1963.

Parallel to the scheme of children's allowance was a tax allowance for each child. In 1984 the government pledged to introduce a unified system of child benefit.[30] This unified system, however, was not introduced but the tax allowance, whose value had been reduced over a period of time, was eventually abolished in 1986 and children's allowance was renamed child benefit.

One of the differences between child benefit and other social welfare payments is that it is paid monthly rather than weekly. Another difference is that changes in the rates of payment of child benefit are treated quite separately from any changes in the weekly social welfare payments.

The number of children for whom child benefit is paid has changed with changes in the number of births. Due to the fall in births in the 1980s, the number of qualified children declined considerably, from 1,187,465 in 1985 to 1,014,340 in 2001, but with the subsequent rise in births this number had increased to 1,156,917 by 2009. The number of large families in receipt of child benefit has declined; by 2009 over three-quarters (76.2 per cent) of families consisted of one or two children.

Child dependant allowance

Qualified child dependants are eligible for child dependant allowance, which is paid to recipients of weekly social welfare payments. As already noted, the Commission on Social Welfare indicated that there were thirty-six different rates of payment, which varied according to the social welfare scheme of the recipient and to the number of children in a family. It recommended that these rates be rationalised. This was implemented over a period commencing in 1988 and was completed in 2007 when a single rate for all children was introduced. The effect of this was to ensure that, irrespective of the social welfare scheme of the adult recipient, the same rate of payment would apply to all qualifying children. There was no increase in the weekly child dependant allowances between 1994 and 2007, when the single rate of €22 was introduced. In 2011 the weekly rate was €29.80.

Family income supplement

The basic objective of the family income supplement, introduced in 1984, was to increase the difference between take-home pay for those on low income and the unemployment payments that those on low pay would be entitled to if they were unemployed. In this way there is a supplement or top-up to take-home pay. At the time of the introduction of family income supplement the perception was that those with large families were only marginally better off when working on low pay by comparison with being in receipt of unemployment support payments, and thus would have little incentive to take up low-paid employment. In Budget 1983, John Bruton, TD, Minister for Finance, indicated that an estimated 20,000 families would benefit from family income supplement. By the end of 1985, after one full year in operation, only 4,664 families had availed of family income supplement. Subsequently, the scheme was widely advertised by the Department of Social Welfare, the eligibility conditions were eased and higher rates of payment were introduced. The number of recipient families has risen steadily from 6,066 in 1989 to 13,143 in 1998, and to 27,798 in 2008. Despite the increased take-up over the past two decades, research has indicated that many potential claimants have little understanding of the scheme or the eligibility requirements.[31]

A unified child income support scheme?

Ideally, the preferred system of child income support would be one that did not have regard to whether the recipient was in receipt of social welfare payments. But to move to that situation would be difficult and costly. The main cost would arise from increasing child benefit to such an extent that it would be possible to abolish child dependant allowances while at the same time ensuring that the families in receipt of them did not experience a drop in total income as a result.

The Fine Gael, Labour and Democratic Left Parties assumed office in December 1994 just as the Child Benefit Review Committee was completing its report for the outgoing government. In their joint programme, *A Government of Renewal*, the three parties pledged they would work towards a basic income system for children by systematic improvements in child benefit and the creation of a child benefit supplement to all social welfare recipients and to low- and middle-income families.

While the precise nature of the child benefit supplements was not clear, government policy in the budgets of 1995 to 1997 enhanced the value of child benefit. At the same time as the child benefit was increased substantially, the child dependant allowances were effectively frozen, with no increases from 1994 until 2007.

Child benefit under review

Child benefit has frequently been the subject of criticism on the grounds that it should be applied more selectively rather than applied to all income groups. Furthermore, the rationale for child benefit has strayed somewhat from its original purpose, and over time various policies have been ascribed to it. The Child Benefit Review Committee (1995) was of the view that child benefit fulfilled a number of roles, the most important of which were:

• assistance to all households with children in recognition of the higher costs incurred;
• the alleviation, without contributing to labour market disincentives, of household poverty associated with children.[32]

Over the past forty years there have been proposals to tax or means-test child benefit, but on each occasion there has been opposition to any change in the universal nature of the payment. In 1969 Charles Haughey, TD, Minister for Finance, proposed a means test but this was not implemented. In 1978 the government Green Paper *Development for Full Employment* proposed taxing child benefit, but this was abandoned in face of widespread opposition. In Budget 1989 Albert Reynolds, TD, Minister for Finance, referred to the unselective nature of child benefit and indicated that the government wished to target resources by confining the payment to families with incomes below a certain level. Nothing became of this proposal either.

An argument against any targeting of child benefit in the past was that it was essentially a payment to mothers for whom it may be the only source of independent income. More recently, child benefit has been viewed as a means of helping to relieve child poverty and of contributing towards the cost of childcare. The childcare issue gained particular prominence in the late 1990s as more women with children participated in the work force. While various suggestions were made as to how this situation might be addressed, the government's decision was to provide capital for the expansion of the number of childcare places rather than directly subsidise the cost of such care to parents through tax allowances. Allied with this, however, was an unprecedented increase in child benefit payments by the Fianna Fáil/Progressive Democrat Government of 1997–2002. During that period the payment for the first and second child increased from €38.09 to €117.60, and the payment for the third and subsequent children increased from €49.52 to €147.30. But the confused purpose of child benefit was evident in Budget 2001 when Charlie McCreevy, TD, Minister for Finance, referred to the diversity of views held in relation to the childcare issue and stated that the government's objective was to offer real choice to parents. According to the minister, the substantial increases in child benefit would therefore help all parents with the cost of rearing their children and represent a major move towards ending child poverty. In other words, the policy was that child benefit would serve a dual purpose: to deal with the costs of childcare and the relief of child poverty.

With the deterioration in public finances in 2008, child benefit once more became a focus for attention. The cost of child benefit in 2008 was €2.5 billion, or 14 per cent of total expenditure, including administration, on social welfare schemes. In the supplementary budget of April 2009 the Minister for Finance, Brian Lenihan, TD, stated that the government did not think that it was fair to pay the same level of benefit to everyone irrespective of their level of income, and he indicated that child benefit would be means-tested or taxed in 2010.

The McCarthy report (2009) indicated that a large saving could be achieved by introducing a standard rate for all children without having to resort to taxing or means-testing, and that this would avoid the legal and administrative problems inherent in either of these two approaches.[33] In Budget 2010 the Minister for Finance, Brian Lenihan, TD, indicated that for 'legal and logistical reasons' it was not possible to either means-test or tax child benefit.[34] Instead, the payment levels were cut across the board with compensatory increases for those on weekly social welfare payments, through the child dependant allowance, and for those on family income supplement. There was a further reduction in 2011 without any compensation for families on weekly social welfare payments.

Reducing expenditure on income maintenance schemes

By 2009 total expenditure on social welfare schemes amounted to €20.5 billion and accounted for 38 per cent of gross current government expenditure. Against a background of deterioration in public finances arising from the fall in GNP, the government embarked on measures to reduce public expenditure across various services. In Budget 2010 Brian Lenihan, TD, Minister for Finance, stated:

> Over the last twelve years, we have increased pension rates by about 120 per cent, unemployment benefits by almost 130 per cent and Child Benefit payments by over 330 per cent. The cost of living has increased by about 40 per cent over the same period. We extended coverage, removed barriers, and increased entitlements such that the level and extent of social support payments has been transformed beyond recognition.[35]

This was a prelude to his announcement of reductions in weekly social welfare payments and in the monthly child benefit. In 2010 reductions of approximately 4 per cent were made in all weekly social welfare payments, with the exception of the state pension. This was the first time in decades that there were no annual increases in weekly payments and that there were also reductions in these payments. Further reductions in weekly payments were made in 2011, with state pensions once again exempted. It is highly probable that further reductions or, at the very least, a freezing of payment levels are likely over the term of the *National Recovery Plan 2011–2014*. The plan provides that social welfare expenditure will be reduced by €2.8 billion. This reduction is to be achieved by a combination of 'greater control measures, labour activation, structural reform measures, a fall in the Live Register and, if necessary, further rate reductions'.[36]

Notes

1. See D. Farley, *Social Insurance and Social Assistance in Ireland* (Institute of Public Administration, Dublin, 1964); Commission on Social Welfare, *Report of the Commission on Social Welfare* (Stationery Office, Dublin, 1986), Chapter 2; M. Cousins, *The Birth of Social Welfare in Ireland, 1922–1952* (Four Courts Press, Dublin, 2003).

2. For an excellent account of the evolution of the income support aspect of the Poor Law system, see S. O'Cinneide, 'The development of home assistance service', *Administration*, Vol. 17, No. 3 (1969).

3. See C. Carney, 'A case study in social policy – the non-contributory old age pension', *Administration*, Vol. 33, No. 4. (1985), pp. 483–527.

4. S. O'Grada, '"The greatest blessing of all": the old age pension in Ireland', *Past and Present*, No. 175, p. 132.

5. See S. O'Cinneide, *A Law for the Poor* (Institute of Public Administration, Dublin, 1970).

6. Quoted in P. Kaim-Caudle, *Comparative Social Policy and Social Security: A Ten Country Study* (Martin Robertson, London, 1973), p. 167.
7. Government of Ireland, *White Paper on Social Security* (Stationery Office, Dublin, 1949), p. 37.
8. Government of Ireland, *Budget 1975* (Stationery Office, Dublin, 1975), p. 23.
9. Farley, op. cit., p. 71.
10. Social Welfare Appeals Office, *Annual Report 2009* (Social Welfare Appeals Office, Dublin, 2010), p. 7.
11. *Relate*, Vol. 9, No. 4 (National Social Service Board, Dublin, 1982), p. 4.
12. Commission on Social Welfare, op. cit., pp. 193–4.
13. Dáil Éireann, 'Vote 48: social welfare (revised estimate)', 20 June 1986, *Dáil Debates*, Vol. 368, No. 834.
14. Social Welfare Appeals Office, *Annual Report 2007* (Social Welfare Appeals Office, Dublin, 2008), p. 15.
15. T. Callan et al., *A Review of the Commission on Social Welfare's Minimum Adequate Income* (Economic and Social Research Institute, Dublin, 1996).
16. Government of Ireland, *Sharing in Progress: National Anti-Poverty Strategy* (Stationery Office, Dublin, 1997), p. 13.
17. National Pensions Board, *Securing Retirement Income: National Pensions Policy Initiative* (National Pensions Board, Dublin, 1998), p. 3.
18. Government of Ireland, *Programme for Prosperity and Fairness* (Stationery Office, Dublin, 2000), p. 80.
19. Government of Ireland, *Final Report of the Social Welfare Benchmarking and Indexation Group* (Stationery Office, Dublin, 2001), p. 61.
20. Government of Ireland, *Building an Inclusive Society: Review of the National Anti-Poverty Strategy under the Programme for Prosperity and Fairness* (Stationery Office, Dublin, 2002), p. 9.
21. Department of the Taoiseach, *Towards 2016: Ten-Year Framework Social Partnership Agreement 2006–2015* (Stationery Office, Dublin, 2006), p. 52.
22. Conference of Religious of Ireland, *Socio-Economic Review 2008: Planning for Progress and Fairness* (Conference of Religious of Ireland, Dublin, 2008), p. 55.
23. Department of Social and Family Affairs, *National Pensions Framework* (Stationery Office, Dublin, 2010), p. 19.
24. For an analysis of the various proposals on a basic income in Ireland, see A. McCashin, *Social Security in Ireland* (Gill and Macmillan, Dublin, 2004), pp. 309–12.
25. 'Paying for social justice', *The Irish Times*, 8 April 1997.
26. Government of Ireland, *Partnership 2000 for Inclusion, Employment and Competitiveness* (Stationery Office, Dublin, 1996), p. 23.
27. Department of the Taoiseach, *Basic Income: A Green Paper* (Stationery Office, Dublin, 2002), p. 44.
28. Conference of Religious of Ireland, op. cit., p. 64.
29. Dáil Éireann, 'Children's Allowances Bill, 1943 – second stage', 23 November 1943, *Dáil Debates*, Vol. 92, No. 27.

30. Government of Ireland, *Building on Reality* (Stationery Office, Dublin, 1984), p. 105.
31. Department of Social and Family Affairs, *Family Income Supplement Uptake Research* (Department of Social and Family Affairs, Dublin, 2008).
32. Department of Social Welfare, *Child Benefit Review: Report to the Minister for Social Welfare* (Department of Social Welfare, Dublin, 1995), p. 4.
33. Government of Ireland, *Report of the Special Group on Public Service Numbers and Expenditure Programmes* (Stationery Office, Dublin, 2009), pp. 189–90.
34. B. Lenihan, *Financial Statement of the Minister for Finance Mr Brian Lenihan TD, 9 December 2009*, available at http://www.budget.gov.ie/Budgets/2010/FinancialStatement.aspx [accessed 20 April 2011].
35. Ibid.
36. Government of Ireland, *The National Recovery Plan 2011–2014* (Stationery Office, Dublin, 2010), p. 11.

3

Housing

Introduction

One of the central features of the Irish housing system is the predominance of owner-occupied or privately owned dwellings. This is due in part to the promotion of owner-occupation by successive governments through various measures. There has been state intervention in housing since the middle of the last century, and such intervention is now very extensive.

At a general level it can be said that government intervention in the housing area is necessary to ensure that certain standards are maintained, that environmental interests are protected and that persons without sufficient income are provided with housing. The provision of adequate housing for all has been a central aim of government policy and has been enunciated in various policy documents over time. The core objective is:

> To enable every household to have available an affordable dwelling of good quality, suited to its needs, in a good environment and, as far as possible, at the tenure of its choice.[1]

The general strategy for realising this aim is that those who can afford to provide for their housing needs should do so through either home ownership or private rented accommodation, and that those who cannot afford housing from their own resources should have access to social housing provided by local authorities or to income support for securing accommodation in the private rented sector.

Administration

The Department of the Environment, Community and Local Government, established in 1924 (as the Department of Local Government and

51

Public Health), is the central authority responsible for national housing policy. It exercises a general supervision over the social, financial and technical aspects of local authority and private housing, and is responsible for the distribution of most of the capital and subsidies for housing provided by the state. Housing policy is implemented in conjunction with local authorities throughout the country. The department also promotes legislation on housing, coordinates the activities of local authorities, has responsibility for legislation on building standards, and liaises with a number of other government departments concerned with aspects of housing.

Evolution of policy and output

In this section the main trends in housing development for over a century are outlined.[2]

Housing prior to 1921

Urban housing
The first series of legislative measures dealing with housing was passed in the 1850s and 1860s. While these and other acts passed in the 1870s provided a legislative basis for a housing drive, little was accomplished except in Dublin city. The Housing of the Working Classes Act, 1890, was a more comprehensive measure that repealed practically all the preceding acts and represented an attempt to deal with the problems of urban housing and slum clearance. The next important piece of legislation dealing with urban housing was the Housing of the Working Classes (Ireland) Act, 1908. This act set up the first subsidy system for urban housing. The Irish Housing Fund was established, a sum of £180,000 was invested, and the income was directed towards the cost of dwellings built after the 1908 act. By 1919, however, only 8,700 houses had been provided under the 1908 act.

The housing situation in Dublin had deteriorated through the latter part of the nineteenth century as former Georgian houses were subdivided into multiple single-room dwellings to house low-income families. These became tenements, and certain districts in the city became 'slumlands'. By 1900 almost 22,000 families (representing one-third of the city's population) lived in single-room dwellings condemned by Dublin Corporation as unfit for occupation.[3]

In 1921 the problem of urban housing still remained unsolved. A survey of housing needs in municipal areas in 1919 estimated that 46,416 houses were required, one-third of them to replace inhabited houses unfit and incapable of being made fit for human habitation.

Rural housing

The first attempts to improve rural housing in Ireland were aimed at getting landlords to take the initiative in building cottages for their own tenants. The Dwellings for Labouring Classes (Ireland) Act, 1860, enabled landlords to obtain loans for the provision of cottages.

The Census of 1881 indicated that there were 215,000 cottiers (landless farm labourers), and the majority of dwellings in which they lived were single-room cabins with mud walls and thatched roofs. Under the Labourers (Ireland) Act, 1883, housing operations were carried out locally by the rural sanitary authorities, the Boards of Guardians, under the general supervision of the Local Government Board for Ireland. The provision of cottages was no longer left to the initiative of individual landlords or farmers. By 1921 approximately 48,000 cottages had been built.

Fahey has indicated that, for decades, the primary focus was on the improvement of rural public housing for farm labourers and that this was a direct link with the process of agrarian reform that ultimately led to tenant farmers becoming owners of land. It was only later (especially with the Housing Act, 1908) that corresponding, though less generous, measures were introduced for the hitherto neglected urban dwellers.[4]

Private housing

The demand for private dwellings was stimulated by the Small Dwellings Acquisition Act, 1899, which enabled local authorities to advance loans for the purchase of existing houses. Another source of finance for house purchase was provided by the building societies; the main piece of legislation governing these societies was passed in 1874. Banks and insurance companies also provided finance in this period. The total number of owner-occupiers at the time, however, was small, and most of the houses were purchased by investors and let to tenants. A significant development was the introduction, under the Housing Act, 1919, of a scheme of grants for persons who constructed houses in accordance with prescribed conditions. The political conditions of the time prevented the extensive use of the scheme. Nevertheless, the scheme marks one of the first steps in direct state aid to the house purchaser, a policy that was sustained throughout the rest of the century and that accounts, in part, for the relatively high proportion of owner-occupied dwellings in Ireland.

Housing in the 1920s

The first real attempt to provide houses on a large scale was made by the Free State Government, which initiated what is referred to as the 'million pound scheme'. Under this scheme local authorities were required to provide £125,000 from rates (local taxation) and to raise a further sum of £375,000 by way of short-term loans from banks, giving a total of £0.5 million. This was matched by £1 million in state aid, and enabled 2,000 houses to be built at an average total cost of £750 per house. The majority of local authority housing provided in the early years of independence was confined to Dublin and Cork.[5]

Under the Housing Act, 1924, grants were again made available to people constructing their own dwellings. This act also empowered local authorities to supplement the state grants by further grants or loans and to provide free or cheap sites for development work. In addition, it provided for the partial remission of rates (local taxation) over nineteen years on grant-aided houses. Reconstruction grants were also made available under the 1924 act.

The housing problem of urban areas, however, remained to be tackled in earnest. A survey carried out by urban authorities in 1929 indicated that almost 44,000 houses were needed, and it highlighted the need for slum clearance.

Housing in the 1930s

The main drive against slums began in the 1930s. The Housing Acts, 1931 and 1932, were particularly important, implementing the recommendations of previous commissions of enquiry on slum clearance and compulsory acquisition of land, and providing greater financial assistance to local authorities for rehousing displaced families.

The output of housing rose steadily during the 1930s, reaching a peak of 17,000 in 1938/9. Between 1931 and 1942 a total of 82,000 dwellings were built. During the same period over 11,000 condemned houses were demolished by local authorities, as well as an unknown number by individuals. This period was one of the most productive in the building of corporation houses in Dublin. The estates of the south-west, centring on Crumlin, which constitute the largest concentration of municipal housing in Dublin, were built at this time. Progress was not confined to Dublin, however, and in the main urban areas overcrowded tenement buildings were replaced by new housing on what was then the outskirts of the built-up area. In smaller towns the same process was continued, mainly in the form of new estates on the fringes.

The housing initiatives of the early 1930s and, in particular, the slum clearance that continued into the 1940s were started by the Fianna Fáil Party, which first came into power in 1932. Fahey has noted that:

> The success of this programme has since gone down in history as one of the great social achievements of the day – and incidentally also as one of the main bases for Fianna Fáil's claim to be a progressive populist party.[6]

Housing in the post-war period

During the period of World War II output of new housing sank to a low level, and only 1,300 dwellings were built in 1946.

A White Paper in 1948 contained an estimate of the number of houses needed. Despite pre-war accomplishments, it was estimated that 61,000 dwellings were required, 44,500 in urban areas and the remainder in rural areas. The major problem was in Dublin, where an estimated 23,500 dwellings were required (approximately 40 per cent of the national need).

The Housing (Amendment) Acts, 1948 to 1952, provided, among other measures, for more generous grants for private dwellings, particularly for people building dwellings for their own occupation, for higher loans to house purchasers and for the strengthening of local authority powers to deal with special housing problems. These measures had a stimulating effect on the housing programme, and in the early 1950s an annual average of 14,500 dwellings were built.

By the late 1950s, however, a downward trend was again evident. This was partly due to the belief (later established to be erroneous) that sufficient progress had been made with meeting housing needs throughout the country. It was also due to cutbacks in local authority capital expenditure on housing. In 1959 the report *Economic Development* stated:

> Private housing needs have been largely met, while local authority housing programmes have already been completed in a number of areas and are expected to be completed in all areas outside Dublin within three or four years.[7]

Between 1956 and 1958, capital expenditure on housing by public authorities was halved from £14.3 million to £7.5 million.[8] In the late 1950s the population was declining by about 10,000 annually, net outward migration was running at over 40,000 annually and some local authority housing estates were reporting vacancies. There was a dramatic rise in the number of vacancies in Dublin Corporation estates from 1954 onwards, reaching a peak of over 1,200 per year between 1958 and 1961 and rapidly declining again later in the 1960s. Output of local authority housing in Dublin declined from a high point of 2,600 in 1951 to 279 in 1961.

Housing in the 1960s

In the 1960s economic growth accelerated and this led to an upsurge in social spending. Furthermore, significant demographic changes occurred, which gave rise to an increased demand for housing, particularly in urban areas.

In 1964 a White Paper, *Housing: Progress and Prospects*, estimated that 50,000 dwellings were required to cater for existing needs and that 8,000 were required for future needs. In the following year the Ballymun housing scheme, one of the largest single housing projects in Europe at the time, was initiated with the Department of Local Government becoming directly involved in housing for the first time. The construction of over 3,000 dwelling units, the majority in high-rise tower blocks, was a formidable achievement and helped to alleviate housing needs in the Dublin area.[9]

In 1969 the government issued another White Paper, *Housing in the Seventies*, which estimated that the number of dwellings required to cater for accumulated needs was 59,000, while the annual prospective need was 9,000 for the period 1966–71 and 11,500 for the mid 1970s.

Housing in the 1970s and 1980s
During the 1960s output of housing increased steadily, and in the early 1970s increased further, reaching what was then a peak of almost 27,000 in 1975. Thereafter there was a slight decline until 1981, when almost 29,000 dwellings were built. Throughout the 1980s there was a steady decline in housing output. Much of this was accounted for by a policy to reduce investment in local authority dwellings and by the increase in emigration that led to reduced demand. In the latter part of the 1980s emigration began to rise steadily, with a net outward migration of over 40,000 in 1988 and 1989. In 1988 the number of housing units built was 15,654, the lowest for two decades.

Housing since 1990
From the beginning of the 1990s output began to steadily increase. This rate accelerated especially from the mid 1990s onwards, and record numbers were achieved in each successive year, reaching 93,419 in 2006. The number built in 2006 was over three times the number built in 1995 (30,575), just over ten years earlier, and was a figure unlikely to be achieved again for a considerable time. In the latter part of the 1990s demand far exceeded supply, leading to unprecedented increases in house prices (see later section in this chapter). This coincided with unparalleled growth in the economy, leading to, among other things, a substantial increase in employment. Output continued to rise up to 2006 before a contraction in the construction sector and a decline in demand led to a sharp drop in housing output by 2008.

The number of dwellings completed for selected years over the past four decades is set out in Table 3.1, which illustrates the large recent annual variation.

Table 3.1: *Output of dwellings, selected years, 1971–2010*

Year	Number of dwellings
1971	15,380
1975	26,892
1981	28,917
1985	23,948
1991	19,652
1995	30,575
2001	52,602
2005	76,954
2006	93,419
2008	51,724
2009	26,420
2010	14,602

Source: Annual *Housing Statistics Bulletin* (Department of the Environment, Community and Local Government).

Housing stock

The total housing stock has more than doubled (120 per cent) in the sixty years following the end of World War II. From 1991 to 2006 it increased by over two-fifths when approximately 456,000 units were added to the housing stock, bringing the total to almost 1.5 million. A feature of the housing stock is the dominance of the owner-occupied or home-ownership sector, which increased its share of the total stock up to the early part of the twenty-first century. The local authority rented sector has declined, and the private rented sector, having declined for several decades, has recently reversed that trend (Table 3.2). The decline of the

Table 3.2: *Tenure structure of housing, selected years, 1946–2006*

Sector	1946	1971	1991	2006
Owner-occupied (%)	52.7	68.8	80.2	74.7
Local authority rented (%)	16.5	15.5	9.7	7.2
Private rented (%)	26.1	13.3	7.1	9.9
Rented voluntary body (%)	–	–	–	3.5
Other (%)	4.7	2.4	3.0	4.7
Total (%)	100.0	100.0	100.0	100.0
No. of housing units (000s)	662	726	1,006	1,462

Source: Census of population (Central Statistics Office).

local authority rented sector is partly accounted for by the relatively high volume of sales of dwellings to tenants, which has brought them into the owner-occupied sector (see later section in this chapter), and by the relatively low output of new dwellings in this sector for the past few decades.

A result of the recent increased output is that the housing stock is relatively new, with 45 per cent built in the 25-year period from 1981 to 2006.

Planning housing need

Planning future housing needs over an extended period can be a difficult exercise because so many factors may affect the outcome. One of the more important factors is demographic change and especially changes in household-forming age groups. Another important factor is the state of the economy and employment prospects, which in turn will have an impact on either immigration or outmigration.

The *National Development Plan 2000–2006* (1999) estimated that 500,000 houses would be required over the period from 2000 to 2010 to meet demand arising from the increased proportion of the population in the household-formation age, falling household sizes, immigration and obsolescence.[10] The plan noted that Ireland's housing stock, at 327 per thousand population, was the lowest in the EU, where the average was 450 per thousand. With the downturn in the economy since 2007 the demand for housing has slowed considerably and, consequently, the output of housing has also declined.

Tenure sectors

In this section the salient features of the different tenure sectors (owner-occupied, local authority and private rented) are outlined.

Owner-occupied sector

By comparison with other European countries Ireland has a relatively high proportion of owner-occupied dwellings.[11] This is due to a number of factors. Chief among these are historical and cultural factors and the schemes of state aid to the owner-occupier. It has been suggested that the legacy of the land-reform measures in the late nineteenth century and early decades of the twentieth century has influenced the pattern of owner-occupation.[12] During that period farmers, who had been tenants of their land, became owner-occupiers.

While it is difficult to measure the extent of the influence of cultural factors on the level of owner-occupation in Ireland, there is little doubt that state intervention has also contributed to Ireland's relatively high proportion of owner-occupiers through a system of financial aid, part of which originated in the latter part of the nineteenth century. This system has included grants, loans provided by local authorities and income tax relief on the interest element of mortgages.

Grants

Since the introduction of grants for the provision of new dwellings in 1919, the grant levels have been increased on several occasions and the system has been altered to respond to the needs of particular sections of the community. In 1977, for example, all previous grant schemes (state and local authority) were rescinded and a new £1,000 grant for first-time buyers of new houses was introduced. In 1985 this grant was increased to £2,000, and to £3,000 in 1993. There was no further increase in the grant, and in 2002 its abolition was announced amid public and political disquiet.

Other forms of grants have been made available in recent decades; for example, the mortgage subsidy scheme and a surrender grant of £5,000 available to local authority tenants who moved into the private sector to purchase a dwelling.

While the grant system has been curtailed in recent years, the provision of such grants in the past undoubtedly helped many people to meet the costs of buying or providing a house, and also provided a stimulus to the production of houses. It could also be argued that, for long periods, the grants system was designed as much to help the building industry as to help persons to acquire houses of their own.

Grants have also been provided from time to time by the state for the reconstruction and improvement of existing houses. These grants have usually operated for certain defined periods. The most recent scheme was introduced in 1985 but was terminated in 1987. Grants for the reconstruction or refurbishment of dwellings for people with disabilities remain.

Income tax relief

The interest element of a mortgage is allowable against income tax, subject to certain limits. This concession to house purchase is a consequence of the income tax code and was not intended as a specific housing subsidy. Prior to 1982 tax relief was available on all forms of interest, but it was then confined to housing and a few other purposes. Over the period from 1992 to 1997 the value of tax relief was gradually reduced to the standard rate of tax (20 per cent in 2003), thus altering the situation whereby those on the highest rate benefited most. The income mortgage-interest tax relief has been subject to various changes in recent years to reflect the changed nature of house prices and the mortgage situation. Budget 2009 provided that relief for first-time buyers would end after seven years.

Other aids
Apart from the grants and the system of tax relief there are a number of other means designed to help owner-occupation. First-time buyers of a new house have not been liable for stamp duty, and in the case of second-hand houses liability for stamp duty only occurred when the price exceeded a certain ceiling, which had been altered to reflect changed circumstances in the housing market.

Financing of private housing
In addition to state and local authority investment in housing, a number of other agencies are involved in the provision of house-purchase loans. Of these, the building societies have played the most important role. Up to the 1970s assurance companies also had a substantial role to play, but their contribution in this area is now almost negligible. In the supplementary budget of 1975 the Minister for Finance, Richie Ryan, TD, directed the associated banks to provide house-purchase loans totalling £40 million over the following two years. This directive was intended to provide a stimulus to the construction industry during a difficult period, as well as providing an additional source of loans to the house purchaser. The banks, while exceeding the figure stipulated by the minister, continued to provide loans beyond this period, and they are now the main source of finance for house purchasers. Up to the 1970s local authorities were also an important source of finance, especially for persons on low or relatively low incomes, but their role as loan providers has declined sharply since then.

Social and affordable housing
The main type of support for those unable to acquire or maintain adequate housing from their own resources is rental accommodation provided mainly by local authorities and also the voluntary and cooperative sector. For several decades the response of local authorities to housing need was to acquire land for development and build new houses for prospective tenants. A fundamental change occurred in the 1990s, and the role of local authorities in meeting housing need became more diverse following the introduction of new policy measures under *A Plan for Social Housing* (see later section in this chapter). Subsequently,

affordable housing supports measures were also introduced to enable persons on moderate incomes to become homeowners. There are now a variety of measures in place for the provision of social and affordable housing. Some of the key features of these various supports are considered in the following sections.

Local authority rented sector
Local authorities provide dwellings mainly for renting to people living in unfit and overcrowded conditions and to those whose income does not allow them to provide adequate accommodation for themselves.

Output of local authority housing
As a proportion of total housing output, the output of local authorities has fluctuated over several decades. In 1949/50 local authority output constituted two-thirds of the total output of 8,113 dwellings. In subsequent years the output constituted one-fifth to one-quarter of the total. All that was to change from the late 1980s onwards as the output began a downward spiral. In 1989, when investment in local authority dwellings was scaled down considerably, output accounted for as little as 4.4 per cent of 18,068 dwellings built. Throughout the 1990s annual output was consistently less than 10 per cent. As housing needs increased in the latter part of the 1990s due to rising house prices, and as the total number of dwellings built began to rise to unprecedented levels, the output of local authority dwellings plummeted even further. In 2006, when total housing output reached a peak of 93,419, only 4,986 local authority dwellings were built (representing 5.3 per cent of the total). In 2008, however, output of local authority completions was maintained while there was a collapse in the number of private dwellings, with the result that the 4,905 local authority houses built accounted for 9.5 per cent of the total of 51,724 dwellings built.

The stock of local authority dwellings available for renting has fluctuated over the past few decades (see Table 3.3). The fact that the stock has not increased continuously over that period is mainly due to the sales of local authority dwellings to tenants (see later section on tenant purchase), thereby removing those dwellings from the stock available for renting. The decline was especially noticeable from the late 1980s due to a particularly attractive purchase scheme introduced in 1988 that resulted in over 28,000 dwellings being taken out of the rented category. It is also due to the relatively low output of local authority dwellings, by historical standards, from the mid 1990s onwards. In recent years the stock has increased so that by 2008 the number (118,396) had slightly exceeded that reached prior to the decline in the late 1980s.

Table 3.3: *Number of local authority dwellings available for renting, selected years, 1975–2008*

Year	No. of dwellings
1975	105,000
1981	104,000
1985	114,364
1988	116,270
1992	93,283
1995	97,219
1999	99,163
2001	102,789
2008	118,396

Source: Annual *Housing Statistics Bulletin* (Department of the Environment, Community and Local Government).

Financing
Prior to 1988 local authorities obtained loans from the Local Loans Fund and were liable for the loan charges (interest and capital repayments). However, their increasing inability to meet these charges and the consequent increase in subsidy to them from the Department of the Environment to meet these charges led to a change in 1988. Since then, capital for the house-building programme of local authorities is made by way of grants rather than fully subsidised loans.

Rents
The majority of local authority dwellings are now let on what is termed a differential rent system, i.e. a rent related to household income. The letting of dwellings at fixed rents was a feature of local authority housing in the past, and the tenants' capacity to pay was not a consideration, irrespective of changes in household income. In 1934 income-related rents were first introduced in Cork city, the rent being based on one-sixth of family income less certain deductions and subject to review with changes in that income. Since 1967 all new lettings of local authority dwellings throughout the country have been let on the differential rent system. In general, minimum rents and, in some cases, maximum rents are set for each dwelling; within this range the tenant pays a proportion of income in rent. If household income increases, so does the rent (up to the maximum set), and if household income is reduced, so also is the rent (down to the minimum set). Rent is normally based on a percentage of the principal earner's assessable income (less certain allowances), while income of other household members may also be taken into account up to a certain limit. In practice, there may be considerable variation

between local authorities throughout the country in the detailed operation of the differential rent system, with, for example, some having abolished a maximum upper limit on rent.

Prior to 1973 differential rent schemes varied from one local authority area to another, principally in regard to allowances deductible from household income. In 1973, however, following a prolonged strike by the National Association of Tenants' Organisations, a new national differential rents scheme was introduced. In effect, subsequent reviews were initiated and the Department of the Environment established the terms of schemes. In 1983 the Minister for the Environment, Liam Kavanagh, TD, decreed that local authorities should themselves decide on the basis of the rent schemes.

Since the introduction nationally of differential rents in 1967, the proportion of local authority dwellings let on these rents has increased steadily, as those on fixed rents were phased out. In 1966/7 just over half (54 per cent) of local authority dwellings were let on fixed rents. By 1990, however, 96 per cent were let on differential rents. No comparable figures have been published in recent years, but it can be assumed that virtually all tenants now pay differential rents.

The total annual rental income has not met the total annual cost of maintenance and management of the local authority stock. Rental income as a proportion of maintenance and management costs was 63 per cent in 1994 and 77 per cent in 2004, the most recent year for which published statistics on the two are available. In 2004 rental income was €202.38 million and maintenance and management costs were €263.22 million.

The average weekly rent of local authority dwellings – €46.85 in 2008 – is relatively low (Table 3.4). Part of the reason for this is that, over a period of time, the higher-income tenants have availed themselves of schemes to purchase their dwellings. As a result, the population in the local authority sector is comprised mainly of either low-income earners or recipients of social welfare payments. Consequently, because of the differential rent scheme, where rent is related to income, few are paying the maximum rents. The report of the *Dublin Lord Mayor's Commission on Housing* (1993) estimated that 80 per cent of the 31,000 rent-paying tenants in the housing stock of the Dublin Corporation area were dependent on social welfare payments as their main source of income. It is likely that a broadly similar situation pertains in other local authority areas throughout the country. The NESC report *Housing in Ireland: Performance and Policy* (2004) noted that 'public tenants have consisted of an increasingly marginalised group'.[13]

Table 3.4: *Rental income of local authority dwellings, selected years, 1975–2008*

	Annual rental income (€ m)	Average weekly rent (€)
1975	11.01	2.02
1980	26.90	5.04
1985	53.41	8.77
1990	57.72	11.76
1995	80.90	16.00
1998	101.49	19.66
1999	109.63	21.26
2001	141.21	26.33
2008	n/a	46.85

Source: Annual *Housing Statistics Bulletin* (Department of the Environment, Community and Local Government).

Tenant purchase schemes
Despite the output of local authority dwellings over several decades, there has not been a commensurate increase in the stock of dwellings, i.e. the total number available for letting (see Table 3.3). This is due to the fact that, since the 1930s, local authorities have operated purchase schemes to allow tenants to purchase their dwellings with a discount on the market or replacement value of the house. For example, between 1970 and 1979 a total of 60,630 local authority dwellings were built while 60,026 were sold through purchase schemes, so there was no net gain to the stock. During the early 1980s the trend was reversed as building exceeded sales. In 1988 a specially attractive purchase scheme was introduced that allowed 40 per cent discount on the market value of a local authority dwelling (50 per cent in the case of those built prior to 1961), together with a £2,000 grant available to purchasers of new houses. The scheme was popularly known within civil service and local authority circles as 'the sale of the century'. It resulted in the sale of 28,241 local authority dwellings between 1989 and 1992. Over the same period the number built was 5,883. The rate of acquisition has slowed since the early 1990s, and there is now an annual number of between 1,000 and 1,500. As already noted in Table 3.3, the net effect of the special purchase scheme in the late 1980s together with a low output of local authority dwellings was to reduce the national stock available for letting.

The total number of local authority dwellings built up to 2008 was 369,247, while the number purchased by tenants was 246,342, representing two-thirds (66.7 per cent) of the total local authority housing stock (Table 3.5).

Table 3.5: *Local authority housing, built and sold*

	Built	Sold
Pre-1964	178,300	74,400
1964–2008	190,947	171,942
Total	369,247	246,342

Sources: T. Fahey, 'Social housing in Ireland: the need for an expanded role?', in *Irish Banking Review* (Autumn 1999), p. 27; Annual *Housing Statistics Bulletin* (Department of the Environment, Community and Local Government).

For several decades, purchase schemes were introduced periodically on a once-off basis with a closing date for applications. From 1994, however, there has been an open-ended scheme in operation so that tenants may apply at any stage. Under the terms of that scheme, a tenant who had been in occupation for over one year could opt to purchase. From the market value of the house there was a discount of 3 per cent per annum for each year of tenancy up to a maximum of 30 per cent, i.e. ten years' tenancy. Budget 2011 provided for a short-term improvement to the scheme that allowed for the discount to be applied to fifteen years' tenancy, resulting in a maximum 45 per cent discount. This would be of benefit to an estimated 45,000 tenancies in place for ten years or more. It was also intimated that the tenant purchase scheme would be terminated and replaced by a new incremental purchase scheme.

The sale of local authority dwellings over a period of time has helped to account for the high proportion of owner-occupied dwellings, but it is a system that has met with some criticism. On the one hand it has been argued that the capacity of local authorities to meet housing needs would be improved in the long run if much less of the stock was sold to tenants and if such sales were at less generous discounts. On the other hand the case has been made that the sale of local authority dwellings encourages better maintenance and improvement of individual dwellings, and therefore of the housing stock; it provides a pool of reasonably priced houses suitable to the needs of first-time purchasers and reduces the maintenance and management burden on the local authorities.[14] Since rental income does not meet total housing maintenance and management costs for local authorities it was once suggested that it would make financial sense for the state to give away the entire local authority stock to tenants free of charge and actually save money in the process.[15]

Priority in letting of dwellings

Prior to the passing of the Housing Act, 1988, local authorities had to establish a scheme of priority in the letting of dwellings so that families or persons most in need of housing received prompt attention. Overall priority was given to families living in dangerous premises, families who became homeless through emergency situations such as fire or flood, families who required housing on medical grounds and families evicted or displaced from areas required for redevelopment.

Some local authorities operate a points system in order to establish priority. In practice, this would apply mainly in the larger urban areas. Up to relatively recently, the highest number of points was generally allocated to those families living in unfit or overcrowded dwellings.

Under the Housing Act, 1988, local authorities are obliged to assess the extent of need for local authority accommodation and to revise their scheme of letting priorities. The aim of the scheme of priorities is to ensure equal opportunity for different categories of need in relation to housing accommodation. The Housing Act, 1988, stipulated that the needs of homeless persons should be provided for. In order to ensure equality of treatment a local authority can set aside a proportion of the dwellings available for renting to particular categories of people, including homeless persons.

Waiting lists

Waiting lists, based on an assessment of housing need carried out by local authorities, have now become an established feature of social housing policy. Between 1981 and 1988 the total number of households on local authority waiting lists fell from 27,000 to 17,700.[16] This decline in need accounts in part for the decline in capital expenditure on local authority housing and the decline in output of local authority dwellings during this period.

In 1989 there was an upturn in the numbers on the waiting lists, and the first assessment of housing needs under the Housing Act, 1988, indicated that 19,376 households (including the homeless and Travellers) qualified for local authority housing. With one exception, each subsequent triennial assessment has indicated an inexorable rise in the waiting list numbers (Table 3.6). By 2002 the numbers had reached 48,413 (an increase of 76 per cent over 1996). Following a drop in numbers in 2005 there was a sharp increase again by 2008. Ironically, this demand for social housing occurred against a background of unprecedented growth in the economy and record levels of total housing output.

In each of the assessments, households are categorised by need. In 1989 and 1991 almost half the households were living in overcrowded or unfit conditions. By 2002, however, the proportions in these combined categories had declined to about 25 per cent (although the actual

Table 3.6: *Assessment of housing needs, selected years, 1989–2008*

Year	Households
1989	19,376
1993	28,624
1996	27,427
1997	39,176
2002	48,413
2005	43,684
2008	56,249

Sources: Department of the Environment, Heritage and Local Government, *A Plan for Social Housing* (Department of the Environment, Heritage and Local Government, Dublin, 1991); Annual *Housing Statistics Bulletin* (Department of the Environment, Community and Local Government).

numbers were far higher than in 1989 or 1991). Affordability became an important issue from the mid 1990s onwards. The highest proportionate increase over the 1989–2002 period was among households in the category 'unable to meet the costs of existing accommodation', which increased from 15 per cent of the total in 1989 to 44 per cent in 2002, and to 57 per cent in 2005.

The factors accounting for the substantial increase in the numbers on the waiting lists for local authority housing include the decline in output of local authority dwellings during the 1990s, the unprecedented rise in house prices from the mid 1990s and the consequent increase in rents in the private rented sector. All of these factors combined to swell the numbers of those unable to provide housing from their own resources.

Voluntary and cooperative housing
The provision of social housing has traditionally been mainly the preserve of local authorities, but voluntary housing activity has grown in importance in recent years to provide rental accommodation for low-income families and for vulnerable people with special needs.

Over the past few decades attention has begun to focus on the issue of accommodation for persons with special needs, such as older people and people with disabilities. This particular type of housing need has been met largely by housing and cooperative organisations providing housing on a non-profit basis. It had been pointed out that Ireland had not shared in the development of the social housing movement which had characterised many European countries and that state support for social housing organisations has been a peripheral aspect of housing policy.[17]

It was not until the 1980s that meaningful funding support became available for voluntary housing activity. Local authorities, in conjunction with the Department of Environment, Community and Local Government, provide support under two separate schemes: the capital assistance scheme and the rental subsidy scheme.

The capital assistance scheme was introduced in 1984 to assist approved voluntary housing associations with the capital funding cost of housing projects for certain categories of persons with special housing needs. Under the scheme, 80 per cent of the capital cost of building or renovating a property for the accommodation in self-contained units for older people and people with disabilities was provided. Subsequently, the scheme was extended to include projects for homeless persons and the level of funding was also increased. The housing associations are responsible for tenancy allocations in consultation with the local authorities. A minimum of 75 per cent of the houses in each project are reserved for persons whose applications for local authority housing have been approved by the local authority, for homeless persons and for local authority tenants and tenant purchasers who return their dwellings to the local authority. The remaining houses in a project are let to people nominated by the housing association. Rents are set having regard to tenants' means and the cost of managing and maintaining the dwellings.

Under the capital loan and subsidy scheme (first introduced as the rental subsidy scheme in 1991), voluntary housing bodies provide housing for renting, particularly to meet the needs of low-income families. At least three-quarters of the dwelling units in a project are let to households that have qualified for local authority housing. Rents are determined by taking account of household earnings and circumstances, and tenants of the houses are centrally involved in the management of their estates.

The Irish Council for Social Housing (ICSH), established in 1982 by housing and hostel organisations in Ireland, acts as a national representative, promotional, information and advisory federation. The ICSH represents over 300 affiliated housing associations and other voluntary organisations involved in housing or hostel services. It seeks to encourage and assist the development of a range of social housing services that complement the housing role of the local authorities and meet the different and changing needs of various groups, such as older persons, the homeless, people with disabilities and families on low incomes.

There are just over 600 voluntary housing associations with approved status from the Department of the Environment, Community and Local Government. However, there is considerable variation among them in the scale of activity. A few large associations, such as Respond! Housing Association and Clúid Housing Association, operate at national level, while a large number of small locality-based associations have provided schemes in towns and villages throughout the country. These associations have provided housing units for a variety of low-income or socially vulnerable groups. While capital assistance is available to social housing organisations, they are responsible for the ongoing running costs such as maintenance, management and social support. These organisations are now an integral part of the social housing sector and play an important role in the provision of rental accommodation in conjunction with local authorities. In 2008 the output from the voluntary housing sector amounted to 1,896 units, or just under 4.0 per cent of total housing output.

Affordable housing
As house prices escalated during the 1990s the problem of access to home ownership became more acute for many. The term 'affordability' assumed greater importance in housing policy, and was also significantly evident in the categories of need in the triennial housing needs assessments by the early 2000s. Affordable houses are those subsidised by the state for eligible first-time buyers who lack the resources to buy on the open market. By 2009 there were four different types of affordable housing schemes: the shared ownership scheme, the affordable housing scheme (1999), the scheme under Part V of the Planning and Development Acts and the affordable housing initiative. While the result was an apparently confusing set of schemes, with each scheme having a different provenance and different procurement system, the main purpose was to increase the supply of affordable housing.

Shared ownership scheme (1991)
Persons in need of housing and who satisfy an income test may be eligible for the shared ownership scheme, which was introduced as one of the elements in *A Plan for Social Housing* (1991). The scheme involves the purchase of a new or second-hand house with the purchaser initially taking at least a 40 per cent stake and renting the remainder from the local authority. The purchaser pays a mortgage for the part they own and pays rent to the local authority for the other part, with a view to taking full ownership of the house.

Affordable housing scheme (1999)
In an attempt to deal with the affordability issue, local authorities provide new houses at a discounted price on their own lands under the affordable

housing scheme. A site subsidy is available from the Department of the Environment, Community and Local Government. Eligibility for this scheme is similar to that for the shared ownership scheme. Procurement under this scheme was acknowledged to be 'a lengthy process, taking at least four to six years from initial concept through to the delivery of completed units'.[18]

Part V affordable housing (2000)
A further affordable housing measure was provided for in the Planning and Development Act, 2000, whereby developers were obliged to provide 20 per cent of dwellings in any development for social housing. This had proved to be a contentious issue and the bill was referred by the President, Mary McAleese, to the Supreme Court for judgement on its constitutionality. The Supreme Court ruled in favour of the section.

The 20 per cent measure did not meet with an enthusiastic response from developers or from potential purchasers of private dwellings who did not favour 'mixed' housing schemes. By the end of 2002 the government was obliged to amend the legislation to allow a more flexible response by developers towards meeting their requirements. The options include the provision of new units on a different site to that of private housing, land swaps with the local authority or the payment of a financial contribution to the local authority for failing to meet their obligations.

Eligibility for the scheme is based on applicants who are in need of accommodation but whose income is not adequate to meet the mortgage repayments on a market-value house.

Affordable housing initiative (2003)
The affordable housing initiative was introduced under *Sustaining Progress: Social Partnership Agreement 2003–2005* (2003) to meet the needs of those who would formerly have been able to purchase a house but who found themselves priced out of the market. The eligibility conditions are the same as those that apply under the Part V scheme. One of the key elements of the initiative was to tap into an additional source of public lands, owned by state bodies, to compensate for the decline in local authority resources, which had been used up under the 1999 scheme. In view of the particular issues of affordability in the greater Dublin area, the Affordable Homes Partnership was established in 2005 to coordinate and accelerate measures for the delivery of affordable housing.

The annual output of houses provided under affordable housing schemes increased from 1,500 in 1994 to 3,200 in 2006. However, the contribution of each of the schemes varied over that period.[19] The take-up of the affordable housing scheme was slow in the first few years, with a total of 398 houses provided by the end of 2001, but picked up thereafter; the delivery of shared ownership housing declined from 2002, and by 2006 was almost half its 1999 level; and the Part V scheme and the affordable housing initiative began to deliver from 2005. By 2008 the total output under these schemes was over 4,500, with the largest contribution coming from the Part V scheme (Table 3.7).

Rental accommodation scheme
Recipients of social welfare payments renting in the private sector can apply for support in the form of a rent supplement under the supplementary welfare allowance (SWA) scheme, which was administered by health boards prior to the establishment of the Health Service Executive (HSE). The scheme was intended to provide short-term income support for those unable to provide from their own resources. Partly as a consequence of the decline in the provision of social housing from the 1980s onwards, the numbers in receipt of the rent supplement increased. Between 1995 and 2005 the number of rent supplement recipients increased from 32,064 to 60,176. Of particular concern was the fact that almost half the recipients were in receipt of the supplement for eighteen months or more.[20]

Against a background of rising numbers of recipients and escalating costs, a decision was taken by government in 2004 to transfer responsibility for housing SWA rent supplement recipients who were deemed to have a long-term housing need to local authorities over a four-year period. This rental accommodation scheme is a collaborative project between the Department of the Environment, Community and Local Government, local authorities, the Department of Social Protection and the community welfare service of the HSE. One of its objectives is to eliminate long-term dependency on the SWA rent supplementation scheme. The scheme is administered by local authorities and is intended to provide an additional source of good-quality rented accommodation for eligible persons.

Total provision under social and affordable housing
In 2008, the year in which the housing boom ended, the total provision under all social and affordable housing measures was 20,223, an increase of 10.3 per cent on the 2007 outturn of 18,341 (Table 3.7). The contribution of each of the different measures varied, with new house completions and the affordable housing measures accounting for almost half (46.8 per cent) of the total in 2008.

Table 3.7: *Social housing provision, 2007–08*

	2007	2008
Local authority houses		
Completions and acquired, including Part V	6,714	5,692
RAS	906	1,600
Regeneration new units	274	–
Total local authority provision	7,894	7,292
Voluntary and cooperative housing		
Capital assistance	593	914
Capital loan	699	620
Part V	393	362
Total voluntary and cooperative provision	1,685	1,896
Other social housing measures		
Vacancies in existing stock	3,350	4,342
Improvement works in lieu of rehousing	67	82
Extensions to local authority houses	254	250
Tenants transferring to RAS	1,171	1,412
Traveller accommodation new units	133	117
Traveller accommodation refurbished units	66	76
Total other social housing measures	5,041	6,279
Total assisted through social housing measures	14,620	15,467
Affordable housing		
Shared ownership	180	139
1999 affordable housing	869	756
Part V affordable housing/AHI	2,304	3,305
AHP (sales completed by AHP)	186	367
Total affordable housing measures	3,539	4,567
Mortgage allowance	182	189
Total social and affordable housing provision	18,341	20,223

RAS = Rental accommodation scheme; AHI = Affordable housing initiative; AHP = Affordable Homes Partnership.

Source: Annual *Housing Statistics Bulletin* (Department of the Environment, Community and Local Government).

Private rented sector

There had been a constant decline in the number of dwellings available for private renting up to the 1990s, when an upturn in this sector occurred. Up to 1982, a distinction could be made within the private rented sector between two categories: dwellings whose rents were controlled (restricted) and those whose rents were uncontrolled (unrestricted). While market forces largely determined the rents of tenants in uncontrolled dwellings, rents were controlled for certain dwellings under various Rent Restrictions Acts, commencing in 1915. The categories of dwellings excluded from rent control were complex but, for example, all furnished lettings and dwellings built since 1941 were excluded.[21]

In 1982 the High Court ruled that sections of the Rent Restrictions Acts were unconstitutional. This decision was appealed to the Supreme Court where the decision of the High Court was upheld. As a result of this, the government was obliged to introduce the Housing Act, 1982, in order to protect the interests of tenants in dwellings that had been subject to rent control. The act provided for security of tenure for existing tenants and also provided a mechanism by which the rents could be reviewed. If landlord and tenant agreed on any increase in rent then there would not be any intervention by the state; otherwise the rent could be established by a district court. For various reasons, this court system was found to be unsatisfactory and was replaced by rent tribunals in 1983.

In order to avoid any hardship that could arise for tenants faced with a substantial increase in rent following decontrol, the Department of Social Welfare introduced a special measure – the rent allowance scheme. This allowance was confined to tenants, mostly older people, in the former rent-controlled dwellings, and was subject to a means test, the maximum allowance being the difference between the old and the new rent. Over the years the number of recipients of this allowance has gradually declined, from 1,348 in 1986 to 192 in 2009.

The general decline in private rented dwellings throughout much of the twentieth century inevitably meant that the needs and potential of this sector were neglected in housing policy. It was not until the 1980s that this was highlighted:

> The Irish private rented sector remains virtually unregulated; its tenants are afforded less protection than any other such group in Europe – and less state subsidies.[22]

For some time, Threshold, a voluntary organisation providing a service for those in the private rented sector, highlighted the lack of government policy in this area. In 1982 it published *Private Rented: The Forgotten Sector*, and it consistently argued, for example, that tenants should have greater security of tenure and that minimum standards of accommodation should be introduced.[23]

In response to these demands, a number of changes were announced in *A Plan for Social Housing* and provided for in the Housing Miscellaneous Provisions Act, 1992. Subsequently, regulations were introduced under this act for rent books (1993), standards for rented dwellings (1993) and registration of rented houses (1996). Together, these changes constituted a Charter for Rented Housing. For a number of reasons, the registration system did not progress satisfactorily, and by 2002 only 25,000 out of an estimated 150,000 accommodation units were registered with local authorities.

Commission on the Private Rented Residential Sector

In 1999 a Commission on the Private Rented Residential Sector was established and its report was published in 2000. The report highlighted what the commission regarded as the two main issues concerning the private rented sector: the first concerned the shortage of suitable accommodation, whether for owner-occupation or renting; the second was the complex issue of providing an appropriate balance of rights between landlords and tenants. The commission proposed the establishment of a Private Residential Tenancies Board (PRTB) to deal with landlord–tenant disputes and to provide for security of tenure of up to four years for tenants who have completed six months' tenancy.

The PRTB was established on an ad hoc basis in 2001 and on a statutory basis in 2004 under the Residential Tenancies Act, 2004. It is responsible for the operation of a national dispute-resolution service for landlords and tenants in the private rented residential sector. It also operates a national registration of private tenancies, a function it has taken over from local authorities, and provides information and policy advice on the private rented sector.

During 2009 almost 1,900 dispute applications were received by the PRTB, with deposit-retention complaints being the single largest category of dispute (51 per cent), followed by cases involving rent arrears (19 per cent). By the end of 2009 there were 234,582 tenancies and 116,577 landlords registered with the PRTB.[24]

Homelessness

Homelessness has been an important issue associated with housing for several decades. In the 1980s the Simon Community and other groups campaigned for government action and legislation. For some time confusion had existed as to which state agency (health board or local authority) had statutory responsibility for providing accommodation for the homeless. In 1983 Senator Brendan Ryan introduced a Homeless Persons Bill in the Seanad in order to bring greater clarity to the situation. However, the government opposed this bill and introduced its own in 1985, but this lapsed with the dissolution of the Dáil in January 1987. The Housing Act, 1988, provided for increased powers of housing authorities regarding accommodation for homeless persons.

The definition of homelessness in section 2 of the Housing Act, 1988, is as follows:

> A person shall be regarded by a housing authority as being homeless for the purpose of this Act if: (a) there is no accommodation available which, in the opinion of the authority, he together with any other person who resides with him or who might reasonably be expected to reside with him, can reasonably occupy or remain in occupation of, or (b) he is living in a hospital, county home, night shelter or other such institution, and is so living because he has no accommodation of the kind referred to in paragraph (a)[25]

The Housing Act, 1988, did not place a statutory duty on local authorities to provide accommodation for homeless persons, but it did empower them, either on their own or in conjunction with other agencies, to provide a range of suitable accommodation. What has emerged as a result of the Housing Act, 1988, is that local authorities have responsibility for the provision of emergency, temporary and permanent accommodation for homeless persons aged over eighteen years, with health boards (now the HSE) having responsibility for the health and in-house care needs of such persons.

In 2000, in response to the growing numbers of homeless persons, the government published *Homelessness – An Integrated Strategy*. The report indicated that in 1999 there were 5,234 homeless persons in the country and that the majority (70 per cent) were in Dublin.[26] The key proposals of the strategy were as follows:

- local authorities and health boards, in full partnership with the voluntary bodies, to draw up action plans on a county-by-county basis to provide a more coherent and integrated delivery of services by all agencies dealing with homelessness;
- homeless forums, comprising of representatives of the local authority and of the health and voluntary sector, to be established in every county;
- local authorities to be responsible for the provision of accommodation, including emergency hostel accommodation, and health boards to be responsible for their in-house care and health needs.

Dublin Homeless Agency

Under the *Integrated Strategy*, and in recognition of the fact that the largest numbers of homeless persons were in Dublin, a partnership body, the Homeless Agency, was established with responsibility for planning, coordination and management of services in Dublin. The board of the agency has representatives from the four local authorities in the Dublin area, the HSE and voluntary agencies. In 2001 the agency published its first three-year action plan, *Shaping the Future*. It indicated that homelessness in Dublin was a persistent problem which had grown in recent years, that there was no overall coordination between the different voluntary and statutory agencies concerned with the provision of services, that there was insufficient emphasis on getting people out of homelessness and that many people were homeless on a long-term basis.[27] The Homeless Agency envisaged that by 2010 long-term homelessness and the need for people to sleep rough would be eliminated in Dublin.

The approach of the Homeless Agency was based on the principle of a continuum of care which would ensure that all the needs of homeless persons were met in an integrated manner and in a way that ensured they moved from homelessness into long-term housing. Unusually, the agency also set an ambitious target for its own demise in time:

> It is not intended that the agency will be a permanent structure. In the effective achievement of its aims, the Homeless Agency will make itself redundant.[28]

The Homeless Agency's third action plan, *A Key to the Door* (2007), for 2007–10, indicated that the level of homelessness in Dublin had notably decreased since the beginning of the first action plan six years previously. It noted that the quality and range of services had improved, leading to a reduction in the number of people experiencing homelessness and sleeping rough.

While the *Integrated Strategy* was aimed at tackling the problems of those already experiencing homelessness, the *Homeless Preventative Strategy* (2002) was focused on the prevention of adult homelessness and was aimed at target groups at risk of homelessness, particularly those leaving custodial or health-related care. For example, it proposed that records would be kept of the number of patients being discharged from psychiatric hospitals and the type of accommodation into which they were being discharged.[29]

A review of the implementation of the national homeless strategies, commissioned by the Department of the Environment, Heritage and

Local Government and published in 2006, noted that fifteen of the twenty-four proposed actions of the *Integrated Strategy* were considered to have been either fully or significantly progressed. It concluded that significant progress had been made in tackling homelessness across a number of fronts, including housing, health and outreach support services, and that these improvements had led to a better understanding of homelessness as a complex issue amongst the general public. It noted that the introduction of the Homeless Agency in Dublin 'has stimulated significant progress with regard to addressing the capital's problems of homelessness'. The review recommended that the integrated and preventative strategies should be amalgamated and revised, and that the revised strategy 'should have an overarching goal to eliminate long-term homelessness in Ireland by a defined date in the future, and include clearly defined objectives, actions, projected outcomes, timescales for delivery and an appropriate monitoring mechanism'.[30]

A revised strategy, *The Way Home*, published in 2008, had six key aims:

i.   prevent homelessness;
ii.   eliminate the need to sleep rough;
iii. eliminate long-term homelessness;
iv.   meet long-term housing needs;
v.   ensure effective services for homeless people;
vi.   better coordinate funding arrangements.[31]

Each strategic aim has a number of actions at both national and local level to ensure that they are achieved. The end of 2010 was set as the target date for the elimination of long-term homelessness – defined as a person being in emergency accommodation for six months or more – and of the need to sleep rough. Following consultation with key stakeholders, *The Way Home* was followed up in 2009 with an implementation plan.[32]

The number of homeless persons declined from 5,581 in 2002 to 3,031 in 2005. Considerable progress was being achieved, especially by the Dublin Homeless Agency. However, the downturn in the economy in 2008, the increase in unemployment and the increase in income-related issues for many households has probably meant the risks on homelessness have increased. For these and other such issues associated with the housing market, it is likely that progress has been slowed somewhat and that the laudable targets of eliminating long-term homelessness and the need to sleep rough by the end of 2010 became more difficult to achieve.

Role of voluntary agencies

Homelessness is an area where voluntary agencies have played a pioneering role. They were the first to provide hostel-type shelter and other forms of accommodation, and some have provided meals for homeless persons for several decades. Some of the voluntary organisations formed the National Campaign for the Homeless and were prominent in pressing for government recognition of the problem of homelessness in the lead up to the Housing Act, 1988. They sought a definition of 'homeless person', a clear identification of the responsibilities of statutory agencies for the care of homeless persons and a requirement that local authorities house homeless persons. As already noted, the 1988 act brought greater clarity on the role of local authorities in relation to homeless persons.

As might be expected, most of the voluntary agencies in this field are located in Dublin, though some, such as the society of St Vincent de Paul and the Simon Community, have facilities for homeless persons outside Dublin also. They also include Focus Ireland, the Capuchin Day Centre and the Vincentian Housing Partnership, as well as a number of voluntary housing associations.

Developments and issues since the 1990s

Over the past two decades the housing market and government policy on housing have undergone many complex changes, some of which have already been touched upon in this chapter. These include a broadening of the role of local authorities in relation to meeting housing need, the increased demand for housing, the successive annual record level of output of new dwellings, the extraordinary house price increases and the response by government to these developments. Before considering these issues and developments it should be noted that it was not until the 1970s that housing policy became subject to critical analysis.

The NESC was the first organisation to analyse housing policy and, to date, it has published a number of specific reports on this topic, as well as considering housing issues in the context of reports on the economy. The 1977 NESC report on housing subsidies was the first attempt to quantify the value of subsidies, both explicit (e.g. grants) and implicit (e.g. income tax relief on the interest element of a mortgage), to the various sectors within the housing system. The report estimated that in 1975 the highest subsidy on a household basis went to those who purchased their local authority dwellings while the average household subsidy varied little between owner-occupier and local authority tenants.[33]

Baker and O'Brien (1979) presented an excellent overview of the housing system with reference to efficiency and equity.[34] They argued that while the system was tolerably efficient at providing accommodation it was also seriously unfair in that it favoured those who already owned or rented houses at the expense of those seeking housing. Some of their recommendations for improvements have been implemented; for example, the greater availability of local authority housing for single persons and the abolition of rent control.

Blackwell (1981) argued that most elements of housing policy did not work to the achievement of either horizontal or vertical equity.[35] Horizontal equity means that households with broadly similar income and household characteristics (e.g. family size) should obtain equal net benefits from the system. Vertical equity is concerned with the implications of policy for those who are not equal and with the extent to which there is a transfer of resources in a progressive manner, i.e. that those on the lowest income should benefit most. In relation to horizontal equity, Blackwell pointed out, for example, that there was a considerable difference in benefit between those purchasing new houses (where grant and stamp duty exemption applied) and those purchasing second-hand houses.

The NESC, in various reports, had consistently questioned the validity of existing policy and had argued for a more balanced housing strategy:

> The central thrust of housing policy has always been the encouragement of owner occupation. In the Council's view, owner occupation per se should not be an end in itself, but one of a series of instruments to achieve the goal of adequate housing, in an acceptable environment, at an affordable price or rent.[36]

The NESC argued that it was necessary to achieve a better balance between tenures and that, while owner-occupation remains the main tenure, the other tenures (local authority, private rented and voluntary/social housing) should play an appropriate role. This, according to the NESC, should be the fundamental aim of housing policy.

Some of the criticisms made by the NESC and others were responded to, in part, in *A Plan for Social Housing*, published by the Department of the Environment, Heritage and Local Government in 1991. The plan was the most comprehensive government statement on housing since the White Paper of 1969, and was a response to the changing housing needs in society. However, it differed fundamentally from previous White Papers, which were primarily concerned with estimating housing need.

A Plan for Social Housing addressed the key issues that had been of concern for some time and proposed far-reaching policy changes, especially in the local authority sector. While reiterating the broad objective of housing policy as enunciated by successive governments, the plan went on to indicate that future strategy would include:

- promoting owner-occupation as a form of tenure preferred by most people;
- developing and implementing responses appropriate to changing social housing need;
- mitigating the extent and effects of social segregation in housing.

The plan provided for a number of policy changes. In relation to local authority housing, for example, it indicated that the approach of local authorities would be broader and more diverse than its traditional role. The new measures envisaged for local authorities included:

- to avoid building large housing estates, which have 'reinforced social segregation with adverse consequences';
- to purchase private houses or existing houses in need of refurbishment where it is more economic than building new houses;
- to carry out improvements to existing local authority dwellings as opposed to providing new houses;
- to introduce a system of shared ownership with tenants in which the local authority would take a 50 per cent share;
- to introduce a new mortgage allowance (over five years) for tenants moving to private houses.

The plan also contained proposals for initiatives in relation to homeless and Travelling people, voluntary and cooperative housing, home ownership and, as already indicated, the private rented sector.[37] The legislative base for some of the policy changes was provided for in the Housing Miscellaneous Provisions Act, 1992.

A review of *A Plan for Social Housing* resulted in *Social Housing – The Way Ahead* (1995). This report recorded progress in relation to different schemes and indicated ways in which these might be improved further.

The two policy reports did nothing to alter the predominant position of owner-occupation. In fact, they reinforced that position by introducing new schemes (shared ownership, mortgage allowance) and continuing existing schemes (tenant-purchase and local authority house-purchase loans).

One of the main changes arising from the two reports was a more diverse role for local authorities in meeting housing need compared with the traditional response of acquiring land and building new, often large, housing estates. While the output of new local authority housing has been relatively low by reference to past trends, housing need has been met by more varied measures since the early 1990s. These include refurbishment of existing stock, purchase of private housing and the shared ownership scheme. However, all the combined measures have still fallen short of meeting housing need, as evidenced by the growth of numbers under the housing assessment needs (see Table 3.6).

House price inflation

In the late 1990s house prices (for both new and second-hand houses) began to rise at an unprecedented level. This applied in particular in the Dublin area but gradually began to affect all parts of the country. The reasons for this increase, according to the NESF, included:

- demographic and household-formation changes;
- economic growth with particular impact on employment growth;
- increased disposable income and lower direct taxes;
- low mortgage-interest rates;
- a shortage of serviced development land;
- increases in the price of development land;
- labour shortages, including those in the planning sections of local authorities;
- investor and general speculative activity;
- immigration.[38]

In the period 1995–2006 the average price of all new houses for which loans were approved increased almost 4.0 times, while the price of second-hand houses in Dublin increased 5.7 times – the largest increase (Table 3.8). In 2007 a downturn in prices commenced and followed through in succeeding years.

In response to the sharp rise in house prices the government commissioned a report from Bacon and Associates (1998), usually referred to as Bacon I. This was followed by two further reports, Bacon II (1999) and Bacon III (2000). In turn, the reports proposed a range of measures on both the supply side and the demand side. Each report was followed by a government policy statement that led to the introduction of measures to improve the situation. Some of these measures were designed to take the heat out of the market, to improve affordability, to curb investor demand and to improve the availability of serviced land.[39]

Table 3.8: *Average house prices, selected years, 1995–2006**

	1995	1997	2001	2006	Increase (%)
New					
National	77,994	102,222	182,863	305,637	291.9
Dublin	86,671	22,036	243,095	405,957	368.4
Second-hand					
National	74,312	102,712	206,117	371,447	399.8
Dublin	88,938	131,258	267,939	512,461	476.2

* For which loans were approved.

Source: Annual *Housing Statistics Bulletin* (Department of the Environment, Community and Local Government).

Some of the measures had a limited impact while others would prove more significant in the long term. Overall, the measures adopted failed to halt house-price inflation.

In 2003, during the housing boom period, an All-Party Oireachtas Committee considered a possible but contentious solution to escalating house prices in the form of regulating the price of development land. The committee did this in response to the Taoiseach's request to revisit a 1974 report (usually referred to as the Kenny report, after the report committee's chairman, Justice Kenny) which recommended that certain areas be designated by the High Court as areas of potential development and that local authorities should have the power to purchase land in these areas within ten years of designation at their existing value plus one-quarter, without regard to their development potential.[40] This recommendation was not implemented partly because it was felt it would have required complex legislation and also because it was felt that it would have constitutional implications. The All-Party Oireachtas Committee's report (2004) concluded that, having regard to modern case law, the principal recommendation of the Kenny report 'would not be found to be unconstitutional'.[41] No progress was made on this issue.

NESC report
In 2004 the NESC published a comprehensive report on housing issues, *Housing In Ireland: Performance and Policy.* The report dealt with a range of issues and challenges in each sector of the housing market. Two of the main areas in the report concerned the achievement of high-quality sustainable developments and the adequate provision of social housing.

The NESC rejected the idea that a greater quantity of housing must be created at the expense of quality development. It argued that 'increased housing quantity and better quality neighbourhoods can be complementary and, indeed, mutually reinforcing'. The report stressed the importance of developing well-designed, sustainable neighbourhoods. According to the NESC, such neighbourhoods have a number of social and economic advantages over the patterns of sprawling suburbs that have characterised suburban development in Ireland in recent decades. These advantages include lower levels of car dependence; inter-generational and social integration; greater independence for young and old people; easier access to social, community and sporting organisations; and higher levels of social and commercial services.

The NESC report acknowledged that 'despite its dynamism, the private market for owner-occupied housing has not met the needs of many and the private rental sector has displayed rent levels that are not affordable for some households'. The report indicated that there was a gap between projected provision of social and affordable housing and the number of households that would be able to achieve home ownership in the private market. It pointed out that the level of social housing provision had fallen too low, and it recommended that the social housing stock should be brought up to 200,000 by the end of 2012. In order to achieve this figure, a net increase of 73,000 social housing units, either owned or managed by local authorities, would be necessary. This implied an addition of about 9,000 units annually, 'a rate that is substantially higher than what has been achieved over the period 2000–2003'. [42] This would bring the social housing stock to about 20 per cent of all private housing as compared with the existing 12 per cent.

The analysis of housing in the NESC report influenced the short, broad-based policy statement *Housing Policy Framework – Building Sustainable Communities* (2005), which set out the government's vision for housing policy for the future, taking account of continued population and economic growth. The statement was followed by a more detailed policy statement the following year. The fundamental aim was to develop the housing sector by delivering more and better-quality housing responses and by doing this in a more strategic way, focused on the building of sustainable communities. The social partnership agreement *Towards 2016* (2006) endorsed the principles set out in the *Housing Policy Framework*.

National Development Plan

The second-largest investment area outlined in the *National Development Plan 2007–2013* was social housing, where proposals included the building or acquisition of 63,000 social housing units from 2007 to 2013 through local authority, voluntary and cooperative housing and the rental accommodation scheme.[43]

Strategic guidance for the delivery of these and other new homes was published by the Department of the Environment, Heritage and Local Government in a statement on housing policy, *Delivering Homes, Sustaining Communities* (2007). It reiterated the commitments made in the *National Development Plan* and the principles outlined in the *Housing Policy Framework*. It accepted the principle of building sustainable communities as outlined in the NESC report (2004) and indicated that 'new housing should be provided in a planned and sustainable fashion, making a positive contribution to the built environment and social integration'. *Delivering Homes, Sustaining Communities* reiterated the importance of home ownership, which 'should be available to as many people as possible where this is their preferred option' and which 'can be an important factor in underpinning social stability and promoting good civic values'. It also proposed the introduction of new schemes to support local authority tenants seeking home ownership, such as an incremental purchase scheme and the sale of flats. [44]

Housing in a changing context

From 2007 the context for housing policy began to change rapidly, and a period of falling demand and falling prices emerged. Prior to this, some economic commentators had contended that the housing boom was an unsustainable 'bubble', while others contended that the pace of development would slow gradually. Differences of opinion arose between those predicting a 'hard landing' and those predicting a 'soft landing' for the housing sector, with consequent implications in either scenario for the general economy. By 2008 some external factors served to trigger an acceleration of the downturn in the construction sector.

For each of the succeeding thirteen years from 1993, when 21,391 housing units were built, an annual record number of units were built, reaching a peak of 93,419 in 2006 (more than four times the output in 1993). By 2010 output had fallen to 14,602 units, the lowest annual number of completions for several decades (see Table 3.1). A sharp deterioration in the state of the public finances led, inter alia, to a reduction in the annual capital housing budget.

Towards the end of the boom period it was obvious that supply had begun to seriously outstrip demand. As a result of the housing bust, local authorities were left with a build up of unsold affordable housing units, which they found difficult to dispose of in a falling market. The Comptroller and Auditor General, in a special value-for-money report, stated that in the light of the changed housing market conditions the rationale for the Affordable Homes Partnership, set up to coordinate the delivery of affordable homes, should be reviewed.[45] The McCarthy report (2009) proposed a number of policy measures for cost savings that would lead to fundamental changes in the system of social and affordable housing, especially the transfer of funding from traditional construction to leasing, rental or purchase of already built dwellings. While this would increase current expenditure, it would also yield better value for money and achieve capital savings.[46]

A special report on the housing situation by the Department of the Environment, Heritage and Local Government in 2010 made for sombre reading. It noted that between 2005 and 2007 the total output of housing units was about 50,000 more than the long-term annual average of 40,000. It pointed out that the timing mismatch between the collapse in demand for housing and the less rapid slowing of output had led to a situation where 'there is now a significant overhang of unsold property'. Estimates suggested that 'total vacancy levels, including holiday homes, is over 300,000, that vacancy excluding holiday homes is over 228,000, and the potential overhang (i.e. the excess vacancy over "normal" levels) is 100,000'. Having noted the relatively short duration of the average upturn and the average downturn in house-price cycles internationally, the report concluded that, since the most recent period of sustained price growth in Ireland was atypically long, 'it is also possible that the current downturn may also be longer or more severe than normal'.[47]

By the end of 2010 it was estimated by various sources that house prices had fallen back to 2002 levels, and were down between 35 and 50 per cent from the peak of the property boom. As might be expected, variation in the levels of both price rise and price decline exist between different geographic areas, and especially between urban and rural areas.

The estimated long-term housing output requirement underlying the government's policy statement *Delivering Homes, Sustaining Communities* was around 600,000 over nine years, or an average of around 65,000 per annum. By 2009 this estimate was revised downward to around 40,000 per annum. A revised national capital plan in 2010 indicated that falling house prices and land values meant that a substantially lower funding allocation for social housing would be required.[48] It also noted that the number of unoccupied dwelling units in the country weakened the case for a construction-centred investment and recommended a greater emphasis on leasing as the only viable medium-term option.

In the aftermath of the house-price collapse it was acknowledged that failures in the banking system during the boom years contributed to supporting 'a credit-fuelled property market and construction frenzy'.[49] A report by the National Institute for Regional and Spatial Analysis in 2010 concluded that failures in the planning system at local authority level had also contributed substantially to the situation. The report was highly critical of the role of the planning system in the housing debacle, and contended that, no matter how much the financial institutions were prepared to lend, construction could not have taken place without rezoning and planning permission.

The report indicated that there were more than 300,000 housing units lying empty and that there were more than 620 'ghost estates', i.e. developments of ten or more units where over 50 per cent are empty or unfinished. It indicated that there was enough excess housing and zoned land nationally to last an average of 16.8 years. According to the report, planning was driven by the demands of developers and speculators, while the government not only failed to adequately oversee, regulate and direct local planning but actively encouraged its excesses through tax incentives and by disregarding its own principles as set out in the *National Spatial Strategy 2002–2020* (2002). It argued that a number of local authorities abjectly failed to manage development and ignored good planning guidelines, regional and national objectives, sensible demographic profiling of potential demand and the fact that much of the land zoned lacked essential services. Others were relatively prudent and, consequently, had low levels of oversupply.

The report concluded that several issues will need to be addressed before the housing market starts to function properly again. For example, supply and demand will need to be harmonised, house prices will have to align more closely to average industrial earnings and there needs to be substantive changes to the planning system.[50]

In the *National Recovery Plan 2011–2014* the government indicated that it would 'take measures to help ensure the effective management of unfinished housing developments'.[51]

Notes

1. Department of the Environment, Heritage and Local Government, *Delivering Homes, Sustaining Communities: Statement on Housing Policy* (Department of the Environment, Heritage and Local Government, Dublin, 2007), p. 17. See also Department of the Environment, Heritage and Local Government, *A Plan for Social Housing* (Department of the Environment, Heritage and Local Government, Dublin, 1991), p. 1. Similar objectives were outlined in Government of Ireland, *White Paper: Housing in the Seventies* (Stationery Office, Dublin, 1969), p. 3.

2.   This section contains a summary of developments up to the mid 1960s as outlined by P.J. Meghan, *Housing in Ireland* (Institute of Public Administration, Dublin, 1966).

3.   K.C. Kearns, *Dublin Tenement Life: An Oral History* (Gill and Macmillan, Dublin, 1994), pp. 7–8.

4.   T. Fahey, 'Housing and local government', in M.E. Daly (ed.), *County and Town: One Hundred Years of Local Government in Ireland* (Institute of Public Administration, Dublin, 2001), pp. 121–2.

5.   D. Ferriter, *'Lovers of Liberty?': Local Government in 20th Century Ireland* (National Archives of Ireland, Dublin, 2001), p. 76.

6.   Fahey, op. cit., p. 123.

7.   Government of Ireland, *Economic Development* (Stationery Office, Dublin, 1959), p. 46.

8.   F. Kennedy, *Public Social Expenditure in Ireland* (Economic and Social Research Institute, Dublin, 1975), p. 15.

9.   See S. Power, 'The development of the Ballymun housing scheme, Dublin 1965–1969', *Irish Geography*, Vol. 33, No. 2 (2000).

10. Government of Ireland, *Ireland, National Development Plan 2000–2006* (Stationery Office, Dublin, 1999), p. 69.

11. See T. Fahey et al., *Housing, Poverty and Wealth in Ireland* (Combat Poverty Agency, Dublin, 2004), pp. 9–10.

12. P. Pfretzschner, *The Dynamics of Irish Housing* (Institute of Public Administration, Dublin, 1965), p. 112.

13. National Economic and Social Council, *Report No. 112, Housing in Ireland: Performance and Policy* (Stationery Office, Dublin, 2004), p. 62.

14. See National Economic and Social Council, *Report No. 87, A Review of Housing Policy* (Stationery Office, Dublin, 1989), pp. 177–81, where the pros and cons of local authority purchase schemes are outlined.

15. P. Tansey, 'Housing subsidies: a case for reform', in J. Blackwell (ed.), *Towards an Efficient and Equitable Housing Policy* (Institute of Public Administration, Dublin, 1989), pp. 31–2.

16. Department of the Environment, Heritage and Local Government, *A Plan for Social Housing*, op. cit., p. 6.

17. Thompson, 'Social Housing', in J. Blackwell and S. Kennedy (eds), *Focus on Homelessness* (Columba Press, Dubin, 1988), pp. 118–19.

18. Affordable Homes Partnership, *Increasing Affordable Housing Supply* (Affordable Homes Partnership, Dublin, 2007), p. 34.

19. Ibid., p. 21.

20. Department of Social and Family Affairs, *Report of the Working Group on the Review of the Supplementary Allowance Scheme* (Stationery Office, Dublin, 2006), pp. 80–1.

21. See T.J. Baker and L.M. O'Brien, *The Irish Housing System: A Critical Overview* (Economic and Social Research Institute, Dublin, 1979), pp. 99–100.

22. B. Harvey and M. Higgins, 'The links between housing and homelessness', in J. Blackwell, op. cit., p. 36.

23. L. O'Brien and B. Dillon, *Private Rented: The Forgotten Sector* (Threshold, Dublin, 1982).

24. Private Residential Tenancies Board, *Annual Report and Accounts 2009*, (Private Residential Tenancies Board, Dublin, 2010), pp. 24, 30.

25. Government of Ireland, *Housing Act, 1988* (Stationery Office, Dublin, 1988).

26. Department of the Environment and Local Government, *Homelessness – An Integrated Strategy* (Department of the Environment and Local Government, Dublin, 2000), pp. 8–9.

27. Homeless Agency, *Shaping the Future: An Action Plan on Homelessness in Dublin 2001–2003* (Homeless Agency, Dublin, 2001), p. 1.

28. Ibid., p. 128.

29. Government of Ireland, *Homeless Preventative Strategy: A Strategy to Prevent Homelessness Among: Patients Leaving Hospital and Mental Health Care, Adult Prisoners and Young Offenders Leaving Custody, Young People Leaving Care* (Stationery Office, Dublin, 2002), p. 19.

30. Government of Ireland, *Review of the Implementation of the Government's Integrated and Preventative Homeless Strategies* (Stationery Office, Dublin, 2006).

31. Department of the Environment, Heritage and Local Government, *The Way Home: A Strategy to Address Adult Homelessness in Ireland 2008–2013*, (Department of the Environment, Heritage and Local Government, Dublin, 2008).

32. Department of the Environment, Heritage and Local Government, *Homeless Strategy: National Implementation Plan* (Department of the Environment, Heritage and Local Government, Dublin, 2009).

33. National Economic and Social Council, *Report No. 23, Report on Housing Subsidies* (Stationery Office, Dublin, 1977), pp. 8–11.

34. Baker and O'Brien, op. cit.

35. J. Blackwell, 'Do housing subsidies show a redistribution to the poor?', in Council for Social Welfare, *Conference on Poverty 1981* (Council for Social Welfare, Dublin, 1981), pp. 225–8.

36. National Economic and Social Council, *Report No. 89, A Strategy for the Nineties: Economic Stability and Structural Change* (Stationery Office, Dublin, 1990), p. 238.

37. Department of the Environment, Heritage and Local Government, *A Plan for Social Housing*, op. cit.

38. National Economic and Social Forum, *Report No. 18, Social and Affordable Housing and Accommodation: Building the Future* (Stationery Office, Dublin, 2000), p. 22.

39. See C. O'Connell, 'The housing market and owner occupation in Ireland', in M. Norris and D. Redmond (eds), *Housing Contemporary Ireland: Housing, Society and Shelter* (Institute of Public Administration, Dublin, 2005), pp. 39–40.

40. Government of Ireland, *Report of the Committee on the Price of Building Land* (Stationery Office, Dublin, 1974).

41. The All-Party Oireachtas Committee on the Constitution, *Ninth Progress Report: Private Property* (Stationery Office, Dublin, 2004).

42. National Economic and Social Council, *Report No. 112, Housing in Ireland: Performance and Policy*, op. cit.

43. Government of Ireland, *National Development Plan 2007–2013* (Stationery Office, Dublin, 2007).

44. Department of the Environment, Heritage and Local Government, *Delivering Homes, Sustaining Communities: Statement on Housing Policy*, op. cit., p. 21.

45. Comptroller and Auditor General, *Special Report: Department of the Environment, Heritage and Local Government. Water Services, Affordable Housing Delivery* (Stationery Office, Dublin, 2009), p. 38. In 2010 the Housing and Sustainable Communities Agency was established on an administrative basis, and will replace the Centre for Housing Research, the Affordable Homes Partnership, the National Building Agency and the Homeless Agency.

46. Government of Ireland, *Report of the Special Group on Public Service Numbers and Expenditure Programmes* (Stationery Office, Dublin, 2009), pp. 93–4.

47. Department of the Environment, Heritage and Local Government, *Housing Market Overview 2009* (Department of the Environment, Heritage and Local Government, Dublin, 2010).

48. Department of Finance, *Infrastructure Investment Priorities 2010–2016: A Financial Framework* (Department of Finance, Dublin, 2010), pp. 34–6.

49. Commission of Investigation into the Banking Sector in Ireland, *The Irish Banking Crisis: Regulatory and Financial Stability Policy 2003–2008, A Report to the Minister for Finance by the Governor of the Central Bank* (Stationery Office, Dublin, 2010), p. 15.

50. R. Kitchin et al., *A Haunted Landscape: Housing and Ghost Estates in Post-Celtic Tiger Ireland. National Institute for Regional and Spatial Analysis, Working Paper 59* (NUI Maynooth, Kildare, 2010).

51. Government of Ireland, *The National Recovery Plan 2011–2014* (Stationery Office, Dublin, 2010), p. 50.

4

Education

Introduction

In many respects, the system of education in Ireland is highly complex. Education is carried out at three levels, and considerable variation exists not only between these but also within each of them. The management of first-level schools differs from that at second level; at first level there are different kinds of primary schools, while at second level there are also distinct subsections. Despite the fact that there is substantial state support at all levels, there are few state schools in the accepted sense. The influence of the churches (especially Catholic) on the development of the education system has been profound.

The present system represents a curious mixture of state and church interests, particularly at first level and in some parts of second level. Secondary schools, for example, are in receipt of various state subsidies yet are privately owned and managed. Apart from the churches, there are various other interest groups, such as the teachers' unions and, more recently, parents' organisations. The presence of these groups, coupled with the fact that until recently there was little legislative basis for education, has meant that it has often been difficult to obtain agreement on policy changes. The following pages will illustrate this.

Since the mid 1960s, some important changes have occurred in the education system. These include the introduction of free post-primary education, the establishment of new institutions such as comprehensive and community schools at second level, and the establishment of regional technical colleges (RTCs; later renamed institutes of technology) and new universities at third level. These developments have been accompanied by increased rates of participation in education.

The Department of Education was established in 1924, renamed the Department of Education and Science in 1997 and renamed the Department of Education and Skills in 2010. For ease of reference, throughout this chapter it will be referred to simply as the Department of Education, except where the formal title is appropriate. The department's mission is 'to provide high-quality education which will enable individuals to achieve their full potential and to participate fully as members of society and contribute to Ireland's social, cultural and economic development'.[1] Most aspects of the administration of the education system are centralised in the Department of Education. The department sets the general regulations for the recognition of schools; prescribes curricula; establishes regulations for the management, resourcing and staffing of schools; and centrally negotiates teachers' salary scales. It has an oversight and policymaking role in relation to all aspects of education.

The main features of each of the three levels, as well as of adult education, are considered in this chapter. Some key issues in education are also considered.

First-level education

Origins of present system
Many basic features of modern Irish primary, or first-level, education can be traced back to the establishment in 1831 of the National Board of Education.[2] Prior to that there was no uniform system of primary education, and while some areas were well served by schools, others had only rudimentary forms of schooling.[3] A number of organisations promoted first-level education in the early decades of the nineteenth century – for example, the Kildare Place Society and Catholic religious orders.

In 1831 the British House of Commons voted a sum of £30,000 towards primary education in Ireland. This money was to be administered by the National Board of Education, which consisted of seven commissioners representing the main religious denominations. The board was given power to contribute to the cost of building schools, pay inspection costs, contribute to teachers' salaries, establish model schools and provide school books. The system aimed to provide for a general secular education for children of different denominations with separate religious instruction outside of normal school hours. The board's intention was to establish a multi-denominational, rather than a denominational, system of education. In other words, it did not favour the funding of schools to pursue a particular religious ethos. Schools run by religious orders were to be given the same assistance as other schools, provided they complied with the rules of the board.

Opposition and lack of cooperation, mainly on religious grounds, hindered the board's early success. In 1837, for example, the religious order of the Irish Christian Brothers withdrew their schools from connection with the board. Four years later, however, Pope Gregory XVI encouraged Catholics to support the national schools. While some of the Catholic hierarchy welcomed the new system, others, notably Dr John MacHale, Archbishop of Tuam, were less enthusiastic and forbade their clergy to cooperate with the board.[4]

The training of teachers for national schools proved to be another contentious issue. In 1837 the board established a training school and three model schools at Marlborough Street, Dublin, where teachers were trained on the principle of the 'mixed system', i.e. the teaching of children of all denominations. The Catholic hierarchy forbade their clerical managers to appoint teachers trained in the model schools to schools under their control. In 1883 the board decided to recognise denominational training colleges, and two Catholic colleges (St Patrick's, Drumcondra, for men and Our Lady of Mercy, Blackrock, for women) were established in Dublin. A Church of Ireland training college for men and women, also in Dublin, was affiliated to the board in the following year. Other Catholic colleges subsequently established included those at Waterford (1891), Belfast (1900) and Limerick (1907).

Notwithstanding its limitations and somewhat tempestuous history, by 1922, when the commissioners of the National Board of Education were replaced by a branch of the newly founded Department of Education under an Irish Minister for Education, the national system could claim credit for considerable achievements.[5] Perhaps the most important consequence of the national system was that it was the chief means by which the country was transformed from one in which illiteracy predominated into one in which most people could read and write: in 1841 over half (53 per cent) the population aged five years and over could neither read nor write, and by 1901 this proportion had declined to 14 per cent. Therefore, in the eradication of mass illiteracy, credit must be given to the national system. The system also ensured that national schools were established in all parts of the country. The number of schools increased from just over 1,000 in 1834 to almost 8,000 in 1921, and the school-going population increased from 107,000 in 1833 to 685,000 in 1891. This occurred despite a decline of over 50 per cent in the total population between 1841 and 1921.

One of the main objectives of the National Board of Education – the establishment of multi-denominational schools – was not achieved. By the time the Irish state was founded, the system of multi-denominational education established in 1831 had become a system of denominational education, and it has remained essentially so ever since. As indicated in the *Rules for National Schools under the Department of Education* (1965), the state gave explicit recognition to the denominational character of these schools well into the twentieth century.

Compulsory schooling

Under the Irish Education Act, 1892, attendance on at least seventy-five days in each half-year was made compulsory for children between the ages of six and fourteen. A number of acceptable excuses for non-attendance were specified by the act, e.g. sickness, harvesting operations, fishing, any other unavoidable cause or the fact that the child was already receiving suitable elementary education. Initially, the application of the act was limited to municipal boroughs and towns, but in 1898 it was extended to all parts of the country. The enforcement of the act was particularly difficult in rural areas. School-attendance committees set up by local authorities helped to enforce the law, but not all local authorities set up such committees.

While the act may not have had the desired effect, it nevertheless brought about a change in school attendance. In 1902 the average yearly attendance was 63 per cent, and this increased to 76 per cent by 1908.

The School Attendance Act, 1926, made further provisions for the enforcement of compulsory schooling and remained the main statute governing school attendance until the Education (Welfare) Act, 2000 (see later section in this chapter).

Management and finance

Initially, the National Board of Education was willing to give special consideration to any joint applications for aid from members of different religious denominations within a parish. In practice, however, where there were sufficient numbers of children of different denominations, the Catholic or non-Catholic clergy or members of religious orders applied for separate aid in building a school. Therefore, the pupils were concentrated in separate schools under local clerical or religious order management. This was the beginning of the managerial system, which survived up to 1975.

Ironically, while the direct administration of primary schools and the appointment and dismissal of teachers remained in the hands of local managers for a long period, the state has always paid a large share of the cost of building schools and paid the teachers' salaries in full. The non-state character of the school was preserved by the provision of a site from local funds together with a local contribution towards the cost of building the school. The state has also contributed towards the maintenance costs of schools. The situation in relation to the subsidy for school buildings up to the late 1990s has been summarised as follows:

> While in theory the State contributes two-thirds of the approved cost of a primary school building, this contribution is open to negotiation, and in the vast majority of cases is very much higher. The system is not entirely satisfactory, since the amount of the State grant provided often depends on the case put forward in respect of local circumstances.[6]

Prior to 1999, the position was that up to 15 per cent of building costs was provided by the patron (a local bishop in the majority of schools; see later section in this chapter), except for special schools for children with learning difficulties (intellectual disabilities) and schools in disadvantaged areas, where the contribution was 5 per cent.

In 1999 Micheál Martin, TD, Minister for Education and Science, announced a fundamental change in capital grants for primary schools that was designed, in part, to relieve fundraising pressures on local communities. The state would now provide the full cost of a site and 95 per cent of the capital cost. While the local community would be responsible for 5 per cent of capital costs, this would be subject to a ceiling of £50,000. However, the most significant change arising from this policy development was that, in future, the state would own the school building; hitherto, the patron was the effective owner of the building. This applies only to new schools built following the change in policy. The new funding system was of significant benefit to multi-denominational schools (see later section in this chapter).

There are also a number of private primary schools, and these do not receive any state subsidy and are totally financed by parents' fees.

In practice, a distinction can be made between primary schools. The majority are referred to as ordinary national schools and are mainly under either Catholic or Protestant clerical patronage. There are also some schools run by religious orders or congregations, mainly in urban areas. In addition, there are special schools for children with disabilities, schools in which the curriculum is taught wholly or mainly through the medium of Irish (gaelscoileanna) and a growing number of multi-denominational schools. There are also a small number of 'model' national schools directly under the control of the Department of Education and Skills.

Suggestions were made in the early 1970s to involve parents and teachers formally in school management, but little became of these until the world oil crisis of 1973 presented the opportunity. The soaring cost of heating oil meant that the state would have to substantially increase its maintenance subsidy to primary schools; otherwise the burden would fall on the local community. In October 1974 Richard Burke, TD, Minister for Education, announced a new scheme of aid towards the maintenance costs of primary schools. Instead of paying schools a proportion of the maintenance costs, a capitation grant of £6 per pupil (to be matched by an amount equivalent to one-quarter of the state grant to be collected locally) would be given only to those schools that had set up joint management committees, composed of four nominees of the patron and two parents, by October 1975. The minister subsequently indicated that teachers should also be represented on these committees. Schools that had not set up the committees would have to accept a lower subsidy from the Department of Education towards the upkeep of their schools. Therefore, from a financial viewpoint, it was in the manager's interest to establish committees. The manner in which management boards were introduced in primary schools has been aptly described as a form of 'gentle blackmail'.[7] It also illustrated the difficulty of making policy changes in the Irish education system. In the absence of a legislative basis, change was normally introduced by agreement among the various interests involved rather than by legislation. In this instance, a financial carrot achieved in one year something that in all probability would otherwise have taken several years to achieve.

While the principle of teacher and parental representation on management boards was accepted, protracted negotiations between the main interests (Irish National Teachers' Organisation, the Catholic hierarchy, the Department of Education and the Catholic Primary School Managers' Association) took place before agreement to establish committees was reached and before the exact functions and composition of the boards of management were agreed. It was not until 1976 that the constitution and rules of procedure for the management boards were published. Following further negotiations, these rules and the composition of boards were subsequently altered in 1981, with further changes occurring in the 1990s. In schools of seven teachers or more, the board is comprised of a total of eight members: two nominees of the patron, two parents elected by other parents, a principal teacher and one other teacher elected by teaching staff, and two others from the local community proposed by the other six (subject to the approval of the patron).

The patron of the school appoints the chairman of the board of management. For the majority of primary schools, the bishop or archbishop (Catholic or Protestant) is normally the patron. The boards are responsible for the maintenance of the school, and up to 2001 they were also responsible for the collection of the local contribution that was introduced as part of the new funding arrangement in 1975. The Primary Education Review Body received submissions that were critical of the management system – e.g. the Department of Education decided on all major matters of policy; the patron played a central role in the appointment of the board, the chairperson, the principal and assistant teachers; and agreements between trade unions and the department further limited the autonomy of the board. Having considered alternative proposals, the review body did not recommend any change in the composition of the boards. Instead, it recommended that the future of the boards be reappraised and strengthened; for example, that they be given greater autonomy in relation to many matters that require the approval of the Department of Education.[8]

The system of funding schools by a capitation grant from the Department of Education coupled with a local contribution of one-quarter of that grant, introduced in 1975, continued into the 1990s. For example, in 1997 the department grant for ordinary schools was £45 per pupil and the local contribution was £10 (a total of £55 per pupil). The local contribution was abolished in 2001. By 2010 the capitation grant was €200 (special schools for children with special needs and gaelscoileanna receive higher capitation grants), but this was reduced by 5 per cent for 2011. The capitation grant is the main source of funding to schools to meet general operating costs, including heating, lighting, cleaning, insurance, painting, teaching aids and other miscellaneous costs.

Under the ancillary services grant scheme, €155 per pupil (in 2010) is provided for caretaking and secretarial services, based on school enrolment.

In 1997 a significant development took place with the introduction of minor capital works grants to primary schools. This grant is to cover such needs as replacement of windows, repair of roofs and purchase of standard furniture. Prior to this, boards of management had to apply to the Department of Education for funding for such purposes.

Rationalisation

A relatively high density of population in the mid-nineteenth century, combined with the fact that education was based on the parish and with the lack of adequate transport, encouraged the building of small primary schools serving a rather limited catchment area. As population declined throughout the latter part of the nineteenth century and the first half of the twentieth century, however, many schools, especially those in rural areas, became vulnerable to closure. Since its establishment, the Department of Education had sought to amalgamate those schools with the smallest number of pupils. In many areas there was considerable opposition to school closures, reflecting the value of the school as a focal point in the local community.

The *Investment in Education* report (1965), produced jointly by the Irish Government and the Organisation for Economic Cooperation and Development (OECD), indicated that, on a cost-effective basis, the one-teacher and two-teacher primary schools were inefficient – for example, in the range of subjects taught and in the rate of pupils' progress through school.[9] This report influenced subsequent policy towards small schools, and an intensive programme of primary school rationalisation was embarked upon. Within a decade (1967 to 1977), 471 one-teacher and 1,186 two-teacher schools were closed or amalgamated. During the same period the total number of primary schools fell from 4,625 to 3,372. In 1925 one-teacher and two-teacher schools had accounted for four-fifths of all primary schools; by 2008 the proportion had fallen to one-seventh (Table 4.1).

Table 4.1: *Small primary schools, selected years, 1925–2008*

	1925	*1967*	*1977*	*1997*	*2008*
(a) Number of one- and two-teacher schools	4,560	2,920	1,263	803	452
(b) Total number of primary schools*	5,700	4,625	3,372	3,186	3,175
(a) as percentage of (b)	80	63	37	25	14

* Special schools for children with disabilities are not included.

Sources: J. Coolahan, *Irish Education: History and Structure* (Institute of Public Administration, Dublin, 1981); statistical reports (Department of Education and Skills).

In 1976 a NESC report questioned the efficacy of closing small rural schools and referred to the trend in Scandinavia where the process of rationalisation had been reversed.[10] In 1977 Peter Barry, TD, Minister for Education, announced that the Department of Education would no longer force the amalgamation of small schools into larger units.[11] Inevitably, the closure and amalgamation of small schools in rural areas has continued, reflecting the continuing decline in population in some of those areas. New schools have continued to be established in the expanding urban areas.

Denominationalism and primary schools

It has already been noted that, despite the intentions of the National Board of Education to establish a non-denominational school structure, a system of denominational schools emerged. The preface to the *Rules for National Schools under the Department of Education* (1965) gave recognition to such schools:

> the State provides for free primary education for children in national schools, and gives explicit recognition to the denominational character of these schools.[12]

In the mid 1970s a movement to establish multi-denominational schools was initiated by some parents in parts of Dublin. The Department of Education was uncooperative while the Catholic Church opposed the concept. The movement was gradually afforded recognition, and state financial support for the establishment of the schools was provided. The first multi-denominational school to open was the Dalkey School Project, Dublin, in 1978. Most of the multi-denominational schools are under the patronage of a representative organisation, Educate Together.

The policy in relation to multi-denominational schools was outlined in the *Programme for Action in Education, 1984–1987*:

> Where the government is convinced that the establishment of a multi-denominational school represents the clear wishes of parents in an area and where such schools can be provided on a viable basis, support will be given to such developments on the same terms that would be available for the establishment of schools under denominational patronage.[13]

Up to 1999, groups of parents who wished to provide a multi-denominational school had to provide a site and up to 15 per cent of the cost of the building (this would have applied to the building of a new school as opposed to the renting of a premise to serve as a school). The change in policy in 1999 regarding funding has made a significant difference to these schools.

Educate Together was established in 1984, and it began acting as a coordinating body for the three multi-denominational schools that existed at that time. Since then, the movement has grown, and by 2010 there were fifty-eight such schools with a number of others at various stages of planning. As compared with the traditional denominational school model, the movement represents greater choice for parents, as well as a response to the growing diversity in Irish society.

In the school year 2009/10 there were 3,165 primary schools (excluding special schools for children with disabilities), and over 90 per cent were under Catholic patronage (Table 4.2).

Table 4.2: *Primary schools by school ethos, 2009/10*

School ethos	No. of schools	% of schools
Catholic*	2,888	91.25
Church of Ireland	181	5.73
Presbyterian	14	0.44
Methodist	1	0.03
Jewish	1	0.03
Inter-denominational	8	0.25
Muslim	2	0.06
Multi-denominational	69	2.18
Quaker	1	0.03
Total	3,165	100.0

* Includes most gaelscoileanna and five model schools of which the Minister for Education and Skills is the patron.

Source: Department of Education and Skills.

School patronage and choice in education

The patronage system in primary education, the continued increase in the school-going population at primary level and the changing nature of Irish society were highlighted in the autumn of 2006 as there was a lack of school places for children of foreign nationals in some parts of the growing urban areas of Dublin. In some instances, where a shortage of places existed, Catholic children were given priority over other children by Catholic schools. In effect, the changing demographic situation had left some non-Catholic children without places. This raised the issue of the denominational control of the majority of primary schools, and led Mary Hanafin, TD, Minister for Education and Science, to pilot a new model of primary school patronage in parts of Dublin.[14] The aim was for these schools, known as community primary schools, to be interdenominational in character, under the patronage of County Dublin Vocational Education Committee (VEC; see later section in this chapter on vocational schools and vocational education committees). This patronage model marked a new departure for a VEC that had traditionally been involved in second-level education and, to a lesser extent, in third level. The minister indicated that the new patronage model would not replace the existing models.

In September 2008 County Dublin VEC opened the first community national school, in Porterstown, Dublin. This marked the first time that a VEC had become involved in primary school education. The Education (Amendment) Bill, 2010, marked a significant development in that it provided for the legislative framework to allow VECs to become involved in the provision of primary education. It provided for the establishment of community national schools under VEC patronage and, in certain circumstances, for a VEC to become patron or joint patron of an existing primary school. However, the bill had not been passed by the time the Dáil was dissolved in February 2011.

Under the traditional denominational model of primary schools, Catholic and Protestant primary schools operate admission policies that require them to give priority to members of their own church, especially in areas where the number of children of school-going age has increased. This obviously constitutes a problem for parents of other or no religion in some areas. In a 2007 policy document the Irish Catholic Bishops' Conference stated that:

> the children of Catholic parents have first claim on admission to Catholic schools. Wherever possible, in keeping with their ethos, and provided they have places and resources, Catholic schools welcome children of other faiths and none.

The conference also acknowledged that Irish society has undergone considerable change and accepted that there should be 'choice and diversity within a national education system' and that 'parents who desire schools under different patronage should, where possible, be facilitated in accessing them'.[15]

In 2009 negotiations commenced between the Department of Education and representatives of Catholic Church patrons with the objective of ensuring that parents should have a choice, as far as possible, about what kind of school their children will attend. In 2010 the department published a study that identified forty-three urban areas, based on demographic and other criteria, where a choice of schools could possibly be provided.[16] The study gave ten random samples from its findings: the towns of Arklow, Athlone, Ballinasloe, Birr, Killarney and Tramore, as well as the Dublin 4 and Dublin 6/8 postal districts, Whitehall on Dublin city's northside and Portmarnock/Malahide, also in Dublin. All or the majority of primary schools in these urban areas are under Catholic patronage. For example, Athlone has fifteen primary schools within five kilometres of the town boundary, and fourteen of the schools have a Catholic ethos. The decision for the church to divest patronage of individual schools ultimately rests with the bishop, as patron, and the Catholic community in the concerned parish, and must follow consultation with parents and staff. It is likely that Church withdrawal from patronage of schools will be a very slow process. Furthermore, about half of the primary schools are small rural schools where it is unlikely there will be any great demand for change.

Second-level education

Second-level education is conducted in four types of schools: secondary, vocational (including community colleges), comprehensive and community. Since the origins, financing, ownership and management structure of these schools differ, each are considered separately in this section.

Secondary schools

While state aid was made available for primary education in 1831, it was not made available for secondary education until 1878, and even then the level of aid was comparatively small. Under the Intermediate Education Act, 1878, the secondary school education system in its present form took shape. The act established the Intermediate Education Board with seven commissioners to administer funds for examination purposes. The word 'intermediate' was taken to imply a system of education between elementary or primary instruction and higher education. Junior, middle and senior grade examinations were established under the act, and results fees were paid to the managers of schools in which candidates passed the examinations. The principal means of obtaining state aid was therefore through success in examinations. On the credit side, the new system imposed a uniform curriculum on secondary schools where variety had predominated. However, since aid available from the state was limited, schools relied heavily on students' fees to meet capital and current costs. Unlike the primary school system, whereby schools could be established in practically every area with state support, the distribution of secondary schools was mainly confined to urban areas. Consequently, many areas of the country lacked secondary schools; the greatest concentration was in the Dublin area and along the east coast generally, while few existed in the province of Connacht.

The Intermediate Education Board was dissolved in 1922, and in 1925 its functions were taken over by the Department of Education. Under the Intermediate Education (Amendment) Act, 1924, the system of paying grants to schools on the results of public examinations was discontinued. Instead, capitation grants were paid to schools for pupils over twelve years of age who followed prescribed courses and who made a certain number of attendances (130 days during the school year). The initial grant was £7 per junior pupil and £10 per senior pupil.

In 1924 the junior, middle and senior grade examinations were replaced by the Intermediate and Leaving Certificate examinations. In 1925, the first year of the new examination system, 2,900 pupils sat the

Intermediate Certificate examination and 995 sat the Leaving Certificate (approximately 54,000 students sat for both the Junior Certificate and Leaving Certificate examinations in 2010).

Incremental salaries for recognised secondary teachers were introduced in 1925 in schools that fulfilled certain conditions regarding size and staffing ratio.

Finance

The Free State Government recognised the private ownership of all secondary schools, and decided to give neither building nor maintenance grants but to help them indirectly by means of capitation grants. An opportunity was therefore lost for redressing the serious imbalance in the distribution of secondary schools. It was not until 1965 that state capital grants were made available for secondary schools.

Up to 1986 the current expenditure of secondary schools was subsidised by a combination of a capitation grant and a supplemental grant (in lieu of fees charged by schools participating in the free post-primary education scheme introduced in 1967). In 1986 these two grants were combined into a capitation grant based on enrolment. The value of the capitation grant in 2010 was €345, and this is used for the general running costs of the school, such as heating and cleaning. The capitation grant was reduced by 5 per cent for 2011. In addition, there is a support services grant (€155 per pupil in 2010) to cover the costs of caretakers and secretaries.

The subsidy for Protestant secondary education is organised on a different basis. The majority of the Protestant secondary schools are not in the free post-primary education scheme, and the Department of Education pays a block grant (€6.5 million in the school year 2009/10) to the Secondary Education Committee, representing the Church of Ireland, the Methodist Church in Ireland, the Presbyterian Church in Ireland and the Religious Society of Friends. The committee distributes the funds, in accordance with a means test, to families who need assistance to send their children to Protestant day or boarding schools.[17]

Free post-primary education scheme

One of the more significant findings of the OECD report *Investment in Education* was that there were serious inequalities between different socio-economic groups in participation in second-level schools. In particular, the report indicated that less than one-third were children of semi-skilled and unskilled workers, while almost three-quarters were the children of professionals, employers, managers and senior salaried employees.[18]

The introduction of the free post-primary education scheme in 1967 was an attempt to ensure equality of access to all seeking education beyond first level. Prior to this, entrance to secondary schools in general depended in part on parents' ability to pay fees. It must also be noted, however, that while all secondary schools charged fees prior to the introduction of the scheme, the ability to pay fees was not a condition of entry to some schools managed by some religious orders. In effect, they operated a free scheme for some pupils from low-income families long before the Department of Education took the initiative.

Under the free post-primary education scheme, secondary schools that opted to discontinue charging school fees for pupils were paid a supplemental grant per pupil equal to the fee charged in the school year 1966/7. The majority of secondary schools agreed to participate in the free scheme.

The free post-primary education scheme also provided for grants towards free school books and accessories for necessitous day pupils. Under the scheme, free transport was also provided for pupils living more than three miles from a school in which free education was available.

A limited scheme of free post-primary education had been under consideration in the Department of Education during the 1960s, and it was intended that such a scheme be introduced in 1970 to coincide with the raising of the school-leaving age to fifteen years. The early introduction of the scheme was due to the intervention of Donogh O'Malley, TD, Minister for Education. Sean O'Connor, Assistant Secretary in the Department of Education at the time, has recounted:

> We, the planners, prepared to introduce free education in tandem with the raising of the school leaving age in 1970 and all our urging and striving for coordination and cooperation had that year as a focal point … I have long been convinced that had matters proceeded according to our plans, when 1970 came, free education would not have been on the agenda at all, or if it had been, it would have been in such attenuated form as scarce to merit the title. Donogh O'Malley shattered our plans and left Ireland in his debt.[19]

The numbers participating in second-level education rose dramatically in the decade following the introduction of free post-primary education, from 148,000 in 1966 to 278,000 in 1976 (an increase of 88 per cent). This was due in part to the increase in the young population at the time, but the participation rate by age also increased (see later section on participation in education). Most of the increased participation must be attributed to the introduction of the free scheme, and the free transport service undoubtedly led to increased participation in rural areas.

Vocational schools

There was little emphasis in Ireland on technical education prior to the early decades of the twentieth century. The Vocational Education Act, 1930, remained the basic statute governing vocational and technical education until the late 1990s, and has provided the framework for development in this area. The development of vocational schools from the 1930s onwards helped to partially redress the regional imbalance in the distribution of secondary schools. The important provisions in the act covered administration and financial arrangements.

Administration

The vocational education system is administered by local VECs subject to the general control of the Minister for Education. Membership of the VEC initially consisted of local authority elected representatives (who constituted the majority) and other representatives of educational, cultural, industrial and commercial interests in the area. A total of thirty-eight VECs were established; one for each county borough (Dublin, Cork, Limerick and Waterford), one for each administrative county and seven for certain urban areas (Bray, Drogheda, Dun Laoghaire, Galway, Sligo, Tralee and Wexford).

The functions of a VEC were to provide, or to assist in the provision of, a system of continuation education and a system of technical education in its area. It could establish schools, employ staff and generally perform all the functions of an education authority, within the general powers conferred by the Vocational Education Act. A VEC's programme was subject to the approval of the Minister for Education but, once the basic educational and financial schemes had been approved, a considerable degree of flexibility and discretion was allowed in regard to the actual organisation of courses. Committees were thus in a position to be responsive to local needs.

The financial arrangements of the Vocational Education Act provided for a local rate contribution and corresponding grant from the state. In the first year, 1931/2, the total cost of vocational education was £303,000, of which the Department of Education contributed two-thirds. In time the local rate contribution declined in importance, particularly following the abolition of rates on private dwellings in 1978. Most of the total cost of vocational education is now met by way of grants from the Department of Education.

The Vocational Education (Amendment) Act, 2001, provided for new structures and accountability, management and financial procedures in order that each VEC could meet the needs of vocational education in their area. The VECs now have corporate status. Although their administrative areas are similar to those of the larger local government bodies, they do not come within that system. Membership of VECs has been broadened under the 2001 act to include parent and staff representatives, and members may also be appointed to represent the interests of students, voluntary organisations, community organisations, Irish language interests and business; local elected representatives still constitute the majority of the membership.

Since 1930 the remit of VECs has increased, particularly in the area of adult education. They are responsible for post-primary education through vocational schools and community colleges. They also have responsibility for further and adult education through Post Leaving Certificate courses (PLCs), youthreach services, the Vocational Training Opportunities Scheme and community education. As indicated in the section on first-level education, the role of VECs in primary education is likely to increase.

Secondary versus vocational schools
Apart from administrative and financing differences between secondary and vocational schools, a number of other important differences have also existed. From the outset, vocational schools were inter-denominational and co-educational, whereas secondary schools were mainly denominational and single-sex institutions. While vocational schools have a more democratic administrative structure, the Church nevertheless has had some influence on the development of the system. At the time of the passing of the Vocational Education Act, 1930, the Catholic hierarchy was given an assurance by Professor John Marcus O'Sullivan, TD, Minister for Education, that the vocational system would not impinge upon the field covered by the denominationally controlled secondary schools.[20] It was intended that the two types of schools would develop quite separately with no overlap between them. Coolahan has noted that in the 1960s:

> Vocational schools were frequently in unequal competition with the local secondary school, each type of school proceeding in splendid isolation from the other.[21]

With the introduction of Leaving Certificate courses in vocational schools in the mid 1960s, the social and educational barriers between the two systems began to be slowly removed. The vocational system, with its emphasis on technical subjects, was popularly regarded as a type of educational cul-de-sac where qualifications led to low-paid occupations; the secondary schools, on the other hand, with their emphasis on academic subjects, were regarded as having higher social status, their qualifications being passports to third-level academic education and more remunerative occupations.

Despite curricular developments, the divisions remained, and were such as to have evoked from Gemma Hussey, TD, Minister for Education, the following remark during a visit to a number of schools in north Kerry in 1984:

> The old snob divisions between vocational and secondary are firmly evident. If I was a dictator they would be all mixed up together.[22]

Comprehensive schools

Apart from inequalities based on social groups, the *Investment in Education* report also indicated that there were inequalities based on geographical location in the participation of children in post-primary education.[23] The reasons for this have already been outlined in the foregoing sections. An attempt to remedy this deficiency was the establishment of comprehensive schools, plans for which were first announced in 1963 by Dr Patrick Hillery, TD, Minister for Education. In his policy statement, the minister referred to:

> areas where the population is so scattered as to make the establishment of a secondary or a vocational school a most unlikely event.[24]

What the minister envisaged was the establishment, in areas where post-primary education was inadequate or non-existent, of schools that would be completely financed by the state. The first four comprehensive schools were established at Cootehill (County Cavan), Carraroe (County Galway), Shannon (County Clare) and Glenties (County Donegal). Each of these schools was sited in rural areas and open to all children within a radius of ten miles.

The comprehensive school also represented an attempt to rectify the division of interest between secondary and vocational schools by combining academic and practical subjects in one broad curriculum. In this way, pupils would be offered an education structured to their needs, abilities and interests.

Protestant comprehensives

Because of the absence of any Protestant equivalent of the Catholic religious orders, which have reinvested members' salaries in the establishment and maintenance of their schools, the cost to Protestants of providing their own secondary schools has been relatively high. The introduction of the concept of a comprehensive school, where capital and current costs would be met fully by the state, presented an opportunity to establish Protestant schools without the burden of heavy costs. Five Protestant comprehensives have been established, but the intake of pupils in these schools is not exclusively Protestant. By the mid 1970s, the total number of comprehensive schools reached sixteen, and this has not increased since then.

The Department of Education meets both capital and current costs of comprehensive schools in full.

Community schools

Another important finding of the *Investment in Education* report was that there were gaps in the efficiency of the educational system in the use of existing educational resources. In particular, the report referred to duplication of resources and staff in secondary and vocational schools. In a statement to the authorities of secondary and vocational schools in 1966, George Colley, TD, Minister for Education, indicated that the two rigidly separated post-primary systems could no longer be maintained, but also that their distinctive character should be retained. He recommended a sharing of accommodation and facilities between schools.[25]

This was taken a stage further when, in 1970, Patrick Faulkner, TD, Minister for Education, announced plans for community schools to be created by agreement rather than legislation. The circular on community schools issued by the minister indicated that in some areas community schools would result from the amalgamation of existing secondary and vocational schools, and in growing suburban areas from the development of a single school rather than the traditional development of separate secondary and vocational schools. The community schools were to be co-educational and non-fee-paying, with enrolments of 400 to 1,000.

The community schools concept seemed a logical development that would help to eliminate many of the obvious deficiencies in the education system at second level. An added attraction was that the capital costs would be covered mainly by the state; in a period of rising costs, this would be an incentive to religious orders to participate in community schools. Another dimension to the community school concept was the involvement of the community. The community schools were to be focal points in the locality, with their facilities being made available to the community outside school hours.

The announcement of plans for community schools gave rise to considerable controversy, and opposition was expressed towards the merging of two distinct educational systems. Much of this was undoubtedly influenced by the higher prestige accorded to secondary schools. In some locations, parents and religious orders objected to the amalgamation of traditional secondary schools with the vocational system. There was also controversy about the deeds of trust (the legal base for the schools in the absence of legislation) that were to be signed by the main parties.

One of the main factors accounting for the acceptance of the community school concept over time was the decline in membership of religious orders. As a result, it was virtually impossible for them to establish new secondary schools as they had in the past and even increasingly difficult for them to retain a significant presence in the existing secondary schools. The decline in membership of religious orders over the past few decades has been a factor in the closure or amalgamation of many secondary schools. Since the late 1960s the number of secondary schools has declined by one-third, and this decline has been partly offset by the increase in comprehensive and, especially, community schools (Table 4.3). In statistics on the number of second-level schools, community and comprehensive schools are grouped together as one category by the Department of Education. In 2009 the breakdown was seventy-six community schools and sixteen comprehensive schools.

Current expenditure in community schools is met entirely by the state.

Table 4.3: *Number of second-level schools, selected years, 1969–2009*

	1969	1976	2000	2009
Secondary	600	532	419	384
Vocational	253	245	247	254
Community and Comprehensive	3	42	85	92
Total	856	819	751	730

Source: Statistical reports (Department of Education and Skills).

Ownership and management of second-level schools

A broad distinction can be made between privately owned and publicly owned second-level schools.

The privately owned schools are secondary schools mostly owned by religious orders (congregations), Catholic dioceses or archdioceses, Protestant boards of governors, individuals or groups. The owners are the patrons/trustees of the school.

The publicly owned schools are vocational schools/community colleges and community and comprehensive schools, where the trustees hold the property in trust for the Minister for Education and Skills.

The local management of second-level schools is far more complex than that at first level where, as noted, boards of management were first introduced in 1975. This complexity arises in part from the very different origins, purpose and ethos of the four categories of schools. To add to the confused situation, there may be differences even within a category, e.g. between Catholic and Protestant secondary schools.

Section 14 (1) of the Education Act, 1998, stipulates that:

> It shall be the duty of a patron, for the purposes of ensuring that a recognised school is managed in a spirit of partnership, to appoint where practicable a board of management the composition of which is agreed between patrons of schools, national associations of parents, recognised school management organisations, recognised trade unions and staff associations representing teachers and the Minister.[26]

The act did not seek to impose a uniform model of boards of management on all second-level schools (achieving agreement on that would have been a difficult task). Instead, it allows flexibility to suit the needs of particular schools. The following is necessarily a summary of the key management features of each category of school, subject to variation at local level:

- Secondary schools – four nominees of the patron/trustees, two elected parents and two elected teachers;
- Vocational schools/community colleges – three nominees of the VEC, two elected parents, two elected teachers, with some variations on this for community colleges;
- Comprehensive schools – originally, a three-member board of management, i.e. the chief executive of the VEC, a diocesan representative (Catholic or Protestant) and an official from the Department of Education (usually a schools inspector); since then, two parents and two teachers have been added;
- Community schools – three nominees of religious orders or the diocese, three nominees of the VEC, two elected parents and two elected teachers.[27]

Rationalisation and regionalisation at second level

A number of developments have occurred in the past few decades that have, to some extent, lessened the distinction between the traditional secondary and vocational schools. Thus, the curriculum in these two types of schools is now broadly the same. Similarly, the establishment of community schools and community colleges has ensured that a single school now exists in some areas where, traditionally, secondary and vocational schools would have been established. In this context, it is reasonable to question whether the present system, with four different types of schools at second level with different administrative and financial arrangements, is justified and whether some further rationalisation is required.

In 1985 the Department of Education published a Green Paper that proposed the abolition of the VECs and their replacement by thirteen local education councils (LECs).[28] These LECs would have a membership representing teachers, parents, school management, youth services, training agencies, trade unions and employers. They would be responsible for coordinating all secondary, vocational, comprehensive and community schools in their area, and for the provision, planning and development of second-level education. The areas to be covered by the LECs would embrace a number of counties in some cases.

The Green Paper pointed out that development in the post-primary education system over the previous two decades had led to the creation of a number of different types of schools, all of which were seeking to provide essentially the same education service to the same public. It indicated that the establishment of a regional body would eliminate friction based on the management structure of schools and would provide a better framework for the rationalisation of post-primary facilities and for the delivery of other services.

There had been proposals for a regional structure prior to this.[29] However, the 1985 Green Paper was the first proposal on regional structures to be published by the Department of Education with the intention of initiating a debate on the subject.

Reaction to the 1985 Green Paper by the various interest groups was not very enthusiastic. The abolition of the VECs was unacceptable to many members of those committees, especially public elected representatives. Similarly, the reaction of the teachers' unions in second-level schools was muted, although the Irish National Teachers' Organisation, representing teachers in primary schools, objected to the plan on the grounds that primary schools were not included in the proposed regional structure. Nothing became of the Green Paper's proposals.

In a White paper, *Charting our Education Future* (1995), regionalisation was raised once again. It proposed the devolution of powers from the Department of Education to ten regional education boards and the establishment of a commission to recommend on the rationalisation of the vocational education system.

The Commission on School Accommodation was set up following publication of the White Paper, and it recommended a reduction from thirty-eight to twenty-one in the number of VECs by the amalgamation of geographic areas.[30] In 1998 the number of VECS was reduced from thirty-eight to thirty-three when five of the smaller urban VECs (Bray, Drogheda, Sligo, Tralee and Wexford) were amalgamated with the relevant county VEC. Further reductions in the number of VECs were subsequently recommended. The McCarthy report recommended that the number be reduced from thirty-three to twenty-two.[31] In 2010 the Minister for Education and Skills, Mary Coughlan, TD, went a step further and announced a reduction from thirty-three to sixteen through the merger of existing VECs; for example, the three VECs for Counties Laois, Offaly and Westmeath would be merged.

The Education Bill, 1997, proposed the establishment of ten regional education boards, covering geographic areas very similar to those of the then regional health boards. Following a change of government, no provision was made for the establishment of regional education boards in the revised Education Bill, 1997.

While regionalisation is no longer on the education agenda, the rationalisation of second-level schools is likely to continue, with amalgamations and a consequent decline in the total number of such schools. The traditional situation in many towns of a secondary school for girls run by a religious order, a secondary school for boys run by a religious order and a co-educational vocational educational school has already changed, and is likely to change further. A report by CORI in 1997 concluded that, within twenty-five years or less, there may not be enough members of religious orders to conduct any school-related function.[32] This process will inevitably lead to a rationalisation of the second-level system at local level.

Third-level education

Third-level education in Ireland may be broadly divided into two sectors: university and non-university.

University sector
There are now seven universities in the Republic:

- University of Dublin with one college, Trinity College;
- National University of Ireland (NUI) with four constituent universities at Dublin, Cork, Galway and Maynooth;
- Dublin City University;
- University of Limerick.

The NUI also has five recognised colleges: the National College of Art and Design, the Royal College of Surgeons, Shannon College of Hotel Management, the Milltown Institute of Theology and Philosophy and the Institute of Public Administration. St Angela's College of Education, Sligo, is a college of NUI Galway.

The following is a brief background to the establishment of the older universities.

Trinity College

University of Dublin received its charter from Elizabeth I in 1591. From the beginning it was identified with English rule and the governing class in Ireland. For much of its history, according to Lyons, Trinity was 'intensely conscious of its position as a bastion of the Ascendancy in general and of Anglicanism in particular'.[33] In 1793 Catholics were admitted to degrees in Trinity College, and by the mid-nineteenth century they constituted about 10 per cent of the undergraduate body. While the formal name is the University of Dublin, it is more commonly referred to as Trinity or Trinity College (attempts to include other colleges were not successful).

The Queen's Colleges

In 1850 a non-denominational university, Queen's University, was established as the degree-awarding body for three Queen's Colleges at Belfast, Galway and Cork. There would be no interference with religious convictions, but the establishment, by private endowment, of a theological school within the colleges was permissible. Opposition to the Queen's Colleges was considerable, particularly from some members of the Irish Catholic hierarchy who feared that lectures in philosophy, history and science were bound to reflect contemporary thought on these subjects. At the Synod of Thurles (1850) the hierarchy condemned the Queen's Colleges and exhorted laymen to avoid them as students or teachers on the grounds that they were dangers to faith and morals. A minority of bishops unsuccessfully appealed against these decisions. Despite ecclesiastical opposition, the three colleges were established.

The Royal University

The University Education (Ireland) Act, 1879, provided for the formation of a new university – the Royal University – and for the dissolution of Queen's University (but not the three Queen's Colleges). The Royal University was modelled on the University of London, which at the time was purely an examining body. Authority was granted to confer degrees on all students irrespective of where they had studied. The religious difficulty was overcome, and Catholics and Protestants presented themselves for examination.

The Catholic University
At the Synod of Thurles a section of the Catholic hierarchy favoured the establishment of a Catholic university styled on that of Louvain, which had been founded with Papal approval in 1834. Dr John Henry Newman, a distinguished Oxford convert to Catholicism, was invited to become rector of the new university, established in 1854. An application by the hierarchy for a charter for the university was unsuccessful, as was an application for state funds. Newman left Ireland in 1858 and the university declined. In 1890 it was placed in the charge of the Jesuits, who administered its affairs until the establishment of the National University in 1908.

The National University of Ireland
The NUI was established by the Irish Universities Act, 1908. In the following year the Royal University was formally dissolved. The act provided for the establishment of two new universities, one in Dublin and one in Belfast. The one in Belfast was to become the Queen's University, replacing the former college of that name. The new NUI, centred in Dublin, was to take over the Queen's Colleges in Cork and Galway as constituent colleges, as well as the new college founded in Dublin to replace the Catholic University. The NUI was further allowed to affiliate institutions that it considered to have a satisfactory standard; this allowed the subsequent entry of Maynooth. No test whatsoever of religious belief was to be permitted for any appointment in either of the universities, thus denying the denominational university that the Catholic hierarchy had long demanded.

St Patrick's College, Maynooth
St Patrick's was founded in 1795 as a seminary for the training of the Catholic clergy. It was the only Catholic educational institution to receive state aid at the time. In 1910, under the provisions of the Irish Universities Act, 1908, the college was given status by the senate of the NUI as a recognised college of the NUI in certain faculties. A decision by the hierarchy to admit lay students to courses at Maynooth in 1966/7 led to the wider use of an institution that had hitherto been confined to the training of priests. Since then, the number of clerical students has declined while the number of lay students has increased steadily. Under the Universities Act, 1997, St Patrick's College remains, but NUI Maynooth has been made into a separate legal entity.

Trinity College in the twentieth century
The future status of Trinity College became a leading question during the early part of the twentieth century. A Royal Commission of 1907 recommended that University of Dublin be enlarged to include the Queen's Colleges, and that a new college acceptable to the Catholic authorities be founded in Dublin. Opposition to this proposal, however, ensured that Trinity maintained its independence when the National University was established in 1908.

At the National Synod of Maynooth in 1875, the Catholic hierarchy had coupled Trinity College with the Queen's Colleges as places forbidden to Catholic students. Yet for many years the bishops took no active steps towards implementing this decision, apart from periodical instructions to priests to refrain from advising parents to send their children to Trinity College. In practice, it was left to the Catholic Archbishop of Dublin to decide under what circumstances attendance of Catholics at Trinity College was permissible: an inability to take the compulsory matriculation qualification in Irish, which was required by the NUI, was regarded as the most common acceptable circumstance. Perhaps the most significant barriers created by the ban were not so much religious as social, and it served to isolate Trinity from the life of the vast majority of the Irish people.

The ban also led to an influx of non-Irish undergraduates. In 1965/6, 27 per cent of Trinity's students were from the UK (excluding Northern Ireland), and a further 9 per cent were from other countries. In the same year Catholics accounted for 20 per cent of the total number of students. In 1967 the board of Trinity College decided to limit the entry of non-Irish students, up to a maximum of 10 per cent, to those who had associations with Ireland or those who belonged to educationally developing countries. This measure partly paved the way for the removal of the ban, which occurred in 1970. By 1975/6, only 3 per cent of Trinity's students were from the UK (excluding Northern Ireland), and a further 6 per cent were from other countries. In the same year Catholics accounted for 65 per cent of students.

Dublin City University/University of Limerick
The former National Institutes for Higher Education, at Limerick and Dublin, were granted university status in 1989. The Higher Education Authority (HEA) first proposed the concept of an institute for Limerick in 1969, and the Institute began functioning in 1972, offering degrees and diplomas with a strong bias towards technology and European studies. The National Institute for Higher Education in Dublin was established in 1975, and the first students were enrolled in 1980. The

two institutes were granted university status in 1989 and became the University of Limerick and Dublin City University.

Non-university sector

The regional institutes of technology (formerly the RTCs), the colleges of the Dublin Institute of Technology (DIT), the teacher-training colleges and a number of other institutions offering courses in areas such as domestic science and commerce provide most further education outside the universities. It is a sector that has grown considerably in the past three decades. Students in this sector now account for 45 per cent of the total at third level.

The idea of RTCs was first referred to in a policy statement on post-primary education in 1963 by Dr Patrick Hillery, TD, Minister for Education.[34] The intention was to arrange for the provision of a limited number of technological colleges with regional status. The proposal was taken further in 1969 by the report of a steering committee on technical education. The report envisaged the colleges, for the most part, as being second-level institutions, but suggested some of them might also provide PLC full-time or equivalent part-time courses over one or two years, leading to higher technician courses.[35] Both the report of the steering committee and the *Investment in Education* report stressed the need for high-level technicians to service a growing industrial sector.

The first RTCs opened in the period 1970–2. While they were originally intended to reinforce the technical dimension of the second-level system, they quickly found themselves called upon to cater increasingly for third-level demand.

The Regional Technical Colleges Act, 1992, gave greater autonomy to the colleges by allowing them their own governing bodies. Hitherto they were effectively subcommittees of their local VEC. During 1997 the status of the RTCs became an issue, and each was redesignated as an institute of technology. The courses in these institutes are now third level and encompass certificate, diploma and degree courses. There are now fourteen institutes of technology, eleven of which originated as RTCs. They are Athlone, Blanchardstown, Carlow, Cork, Dundalk, Dun Laoghaire, Galway–Mayo, Letterkenny, Limerick, Sligo, Tallaght, Tralee, Waterford and the DIT.

Dublin Institute of Technology

The DIT was established informally in 1978 to bring greater coordination to the work of six third-level colleges of the City of Dublin VEC. The six colleges are the Colleges of Technology in Bolton Street and Kevin Street and the Colleges of Catering, of Commerce, of

Marketing and Design, and of Music. The Dublin Institute of Technology Act, 1992, gave statutory recognition to the development and expanding role of the institute. The DIT has had degree-awarding powers since 1998/9.

Colleges of education
There are five colleges of education for primary school teachers: St Patrick's, Drumcondra; Church of Ireland College, Rathmines; St Mary's, Marino; Froebel College, Blackrock; and Mary Immaculate College in Limerick (Carysfort Teacher Training College, Dublin, established in 1883, was closed in 1987). There are two colleges for home economics (St Catherine's in Dublin and St Angela's in Sligo). Thomond College (Limerick) is a specialist college for teachers of physical education and crafts. Both Mary Immaculate College and Thomond College were incorporated into the University of Limerick in 1991. St Patrick's College, Drumcondra, was included within Dublin City University in 1993. Teachers of art are trained in the National College of Art and Design, Dublin. The colleges of education and the two colleges of home economics are associated with the universities for their degree awards.

As already indicated, two other institutions were part of the non-university sector – the National Institutes for Higher Education at Limerick and Dublin – until they achieved university status in 1989.

Other third-level bodies
Apart from the universities, institutes of technology and other teaching institutions, there are a number of other bodies that play key roles in the development of third-level education, notably the Higher Education and Training Awards Council (HETAC) and the HEA.

Higher Education and Training Awards Council
To meet the demand for qualifications in third-level institutions outside of universities, the National Council for Educational Awards (NCEA) was set up in 1972 on an ad hoc basis pending the passing of legislation to establish it on a statutory basis. Its function was to approve courses and grant awards outside the university sector. Following a period of uncertainty concerning the NCEA's future in the mid 1970s, the NCEA Act was passed in 1978 and came into effect in 1980. The NCEA was responsible for the coordination, development and promotion of technical, industrial, scientific, technological and commercial education and of education in art and design outside the universities.

HETAC was established in 2001 under the Qualifications (Education and Training) Act, 1999. It is the legal successor to the NCEA. Awards made by the former NCEA are deemed to be HETAC awards. Essentially, HETAC is the qualifications-awarding body for third-level educational and training institutions outside the university sector.

Higher Education Authority
The HEA was established in 1968 on the recommendation of the Commission of Higher Education (1967), but it was not until 1972 that it became a statutory body under the Higher Education Act, 1971. The HEA is the statutory planning and policy development body for higher education and research in Ireland. It has wide advisory powers throughout the whole of the third-level education sector.

The main source of funding for third-level institutions are state grants, which are channelled to them through the HEA.

Grants and fees at third level
The *Commission on Higher Education* report (1967) contained surveys which indicated that children of manual workers comprised less than one-tenth of university students, and that farmers' children comprised not more than two-tenths, with the children of non-manual workers accounting for the remainder. In considering various schemes of financial aid, the commission affirmed the principle 'that no qualified student should be denied the opportunity of higher education through lack of means'.[36] The Local Authority (Higher Education Grant) Act, 1968, provided for such a scheme, with grants available to students who reach a required standard in the Leaving Certificate examination and whose parents satisfy a means test. The grant, administered by local authorities, has operated on a sliding scale related to parental income and the number of children in the family. It also distinguished between students living within commuting distances of third-level centres and those living outside of commuting distances.

In 1995 Niamh Bhreathnach, TD, Minister for Education, announced the phased abolition of undergraduate fees over the academic years 1995/6 and 1996/7, to be financed in part by the phasing out of covenants that provided tax relief to parents who took out such covenants in favour of their children. By 1995 approximately two-thirds of students were not paying fees, with some in receipt of grants and others pursuing courses mainly in institutes of technology funded by the European Social Fund grants. The maintenance element of the higher-education grants (subject to a means test) remained as an important source for many students following the abolition of third-level fees.

There was no groundswell of opinion in favour of the abolition of third-level fees. If anything, the view among education analysts was that it represented a windfall to the middle- and higher-income groups and that it would do little to further participation in third level by those from lower-income groups. While fees were abolished, a student services charge was introduced and the level of this charge increased in subsequent years.

By the latter part of 2002, Noel Dempsey, TD, Minister for Education and Science, was having second thoughts about free third-level education. This apparently had as much to do with the need to reduce public expenditure as with a concern that lower socio-economic groups had not reaped the benefit of the abolition of fees by increased participation (see later section on participation at third level). It should be noted that in introducing the free fees initiative Niamh Bhreathnach made no claims that it would lead to greater participation among lower socio-economic groups. Considerable controversy ensued from Noel Dempsey's suggestion to revisit the fees issue. He initiated a review on the need to broaden access to and improve equity in third-level education, which was completed in 2003. The review considered various aspects of third level, including expenditure and participation, and included a survey of student-support systems in a number of other countries. It noted that the free fees initiative had no impact on promoting equity or broadening access to higher education for the lowest socio-economic groups. The review presented a series of options based on the introduction of fee contributions across a range of income bands and concluded that 'the more that students from higher-earning families can contribute towards the cost of tuition fees, the more money will be made available to improve supports for students from lower-income families'.[37] The review proposed retaining free fees for students of middle-income families. In the event, fees were not reintroduced.

In 2008 the issue of third-level fees was raised once again, this time by Batt O'Keefe, TD, Minister for Education and Science, and in a context of the need to increase funding of third-level education and to reduce public expenditure due to the economic downturn. Among the options being considered was the introduction of a student loan scheme (see later section on the Hunt report).

Rationalisation of structures at third level

For over three decades, there has been debate and controversy surrounding the status of different third-level institutions.[38] Between 1967 and 1977 a variety of proposals and counterproposals were put forward, either by the Minister for Education or by other sources such as the *Commission on Higher Education* report (1967) and the HEA. Essentially, these proposals were concerned with the number of universities and with which colleges should have university status. The classic examples of the bewildering changes and proposals were those made by Richard Burke, TD, Minister for Education. In 1974 he indicated that Trinity College would retain its status as a separate university, that University College Dublin (UCD) would become an independent university and that the NUI would remain (with constituent colleges in Cork and Galway), i.e. there would be three universities. In 1976, however, in a complete turnabout in policy, he announced that there would be five universities – Trinity, UCD, University College Cork (UCC), University College Galway (UCG) and Maynooth.

The results of a national referendum on the seventh amendment to the Constitution, held in 1979, made it possible for the government to introduce legislation providing for the abolition of the NUI and the establishment of independent universities at UCD, UCC and UCG.

As a result of various pieces of legislation, many changes occurred from the late 1980s onwards. These included the establishment of Dublin City University and the University of Limerick (1989), the establishment of the four constituent universities of the NUI (1997), the granting of autonomy to the DIT and the RTCs (1992), the redesignation of the RTCs as institutes of technology (1998), the abolition of the NCEA and its replacement by HETAC.

Despite these changes, which have brought about a certain amount of rationalisation, the debate has continued on issues such as autonomy and degree-awarding functions, especially in the non-university sector.

The National Strategy for Higher Education to 2030

In 2009 the government established a strategy group, under the chairmanship of Dr Colin Hunt, to review third-level education in a changing environment. The group's report, usually referred to as the Hunt report, was published in 2011 and set out a 20-year strategy for the third-level sector. It noted that the system had witnessed exceptional development in the recent past, moving from one that was confined to a social elite to one of widespread participation. The report estimated, based on projections, that the demand for higher education would increase by over 70 per cent over the coming decades and that this demand would be driven by a rising demographic of school leavers together with an increase in adult students and international students. It also identified the need for a more diverse range of both full- and part-time programmes, on and off campus, and more entry routes into higher education. Two key aspects of the report's recommendations concerned funding and structures.

The Hunt report had a particular focus on the challenge of finding a sustainable long-term funding base for third level. It concluded that the sector had a requirement of €500 million per annum to keep pace with student demand and to meet government targets for the economy. Since current funding of the sector is largely dependent on the state, it concluded that this situation was unsustainable. While recognising that certain efficiencies could be achieved within the system, it also recognised that there was no alternative to 'direct student contribution, based on a combination of upfront fees and an income-contingent loan scheme'.[39] The recommendation regarding fees was partly met when Budget 2011 provided for an increase in the student contribution (formerly the registration charge) from €1,500 to €2,000. Options concerning the possible introduction of a student-loan scheme had already been considered at some length in a previous report.[40] The Hunt report therefore did not consider how such a scheme might work, and recommended that the design of an appropriate loan scheme for Ireland be left to an expert group.

In order to ensure that the system can deliver on the necessary range of educational provision and of student access and choice, the Hunt report set out a policy framework for the roles and relationships across the network of higher-education institutions. It recommended that institutions should cooperate on a regional cluster basis and indicated that no new universities should be recognised under Section 9 of the Universities Act, 1997. However, it also recommended that the regional amalgamation of institutes of technology be promoted and their future redesignation as technological universities be provided for.

The Fine Gael/Labour *Programme for Government* (2011) contained a commitment to review the recommendations of the Hunt report.

Adult education

With the introduction of important developments in the Irish education system at all levels during the 1960s and early 1970s, it was inevitable that attention would be focused on adult education and, more specifically, on those who, for whatever reason, had terminated their full-time education at an early age.

Formal adult education courses are mainly provided by statutory agencies, notably the VECs. Many other organisations and institutions, both statutory and voluntary, are involved in adult education. These provide a variety of courses from basic literacy to leisure-type courses.

A number of policy reports on adult education have been published over the past few decades, including a White Paper in 2000. One report,

Adult Education in Ireland (1973), estimated that 10 per cent of the adult population participated annually in adult education, indicated that the expenditure on adult education was inadequate to meet even existing needs and recommended separate budgetary provision by the Department of Education. Among its main structural recommendations was the establishment of county education committees.[41]

The *Report of the Commission on Adult Education* was published a decade later, in 1984. Its findings indicated that the group which had not participated in any form of education since completing their initial education had within it disproportionately high numbers of older and working-class people and rural dwellers, i.e. those who had, in general, benefited least from initial education compared with their younger, middle-class and urban counterparts. The commission recommended that local adult education boards be established under the VECs with a separate budget to enable priorities to be established on a local basis. It also recommended the establishment of a national education council.[42]

Some progress was made, especially with the appointment of adult education organisers in 1979 under the VECs and the establishment of adult education boards in each VEC area in 1984. However, criticism of the lack of investment in the sector continued.

In a 1989 report, Aontas, the National Adult Learning Organisation, which represents statutory and voluntary bodies involved in adult education, stated:

> Adult education in Ireland is underdeveloped ... it is more oriented in range and practice towards the middle classes following hobby and leisure pursuits than a direct means towards improving their life chances. Often those who have most to benefit tend to be excluded.[43]

A Green Paper was published in 1998 and was followed by a White Paper in 2000.[44] The White Paper, *Learning for Life*, defined adult education as 'systematic learning undertaken by adults who return to learning having concluded initial education or training'. It was critical of the lack of priority given to the sector and the inadequate level of investment by successive governments. Of the 1984 commission's report, it noted that:

> it was to have little impact on an education system already straining to cope with a greatly expanded provision for a rapidly increasing youth population and the financial crises of the mid-1980s.[45]

The White Paper proposed the establishment of a statutory agency, the National Adult Learning Council, which would have responsibility for framing and implementing policy, and thirty-three Local Adult Learning Boards. It also proposed increased funding. This White Paper was widely welcomed in adult education circles.

The National Adult Learning Council was established on an ad hoc basis in 2002 pending its establishment as an executive agency of the Department of Education, but it had ceased to function by 2004. The expectations raised in the wake of the White Paper of 2000 of a revitalised and prioritised role for adult education have not been met.

Participation in education

The numbers of full-time students at each level of education and as a proportion of the total have fluctuated over the past forty years or so due to demographic reasons and other factors. The high number of births in the 1970s is reflected in the growth in numbers of pupils enrolled at first level. However, as the number of births declined from the early 1980s until the mid 1990s, so also did the numbers attending first level (Table 4.4).

Table 4.4: *Enrolments of full-time students in institutions aided by the Department of Education and Science (000s), selected years, 1965–2009*

Level	1965/6	1975/6	1985/6	1995/6	2009/10
First	481 (76.1%)	528 (63.8%)	567 (59.4%)	479 (50.7%)	506 (49.9%)
Second	132 (20.9%)	268 (32.4%)	335 (35.0%)	370 (39.2%)	351 (34.6%)
Third	19 (3.0%)	32 (3.8%)	53 (5.6%)	95 (10.1%)	157 (15.5%)
Total	632 (100.0%)	828 (100.0%)	955 (100.0%)	944 (100.0%)	1,014 (100.0%)

Source: Statistical reports (Department of Education and Skills).

In the mid 1960s first-level students accounted for three-quarters of all full-time students; forty years later, however, due to various factors such as increased participation in education by age, they accounted for half of the full-time student population. The numbers at third level have increased consistently over the forty-year period, and their percentage share has increased from a low base of 3 per cent to 15 per cent over the same period.

On the basis of the figures in Table 4.4, just over one-fifth of the total population were in full-time education in 2009.

Participation by age

While there has been a general increase in the numbers attending second and third level, it is more relevant to examine trends in participation rates. From the mid 1960s, prior to the introduction of free post-primary education, the participation rates for those aged fifteen to eighteen years increased remarkably up to the mid 1990s (Table 4.5). Since then, the rate of progress has halted and further improvement in participation by age is likely to be more difficult to achieve.

Table 4.5: *Participation in full-time education by age, selected years, 1966–99*

Age	1966	1974	1988	1995	1999
15	54.2	77.5	97.1	95.7	96.0
16	39.0	60.4	90.3	91.1	91.6
17	27.3	43.2	74.2	81.9	80.5
18	14.7	22.4	48.3	63.6	63.2
19	9.6	12.5	28.5	47.5	47.3

Source: Statistical reports (Department of Education and Skills).

Participation in third level

Measures introduced in the 1960s, such as the free post-primary education scheme, have ensured that second level is accessible to all students. However, despite these and other developments, the problem of early school leavers has persisted. While education is compulsory between the ages of six and sixteen years, some children still drop out of the education system before the end of primary school or do not go on to post-primary schools. A report by the NESF in 2002 estimated that 1,000 children per year do not transfer from primary to post-primary school.[46] The NESF report also indicated that some 12,000 young people who commence second-level education leave school without sitting the Leaving Certificate examination; of these, some 2,400 leave before the Junior Certificate examination. The report also commented that 'there is a persistent 3 per cent of the school population for whom the education system is failing as they leave with no qualifications'.[47]

Participation at third level is very different to that at either first or second level, and it is at this level also that disparities exist in relation to participation by students from different social classes. In its review of participation in education from first through to third level the *Investment in Education* report noted in relation to third level that 'by this stage the disparity between the social groups has become most marked and the strong association between university entrance and social group is unmistakable'.[48] It should be noted that many developments took place subsequent to the *Investment in Education* report that had the effect of improving access to higher education. These included the introduction of higher-education grants in 1968 and the provision of additional places at third level, especially in the non-university sector.

One of the first surveys of entrants to third-level education following the introduction of higher-education grants in 1968 was conducted for the Dublin area in 1978/9. This survey indicated that about three-quarters of entrants came from the four higher socio-economic groups despite the fact that these groups constituted only one-fifth of the population of Dublin.[49] The study also revealed distinct geographic differences within Dublin based on postal districts, reflecting the socio-economic composition of the population in different geographic areas.

Beginning in 1980, national surveys commissioned by the HEA have been carried out every six years on participation in third-level education. As might be expected, admission among the relevant age group (seventeen to eighteen years old) has increased substantially since the first survey (Table 4.6). Over the approximately twenty-year period, the admission rate increased from 20.0 per cent to 55.0 per cent, i.e. almost three times the proportion of students in the relevant age group were going to third-level institutions in 2004 as compared with 1980. In view of this rate of progress, a target of 72 per cent participation for the relevant cohort was set for 2020 by the HEA (see section on improving access to third level).

Each of the surveys conducted so far has highlighted the fact that students from the higher socio-economic groups have gone on to third

Table 4.6: *National rate of admission to higher-education institutions, selected years, 1980–2004**

Year	Rate of admission (%)
1980	20.0
1986	25.0
1992	35.9
1998	44.4
2004	55.0

* Admission from relevant age cohort.

Sources: P. Clancy, *College Entry in Focus: A Fourth National Survey of Access to Higher Education* (Higher Education Authority, Dublin, 2001); P.J. O'Connell et al., *Who Went to College in 2004? A National Survey of New Entrants to Higher Education* (Higher Education Authority, Dublin, 2006).

level in greater numbers than their proportion in the national population, while the reverse has been the case for those students from the lower socio-economic groups. Put another way, some groups are over-represented at third-level while others are under-represented. This has been the case since the first survey was carried out in 1980 and, while there has been some increased participation from the lower socio-economic groups, the latest survey, for 2004, has confirmed that disparities continue to exist (see Table 4.7).

Table 4.7: *Participation of new entrants to third-level institutions, 2004, by socio-economic group of father*

Father's socio-economic group	New entrants (%)	National population, 15–17 years (%)	Participation ratio*
Employer and manager	23.1	19.5	1.2
Higher professional	11.1	4.5	2.5
Lower professional	11.5	9.8	1.2
Non-manual	8.9	18.1	0.5
Skilled manual	13.4	14.9	0.9
Semi-skilled	5.7	10.5	0.5
Unskilled	5.0	6.7	0.7
Own account	8.2	6.9	1.2
Farmers	12.7	7.8	1.6
Agricultural workers	0.4	1.3	0.3

* The participation ratio is calculated by relating the number of entrants by socio-economic group to the national population in that group. Where the ratio is 1.0, the socio-economic group is proportionately represented; where it exceeds 1.0, the group is over-represented; and where it is less than 1.0, the group is under-represented.

Source: P.J. O'Connell et al., *Who Went to College in 2004? A National Survey of New Entrants to Higher Education* (Higher Education Authority, Dublin, 2006), adapted from Table 3.6.

The survey for 2004 noted that:

> The children of higher professionals are substantially over-represented among new entrants, relative to their share of the underlying population. The children of farmers are also over-represented relative to the population share ... The children of employers and managers, lower professionals, skilled manual workers and own account workers are distributed in rough proportion to their shares of the population. The participation ratios in respect of non-manual workers fall below 1, indicating that their children are under-represented among new entrants to higher education, relative to their share of the population.[50]

This survey also noted other features, some of which were broadly in line with previous surveys:

- great variation in participation by county, with the counties along the western seaboard having the highest participation, e.g. Mayo, at 66.8 per cent, and Kerry, at 67.0 per cent, were well above the national average of 55.0 per cent;
- great variation in participation among postal districts in Dublin, with those on the south side of Dublin having the highest participation, e.g. Dublin 14 (Rathfarnham/Clonskeagh), at 86.5 per cent, and Dublin 18 (Foxrock/Glencullen), at 83.2 per cent, were well above the national average of 55.0 per cent, while Dublin 10 (Ballyfermot/Chapelizod), at 11.7 per cent, was well below the national average;
- secondary schools were the main source of new entrants for all college types, accounting for 61 per cent of new entrants in institutes of technology and up to 70 per cent of university entrants;
- the transfer rates from Leaving Certificate students to third-level institutions were highest from fee-paying secondary schools (86.7 per cent), followed by non-fee-paying secondary schools (72.6 per cent), comprehensive/community schools (62.2 per cent) and vocational schools (54.8 per cent);
- the majority of new entrants (54 per cent) were female;
- the average age of new entrants is increasing over time – this is a result of a marked decline in the number of 17-year-olds and a substantial increase in students aged over 20 years, including mature students.

In its conclusions, the survey refers to two patterns: continuity and change. Continuity is indicated by persistent social inequalities in access to higher education. Change is indicated by some evidence of a narrowing of relative social inequalities as more advantaged groups reach a 'saturation point' in their levels of participation in higher education and the children of manual workers increase their participation rates.

Improving access to third level
In September 2000 an action group was established by Michael Woods, TD, Minister for Education and Science, to advise on the most appropriate means of increasing third-level participation of students from disadvantaged backgrounds, students with disabilities and mature students. The report of the group, *Report of the Action Group on Access to Third Level Education* (2001), contained over seventy recommendations, including a substantial increase in the rate of maintenance grants and the participation targets for students with disabilities and mature students.[51]

Concern with access to third level was also reflected in the establishment in 2003 of a dedicated national office to promote equity of access. The National Office for Equity of Access to Higher Education, based in the HEA, liaises with all publicly funded higher-education institutions. A three-year national strategy, *Achieving Equity of Access to Higher Education* (2004), set goals to be achieved, and the 2006 annual report noted considerable progress in the achievement of national participation targets.[52] This was followed by a six-year plan, *National Plan for Equity of Access to Higher Education 2008–2013*, which noted that the targets set in 2001 and endorsed in the 2004 strategy had been achieved and exceeded for students with a disability, for students facing social and economic barriers and for mature students in full-time higher education.[53] One of the key objectives of the plan was to mainstream approaches to improving access to higher education. The plan set ambitious targets, which included the following:

- a national participation rate of 72 per cent of the relevant age cohort to be achieved by 2020 (55 per cent in 2004);
- all socio-economic groups to have entry rates of at least 54 per cent by 2020 ('non-manual' group at 27 per cent and 'semi-skilled and unskilled manual' group at 33 per cent in 2004);
- mature students to comprise at least 20 per cent of total full-time entrants by 2013 (13 per cent in 2006);
- the number of students with sensory, physical and multiple disabilities in higher education to be doubled by 2013.

The plan identified a number of challenges in meeting its targets, such as the need for joined-up strategies across education levels and across government departments and the special attention required for the persistently poor participation by low- to middle-income working families.

Expenditure by level

For some time the per capita expenditure at first level (i.e. during the years of compulsory schooling) has traditionally been much less than that at second level and significantly less than that at third level. However, the differential has narrowed considerably over the past two decades (Table 4.8). By 2008 expenditure for third-level students was less than twice that for first-level students as compared with a five-fold differential in 1980.

Increased expenditure and support at first level has been advocated as a means of ensuring greater equality of opportunity in education and

Table 4.8: *Public expenditure (per capita) on education at first, second and third level, selected years, 1980–2008*

	1980		1995		2000		2008	
	(€)	*Ratio*	*(€)*	*Ratio*	*(€)*	*Ratio*	*(€)*	*Ratio*
First level	430	1.0	1,640	1.0	2,181	1.0	6,546	1.0
Second level	826	1.9	2,385	1.5	3,325	1.5	9,447	1.4
Third level	2,151	5.0	5,050	3.1	4,604	2.1	11,368	1.7

Sources: National Planning Board, *Proposal for Plan 1984–1987* (Stationery Office, Dublin, 1984), p. 291; Statistical reports (Department of Education and Science).

of mitigating the effects of educational disadvantage. In this context, there has been a progressive improvement in the funding for this level over the past two decades.

Educational disadvantage

Section 32 (9) of the Education Act, 1998, defined educational disadvantage as 'the impediments to education arising from social or economic disadvantage which prevents students from deriving appropriate benefit from education in schools'.[54]

From the mid 1980s specific measures were introduced to lessen the incidence of educational advantage. The principal means initially was through the Disadvantaged Areas Scheme (1984) whereby certain schools were designated as being disadvantaged. Initially, 33 primary schools were included in the scheme. Further schools were designated periodically as resources permitted, and by 2000 the number exceeded 300. These schools received higher capitation grants than those given to the ordinary primary schools, and there was a concerted effort to reduce the pupil–teacher ratio.

In 2000 the Disadvantaged Areas Scheme was incorporated into the Giving Children an Even Break programme, under which there was a target of 'individuals at risk' in schools rather than the previous method of designating additional schools. The support provided was related to the degree of concentration of pupils with educational disadvantage. Schools qualifying were in areas of high unemployment and generally concentrated in large urban areas.

A number of other initiatives were introduced, some on a pilot basis. The Home Liaison Scheme was established in 1990 and extended in 1999 to all designated disadvantaged schools. It involved a preventative strategy that promoted active cooperation between home, school and relevant community agencies in promoting the educational interests of children. By 2001 there were 309 primary schools and 190 second-level schools participating in the scheme.

Breaking the Cycle was yet another scheme, which commenced in 1996, with the pilot phase ending in 2001. Features of the scheme included a reduction to 15:1 in the pupil–teacher ratio in the junior classes in urban areas and the provision of a local coordinator to clusters of schools in rural areas to provide support to pupils at risk of early school leaving. All schools in this scheme, which qualified for special financial-support packages, became included in the Giving Children an Even Break programme.

Since the mid 1980s a number of separate schemes to tackle educational disadvantage were put in place, with some schools benefiting from just one of these schemes and others benefiting from more than one. In a special value-for-money report in 2006 the Comptroller and Auditor General indicated that 'the picture presented was one of a patchwork of schemes each attempting to address aspects of disadvantage'.[55] In attempting to assess the impact of the initiatives, the report expressed disappointment at the rate of improvement in literacy and numeracy levels and absenteeism. It suggested that there was a need for greater coordination and joined-up approaches among the agencies involved in addressing disadvantage. It recommended that, in order to evaluate the effectiveness of any future programme, it would be necessary to set targets for literacy, numeracy and school attendance.

In keeping with a growing commitment by government, an Educational Disadvantage Committee was established in 2002 under the Education Act, 1998. The committee's role was to advise the Minister for Education and Science on policies and strategies to be adopted to identify and correct educational disadvantage. In order to facilitate participation by a wide range of education interests, a larger Educational Disadvantage Forum was established that would work in close tandem with the committee and would primarily provide a means, through public meetings, for all those involved in educational dis-advantage to make their views known.

A comprehensive report of the Educational Disadvantage Committee was submitted to the minister in 2005. The committee acknowledged that 'it is clear that there are no simple or quick solutions: all the research evidence suggests that effective approaches are as complex and multifaceted as the problem itself'. The committee had difficulty with the definition of educational disadvantage in the Education Act, 1998, 'which sees educational disadvantage in the formal school context and does not refer to other settings', nor does it 'take adequate account of the evidence from national and international research that an integrated approach is a better way of dealing with educational disadvantage and of promoting lifelong learning for all'. The committee recognised that the problem of educational disadvantage cannot be solved in mainstream school-based educational programmes alone, and it proposed a new strategy that placed the solutions to educational disadvantage within an inclusive lifelong-learning framework. From its analysis of various programmes, initiatives and projects, the committee concluded that 'it is clear that services to address educational disadvantage in Ireland are moving, albeit slowly, towards a more integrated model'.[56]

Before the reports of the Comptroller and Auditor General and of the Educational Disadvantage Committee were published, the Department of Education had begun a consolidation process of the various schemes or programmes with the introduction of a new plan, *Delivering Equality of Opportunity in Schools*, to be implemented on a phased basis between 2005 and 2010. The core elements of the plan comprise:

• a standardised system for identifying, and regularly reviewing, levels of disadvantage;
• a new integrated school support programme that will bring together, and build upon, existing interventions for schools and school clusters/communities;
• the differences between urban and rural disadvantage will be taken into account in targeting actions under the programme.[57]

About 600 primary and 150 second-level schools were to be included in the new school support programme.

National Educational Welfare Board
Up to 2002 the monitoring of attendance at school was the responsibility of special departments of local authorities in the larger urban areas, and the responsibility of the Garda Síochána elsewhere. It was felt that this function would be better administered under an agency with a national remit. The National Educational Welfare Board (NEWB) was established on a statutory basis in 2002 under the Education (Welfare) Act, 2000. The mission of the NEWB is to maximise the level of educational participation of children and young people by ensuring that each child is attending school or otherwise participating in an appropriate education.

Since the commencement of the Education (Welfare) Act, 2000, schools are obliged by law to submit a report to the NEWB on the levels of school attendance. Within a few years there was a large increase in the number of schools responding to the NEWB's *Annual School Attendance Report*. One of the first requisites was to establish a database on non-attendance. Analysis of data up to 2005/06 indicated a number of important features:

- The percentage of student days lost through absence is running at over 6 per cent in primary schools and around 8 per cent in post-primary schools. Over 55,000 students miss school each day, consisting of approximately 27,000 primary and 28,000 post-primary students. This represents a loss of 12 school days per student per year in primary school, and 13 school days per year in post-primary school.
- About 11 per cent of primary school students (one in ten) and 17 per cent of post-primary students (one in six) are absent for 20 days or more during the school year. This is close to 50,000 primary school students and over 55,000 post-primary students.[58]

The analysis also indicated that rates of regular non-attendance in primary schools are higher in urban areas, expulsions are rare, suspensions occur mostly in second-level schools and rates of non-attendance are highest in vocational schools. The link between poor attendance and economic and social disadvantage is also indicated. Primary schools with high non-attendance are likely to have a high proportion of students living in local authority accommodation, in lone-parent families or in families where the main earner is unemployed. At post-primary level, non-attendance is strongly linked to high ratings for socio-economic disadvantage, with high rates of drop out in junior and senior cycle and poorer performance in the Junior Certificate examination.

Evolution of policy

Reference has been made at the beginning of this chapter to the lack, until recently, of a comprehensive legislative base for the education system. This in itself has, at times, hindered the development of education policy.

Sean O'Connor, former Secretary of the Department of Education, has pointed out that it is only since the early 1960s that the Minister for Education and the Department of Education began to take a lead role in policy formation. Up to then the department seemed content to leave the control of the system to the three main interest groups – the church, teachers' unions and parents. O'Connor indicates that, of these groups, the church exerted the most decisive influence, the teachers' unions were mainly concerned with working conditions and remuneration, and parents only became involved to protest at inadequate facilities in their local school.[59]

Even when the department or the minister assumed a lead role in policymaking, difficulties could still arise in obtaining agreement among the various interests. The problems associated with the establishment of management boards in primary schools in the mid 1970s exemplify the difficulties of effecting change by agreement. Similar problems arose in relation to community schools.

Part of the problem was that until the Education Act, 1998, there was an absence of a general legislative framework. The system was therefore open to the criticism that decisions were being made without reference to the Oireachtas. Successive Ministers for Education issued circulars and regulations as administrative measures, but these did not have a statutory basis.

Until recently, much of the analysis that influenced developments was contained in reports of independent review bodies, such as *Investment in Education* (1965), which was carried out by the OECD. Policy documents emanating from the Department of Education itself had been few enough in number until recent years.

The White Paper *Educational Development* (1980), which had been promised since 1973, had been expected to deal with a range of fundamental issues in the education system. The general reaction to the White Paper, however, was one of disappointment. The following extract from an editorial in *The Irish Press* summarised the popular criticism:

> The White Paper is open to serious criticism for what it does not contain. There is no timescale or costing on the proposals and insufficient government commitment to their implementation.[60]

In contrast to the White Paper, the reaction to the *Programme for Action in Education, 1984–87*, published by the Department of Education following submissions from different interest groups, was more positive. It spelled out a whole series of issues that the government intended to tackle and at the same time left scope for further discussion and consultation.

The 1990s
The education system was subject to a level of scrutiny and debate on an unprecedented scale during the 1990s.[61] It was a decade in which various policy reports were produced and widely discussed with

proposals and counterproposals being made. It was also a decade in which all of the interest groups in education were consulted, and voiced their views. It had the classic policy pathway of a Green Paper, followed by a White Paper, culminating in legislation.

In 1990 Mary O'Rourke, TD, Minister for Education, announced her intention to issue a White Paper, to be followed by public discussion and an Education Act. The social partnership agreement *Programme for Economic and Social Progress* (1991) reiterated these views but added that a Green Paper, comprehensive in its coverage, would be published in 1991, affording the opportunity to all parties to offer views prior to the publication of a White Paper in 1992 and the introduction of an Education Act.[62]

Following two changes of ministers and leaks of drafts to the media, the Green Paper, *Education for a Changing World*, was finally published in 1992 by Seamus Brennan, TD, Minister for Education. Among the main proposals were the devolution of power from the Department of Education to school boards, which would have to produce a school plan and issue an annual report on its work; the raising of the school-leaving age from fifteen to sixteen years; and the establishment of boards of management in all primary and second-level schools.

A period of consultation between the various interest groups followed the publication of the Green Paper. The National Education Convention held in Dublin Castle in 1993 represented a new departure in education: it was the first time that representatives of the Department of Education, the churches, the teachers' unions and parents had come together to tease out issues of common concern. This laid the foundation for the White Paper, *Charting our Education Future*, published in 1995. Among the key proposals of the White Paper were:

- the devolution of powers from the Department of Education to ten regional education boards;
- the establishment of a commission to recommend on the rationalisation of the vocational education system;
- the underpinning of the rights and responsibilities of school boards of management by legislation;
- the extension of the remit of the HEA to all publicly funded third-level institutions;
- the raising of the school-leaving age from fifteen to sixteen years.

Reaction to the White Paper was generally positive. Criticism related to the failure to provide an indication of the cost of the proposals or of how they were to be funded. As already noted elsewhere in this chapter, the vocational education system was rationalised, with the reduction of VECs from thirty-eight to thirty-three in 1998.

Education Act, 1998

An Education Bill to give legislative effect to the main proposals in *Charting Our Education Future* was published in January 1997. As previously mentioned, it proposed the establishment of ten regional education boards, covering geographic areas very similar to the then health boards. The bill also proposed to establish school boards of management on a statutory basis. Opposition to sections of the bill came mainly from the various Churches who, in an unprecedented move, came together to issue a joint statement. Their main cause of concern was the perceived lessening of the role of the patron in the management of schools. Fianna Fáil and the Progressive Democrats, the opposition parties in the Dáil, also opposed the bill for a variety of reasons and promised that, in government, they would abolish the regional education boards if they were established. In the event, the bill was not passed before a general election was called in May 1997 and, along with other bills, consequently lapsed.

Following a change of government in June 1997, a revised Education Bill was published in December 1997. It did not provide for the establishment of regional education boards. The Education Act, 1998, set out the role and responsibilities of the various stakeholders in education such as students, teachers, parents and boards of management. For example, the act recognises patrons as the owners of schools, recognises the National Parents Council and recognises that parents, teachers and patrons have a right to be involved in the management of their schools. Throughout the act there is a strong emphasis on the notion of partnership between all the interests in education.

It could be argued that the Education Act, 1998, did not meet the expectations of fundamental change in the system that the discussion arising from the Green and White Papers had generated. However, it can be said that the act 'remains the most significant piece of legislation enacted for the educational system, which was put on a statutory basis for the first time'.[63]

Decentralisation issues

While the establishment of regional education boards was effectively abandoned with the change of government in 1997, the issues that gave rise to the proposal remained.

In 2000 a review of the operation of the Department of Education, carried out by Sean Cromien, former Secretary General of the Department of Finance, was highly critical of certain aspects of the department. The report referred to the department as 'overwhelmed with detailed day-to-day work which has to be given priority over long-term strategic thinking' and, quoting a member of senior management, where 'the urgent drives out the important'. The Cromien report indicated that the 'problem for the Department has been that it is so centralised that this leads to a degree of dependence by its clients which is quite exceptional', and that this dependence appears to be encouraged by the department through its 'willingness to respond to every claim on its time and attention'. The report recommended that specialist bodies, such as a schools examinations agency, be established to take the burden off the department, which could then concentrate on policy and strategic planning. It also recommended the establishment of a network of local offices that initially would provide information and integrated services but that ultimately could have a decision-making function. It recognised that this process would take some time. While not going down the road of regionalisation (the issue as such was not considered), the recommendations of the Cromien report represented a strong signal in that direction.[64]

In 2001 Michael Woods, TD, Minister for Education and Science, announced a number of fundamental reforms that would reduce the detailed workload of the department and allow it to concentrate on key areas of policy. These included:

- the establishment of an independent examinations agency;
- the establishment of a network of regional offices, which would be a first point of contact for schools;
- education services for children with disabilities to be taken over by a new body, the National Council for Special Education (NCSE; see section on people with disabilities, Chapter 6);
- an extension of the remit of the HEA to include funding and coordination of all publicly funded third-level colleges (this would include the institutes of technology, which were then funded by the department).

In the event, these changes did take place. The State Examinations Commission was established by statutory order in 2003, and is now responsible for the operation of all aspects of the established Leaving Certificate, Leaving Certificate Applied and Junior Certificate examinations. The NCSE was established under the Persons with Special

Educational Needs Act, 2004, and its functions include the provision of a range of services at local and national level to meet the educational needs of children with disabilities. Regional offices of the department were also established in twelve locations, and the HEA assumed responsibility for funding the institutes of technology.

Ironically, within a few years of the establishment of some education agencies to counter what was considered as the excessive centralisation of the department's activities, the McCarthy report recommended that some recently established agencies, such as the NCSE, the NEWB and the HEA, be absorbed back into the Department of Education.[65]

Notes

1. Department of Education and Science, *Statement of Strategy 2005–2007* (Department of Education and Science, Dublin, 2005).
2. There are many excellent works dealing with the development of first-level education and the education system in general. The most comprehensive is J. Coolahan, *Irish Education: History and Structure* (Institute of Public Administration, Dublin, 1981). Other works include D.H. Akenson, *The Irish Education Experiment* (Routledge and Kegan Paul, London, 1970), which deals with the national system of education in the nineteenth century; N. Atkinson, *Irish Education, A History of Education Institutions* (Hodges Figges, Dublin, 1969); P.J. Dowling, *A History of Irish Education* (Mercier Press, Cork, 1971); F.S.L. Lyons, *Ireland Since the Famine* (Fontana, London, 1973), relevant sections; J. Lee, *The Modernisation of Irish Society, 1848–1919* (Gill and Macmillan, Dublin, 1973), Chapter 1; T.J. McElligot, *Education in Ireland* (Institute of Public Administration, Dublin, 1966).
3. See P.J. Dowling, *The Hedge Schools of Ireland* (Mercier Press, Cork, 1968).
4. See M. Mulryan Moloney, *Nineteenth-Century Elementary Education in the Archdiocese of Tuam* (Maynooth Studies in Irish Local History, No. 36) (Irish Academic Press, Dublin, 2001).
5. Akenson, op. cit., Chapter 1.
6. Primary Education Review Body, *Report of the Primary Education Review Body* (Stationery Office, Dublin, 1990), p. 93.
7. J. Armstrong, 'Friendly persuasion or gentle blackmail', *The Irish Times*, 21 October 1974.
8. Primary Education Review Body, op. cit., p. 36.
9. Government of Ireland/OECD, *Investment in Education* (Stationery Office, Dublin, 1965), pp. 225–66.
10. National Economic and Social Council, *Report No. 19, Rural Areas: Social Planning Problems* (Stationery Office, Dublin, 1976), pp. 52–3.
11. D. Musgrave, 'Small schools are beautiful after all', *The Irish Times*, 8 February 1977.

12. Government of Ireland, *Rules for National Schools under the Department of Education* (Stationery Office, Dublin, 1965), p. 8.

13. Government of Ireland, *Programme for Action in Education, 1984–1987*, (Stationery Office, Dublin, 1984), p. 16.

14. Office of the Minister for Education and Science, *Press Release: Minister Hanafin Announces New Community National Schools for Two Dublin Locations – Responding to Diverse needs of a Changing Society* (Department of Education and Science, Dublin, 13 December 2007).

15. Irish Catholic Bishops' Conference, *Catholic Primary Schools: A Policy for Provision into the Future* (Veritas, Dublin, 2007), p. 3.

16. Department of Education and Skills, *Information on Areas for Possible Divesting of Patronage of Primary Schools* (Department of Education and Skills, Dublin, 2010).

17. The block grant is calculated by reference to a complex formula that takes account of the number of day pupils and boarding pupils in Protestant schools.

18. Government of Ireland/OECD, op. cit., p. 150.

19. S. O'Connor, *A Troubled Sky: Reflections on the Irish Educational Scene, 1957–1968* (Educational Research Centre, St Patrick's College, Dublin, 1986), p. 193.

20. J.H. Whyte, *Church and State in Modern Ireland, 1923–1970* (Gill and Macmillan, Dublin, 1971), p. 38.

21. Coolahan, op. cit., p. 103.

22. G. Hussey, *At the Cutting Edge: Cabinet Diaries 1982–1987* (Gill and Macmillan, Dublin, 1990), p. 128.

23. Government of Ireland/OECD, op. cit., pp. 154–68.

24. OECD, *Review of National Policies for Education: Ireland* (OECD, Paris, 1969), Appendix iv, p. 122.

25. Ibid., p. 129.

26. Government of Ireland, *Education Act, 1998* (Stationery Office, Dublin, 1998).

27. For further details, see Commission on School Accommodation, *Amalgamation of Second-Level Schools* (Commission on School Accommodation, Dublin, 2001), pp. 59–64; and Commission on School Accommodation, *Criteria and Procedures for the Recognition of New Second Level Schools* (Commission on School Accommodation, Dublin, 2004), p. 75.

28. Government of Ireland, *Green Paper: Partners in Education* (Stationery Office, Dublin, 1985).

29. J. Walsh, *A New Partnership in Education: From Consultation to Legislation in the Nineties* (Institute of Public Administration, Dublin, 1999), pp. 46–60.

30. Commission on School Accommodation, *Rationalisation of Vocational Education Committees* (Commission on School Accommodation, Dublin, 1996).

31. Government of Ireland, *Report of the Special Group on Public Service Numbers and Expenditure Programmes* (Stationery Office, Dublin, 2009), p. 62.

32.   Conference of Religious of Ireland, *Religious Congregations in Irish Education – A Role for the Future?* (Education Commission, Conference of Religious of Ireland, Dublin, 1997), p. 9.

33.   Lyons, op. cit., p. 93.

34.   OECD, op. cit., pp. 124–5.

35.   Steering Committee on Technical Education, *Report to the Minister for Education on Regional Technical Colleges* (Stationery Office, Dublin, 1969).

36.   Commission on Higher Education, *Commission on Higher Education, 1960–67*, Vol. 2 (Stationery Office, Dublin, 1967), p. 765.

37.   Department of Education and Science, *Supporting Equity in Education: A Report to the Minister for Education and Science* (Department of Education and Science, Dublin, 2003).

38.   For an excellent overview of the various policy issues and developments in the third-level sector, see T. White, *Investing in People: Higher Education in Ireland from 1960 to 2000* (Institute of Public Administration, Dublin, 2001).

39.   Department of Education and Skills, *National Strategy for Higher Education to 2030* (Stationery Office, Dublin, 2011).

40.   Department of Education and Science, *Policy Options for New Student Contributions in Higher Education, Report to the Minister for Education and Science* (Department of Education and Science, Dublin, 2009).

41.   Government of Ireland, *Adult Education in Ireland* (Stationery Office, Dublin, 1973).

42.   Commission on Adult Education, *Lifelong Learning: Report of the Commission on Adult Education* (Stationery Office, Dublin, 1984), p. 9.

43.   M. Bassett et al., *For Adults Only: A Case for Adult Education in Ireland* (Aontas, Dublin, 1989), p. 44.

44.   Government of Ireland, *Green Paper: Adult Education in an Era of Lifelong Learning* (Stationery Office, Dublin, 1998); Government of Ireland, *Learning for Life: White Paper on Adult Education* (Stationery Office, Dublin, 2000).

45.   Government of Ireland, *Learning for Life*, op. cit., p. 54.

46.   National Economic and Social Forum, *Report No. 24, Early School Leavers* (Stationery Office, Dublin, 2002), p. 31.

47.   Ibid., pp. 37–8.

48.   Government of Ireland/OECD, op. cit., p. 173.

49.   P. Clancy and C. Benson, *Higher Education in Dublin: A Study of Some Emerging Needs* (Higher Education Authority, Dublin, 1979), pp. 13–16.

50.   P.J. O'Connell et al., *Who Went to College in 2004? A National Survey of New Entrants to Higher Education* (Higher Education Authority, Dublin, 2006), p. 47.

51.   Action Group on Access to Third Level Education, *Report of the Action Group on Access to Third Level Education* (Stationery Office, Dublin, 2001).

52.   Higher Education Authority (National Access Office), *Achieving Equity of Access to Higher Education, Action Plan 2005–2007* (Higher Education Authority, Dublin, 2004).

53.   Higher Education Authority (National Access Office), *National Plan for Equity of Access to Higher Education 2008–2013* (Higher Education Authority, Dublin, 2008), pp. 29–30.

54. Government of Ireland, *Education Act, 1998*, op. cit.

55. Comptroller and Auditor General, *Educational Disadvantage Initiatives in the Primary Sector, VFM Report 54* (Comptroller and Auditor General, Dublin, 2006), p. 8.

56. Educational Disadvantage Committee, *Moving Beyond Educational Disadvantage, Report of the Educational Disadvantage Committee 2002–2005* (Department of Education and Science, Dublin, 2005), p. 10.

57. Department of Education and Science, *Delivering Equality of Opportunity in Schools: An Action Plan for Educational Inclusion* (Department of Education and Science, Dublin, 2005), p. 9.

58. Educational Research Centre, *Analysis of School Attendance Data in Primary and Post-Primary Schools, 2003/4 to 2005/6: Report to the National Educational Welfare Board* (Educational Research Centre, Dublin, 2008), p. 4.

59. O'Connor, op. cit., Chapter 1.

60. *Irish Press*, 19 December 1980.

61. For an excellent comprehensive overview of this period, see Walsh, op. cit.

62. Government of Ireland, *Programme for Economic and Social Progress* (Stationery Office, Dublin, 1991), pp. 33–4.

63. Walsh, op. cit., p. 208.

64. Department of Education and Science, *Review of Department's Operations, Systems and Staffing Needs* (Department of Education and Science, Dublin, 2000).

65. Government of Ireland, *Report of the Special Group on Public Service Numbers and Expenditure Programmes*, op. cit., pp. 67–8, 72–3.

5

Health Services

Introduction

Health policy is the responsibility of the Department of Health, and health and personal social services are delivered by the HSE. The department originated as the Department of Local Government and Public Health in 1924. The Department of Health was established in 1947 and fifty years later, in 1997, its name was altered to the Department of Health and Children. In 2011 the department reverted to its former name, the Department of Health, and functions relating to child welfare were assigned to the new Department of Children. The HSE organisation is a relatively recent creation, having replaced and taken over the functions of former regional health boards and some other agencies in 2005.

Health is one of the main areas of public expenditure. The gross public non-capital health expenditure was €14.4 billion in 2010.

Eligibility for health services is based on a two-tier system, with about one-third of the population entitled to all services free of charge and the remainder having to pay for services. Private health care has become an integral part of the system, and about half the population are now covered by private health insurance.

The health services were subject to extensive review in the 1960s, which led to the landmark Health Act, 1970. Against a background of expenditure restraints and, more recently, of an emphasis on value for money, further reviews and policy formulation have taken place. Two of the more important documents to emerge from this process have been the *Report of the Commission on Health Funding* (1989) and the *Health Strategy: Quality and Fairness, A Health System for You* (2001). Since these two documents will be referred to in different sections, a brief context is given here.

The Commission on Health Funding was established in 1987 against a background of public-expenditure cutbacks in the health services and growing disquiet among health service unions and the public at large with the consequences of these cutbacks. The establishment of the commission must also be viewed against a background of reviews in other countries, stemming from a concern with the performance of health services and, in particular, the efficient use of resources. The commission's report examined not only the financing of the health services but also the administration and delivery of services, the quality of services and the mix of public and private health care, and made appropriate recommendations.

Despite a substantial increase in funding of the health services in the late 1990s, there was public disquiet with many aspects, particularly the mix of public and private care in hospitals, which gave rise to unacceptable waiting lists for public patients. It was against this background that a national strategy was prepared in consultation with the main providers of services. The report *Health Strategy: Quality and Fairness, A Health System for You* represented a comprehensive blueprint for developments for reform of the health services over a ten-year period, setting out core principles, national goals and objectives for implementation through 121 actions. In this, it was a far more systematic, comprehensive and goal-oriented strategy than a previous strategy statement, *Shaping a Healthier Future* (1994). The *Health Strategy* established four guiding principles: equity, people-centredness, quality and accountability. It dealt with proposed targets, developments and reforms across a range of services. It will be referred to simply as the *Health Strategy* throughout this chapter.

Evolution of services

As in the case of income maintenance and other social services, the Irish health services evolved over a period of time. Consequently, only a summary of the key developments up to the 1970s is given as background to the present system in this section.

Services in the nineteenth century
It is possible to distinguish between four different elements of health services in the nineteenth century. These were hospital services, mental hospital services, dispensary services and prevention services.[1]

The hospital system had emerged over a period, with some voluntary hospitals established in the eighteenth century. These were established initially by philanthropic individuals and later by religious orders. The hospitals, usually located in the larger urban areas, mostly Dublin, were independent of state control. They provided a service well into the twentieth century, and some continue to play a vital role in the national hospital system. They include a number of hospitals in Dublin, such as Dr Steevens' Hospital and the Mater Misericordiae Hospital, and others in Cork, such as the North Infirmary. Many of the smaller voluntary hospitals were closed in the late 1980s (see later section in this chapter). In addition to the voluntary hospitals, a network of public infirmaries and fever hospitals were developed in the nineteenth century. By the 1830s there were approximately twenty county infirmaries and seventy fever hospitals. A further strand in the hospital system was the workhouse, whose medical role gained in importance as the numbers in the workhouses declined towards the latter part of the nineteenth century.

Treatment of mental illness was confined to lunatic asylums. A small number of large asylums were established in the nineteenth century. Among these was the Richmond Institution at Grangegorman in Dublin, which was established in 1815 and continued to function well into the twentieth century as St Brendan's Hospital.[2] In addition to these large institutions, district asylums were established in almost all counties.

As already noted in Chapter 1, the central feature of the Poor Law system, established in Ireland in 1838, was the workhouse. However, some other services were developed outside the workhouse, and one of the most notable was the dispensary system. Under this system, introduced under the Poor Relief Act, 1851, a network of dispensary districts was established throughout the country. In each of these districts a doctor was employed to provide a free service to the poor of the area. This dispensary system continued up to 1972 and was the forerunner of the present choice-of-doctor scheme for medical card holders.

For a variety of reasons, the preventive services were limited throughout most of the nineteenth century, with the result that outbreaks of infectious diseases wrought havoc. For example, a cholera outbreak in the early 1830s affected large parts of the country, especially Dublin, with devastating consequences – at least 25,000 died in 1832–3, creating widespread panic and social disruption.[3] The cause was unknown and there was no known effective treatment; the link between cholera and polluted water supplies only became established over several decades. By the latter part of the nineteenth century the connection between public and personal hygiene and the transmission of disease became firmly established by scientists. This, together with the work of public health reformers, resulted in the Public Health Act, 1878, which introduced measures to ensure proper sanitation, clean water supplies and food-hygiene controls in order to prevent the spread of infectious diseases. Subsequent advances were such that by about 1900 'large scale epidemic disease had become history'.[4]

Services in the twentieth century

Apart from the evolutionary development of the above and allied services to meet changed circumstances and advances in medicine, a number of broad trends were discernible in the health services throughout the twentieth century.

Firstly, there was a gradual shift away from the community as a focus of health care to the health needs of the individual. For example, some of the early measures in the nineteenth century were designed not so much to promote health as to prevent community-wide catastrophes caused by the spread of infectious diseases. Similarly, the emphasis for mental illness was on protecting society rather than rehabilitating the individual.

Secondly, the state became more and more directly involved in the planning and provision of health care. This did not occur without controversy and opposition, mainly from the Catholic Church and the medical profession. The classic instance of this was the Mother and Child Scheme that Dr Noel Browne, Minister for Health (1948–51), proposed to introduce. The Catholic hierarchy opposed the scheme (which would have provided free health service for women before, during and after childbirth and for children up to sixteen years) on the grounds that it represented undue state intervention. The medical profession opposed the scheme because it did not want a comprehensive state health service, preferring instead a mix of public and private.[5]

Thirdly, there was a move away from local administration to a more centralised model. The large numbers of local administrative units in the nineteenth and early twentieth centuries were gradually rationalised. The number of such units was reduced from ninety in the 1920s to eight following the Health Act, 1970 (see later section in this chapter). At central level, the Department of Health emerged as a separate government department out of the former Department of Local Government and Public Health.

Fourthly, the administrative changes at local and regional level reflected a change in funding from local taxation (rates) to central funding. At the beginning of the twentieth century the health services were largely funded from local taxation, a situation whose shortcomings became increasingly apparent. A gradual shift towards central funding occurred over several decades so that by the late 1970s local taxation no longer made a contribution to financing and the services were funded almost entirely through the exchequer from general taxation and a special health levy.

The above trends have been summarised by Barrington:

> In 1900, governmental responsibility for the health of the population was
> limited to controlling outbreaks of the most serious epidemic diseases and
> ensuring access by the poor to general practitioner services and Poor Law
> infirmaries. By 1970, government had accepted responsibility for providing a
> high standard of medical care for all sections of the population at no or at a
> heavily subsidised cost to the recipient.[6]

In many ways the Health Act, 1970, marked a watershed in the
development of the modern health system with changes in
administrative structures and some key services.

Evolution of administrative structures

The evolution of the administrative structures for health care in Ireland
up to the 1980s has been outlined by Hensey in admirable detail.[7]
Consequently, only the major developments up to that period are
reviewed here.

State services were first provided in a rudimentary form under the
Poor Law (Ireland) Act, 1838. The Poor Law administration provided
infirmaries and other forms of medical care in association with the
workhouses established in each Poor Law Union. Unions were
administrative units, and the total number covering the present area of
the Republic was 126.

In 1872 the Irish Poor Law Commissioners were abolished and
replaced by the Irish Local Government Board, which assumed control
of both Poor Law and health services. Central control became more
pronounced following independence when, in 1924, the Department of
Local Government and Public Health was established. In 1947 this
department was effectively divided and three separate departments
emerged – the Departments of Local Government, Health and Social
Welfare.

At local level the administrative structure for health services remained
highly complex throughout the nineteenth century and well into the
twentieth century. There were a number of agencies with responsibility
for various aspects of health care; boards of guardians, for example,
which had been established in each Poor Law Union, continued in
existence until 1923. By 1940 most health functions at local level had
been transferred to county councils, and the county manager became
responsible for the formulation of local policy on health services. The
transfer of responsibility for all health services to local authorities was
completed in 1947 when they assumed responsibility in urban areas for

preventive health services, which up to then had been the domain of urban district councils. In 1947 there were thirty-one health authorities, corresponding to the same number of county councils and county boroughs. In 1960, however, this number was reduced to twenty-seven when unified health authorities were established within the four counties containing the main cities of Dublin, Cork, Limerick and Waterford; the health functions of Dublin County Council and Dublin City Borough, for example, were amalgamated. The trend towards a reduction in the number of authorities with responsibility for health services was taken a stage further when the Health Act, 1970, provided for the establishment of eight regional boards.

The reasons for the regionalisation of health functions were outlined in a White Paper in 1966.[8] They were based mainly on the following considerations:

- The state had taken over the major share of the costs, which were increasing substantially every year. It was therefore desirable to have a new administrative framework to combine national and local interests.
- It was becoming more and more obvious that in order to develop the medical service itself, especially in relation to acute hospital care, it would be necessary to have the organisation on an inter-county basis. It was clear that the county as a unit was unsuitable; it was too small an area for the provision of a comprehensive hospital service.
- The removal of health affairs from the general local authority sphere had been foreshadowed as far back as 1947 when the Department of Health was separated from the Department of Local Government and Public Health and set up as a separate ministry.

Under the provisions of the Health Act, 1970, the administrative structure of the health services was changed as from 1 April 1970. From that date the health services were administered by eight health boards, each covering a number of counties; for example, the Eastern Health Board area covered the counties of Dublin, Kildare and Wicklow, while the Western Health Board area covered the counties of Galway, Mayo and Roscommon.

The population of the regions varied, with the Eastern Health Board area, for example, having a population approximately six times that of either the Midland or North Western Health Board areas in 1971. However, the density of population and the location of existing facilities, especially hospitals, explain some of these differences.

The membership of each health board represented a combination of three main interests:

i.   elected representatives drawn from county councils and borough councils, accounting for more than half the membership;
ii. professional representatives of the medical, nursing, dental and pharmaceutical interests, who are mostly officers of the board;
iii. nominees of the Minister for Health, of which there were three on each board.

In the discussions leading to the Health Act, 1970, Erskine Childers, TD, Minister for Health, had yielded to political pressure by conceding just over half the membership of health boards to local elected representatives.[9] In the majority of cases, a local elected representative has been chairperson of each health board (a non-executive position filled on an annual basis).

In 2000 the Eastern Regional Health Authority (ERHA) replaced the Eastern Health Board, and there were a number of consequential changes to the structures in the eastern region as well as to membership of the authority (see later section).

Other agencies

The administrative organisation of the health services under the Health Act, 1970, also provided for the establishment of other agencies. These included Comhairle na nOspidéal, three regional hospital boards (to be based in Dublin, Cork and Galway) and advisory committees.

The functions of Comhairle na nOspidéal included regulating the number and type of consultant medical staff and certain other staff in the hospitals, and advising the Minister for Health on matters relating to the organisation and operation of hospital services.

The regional hospital boards, whose establishment had been recommended in the *Report of the Consultative Council on the General Hospital Services* (1968), were charged with the general organisation and development of hospital services in an efficient manner by the health boards and voluntary organisations. They were not to be concerned with the day-to-day running of the hospitals. These boards were never fully activated.

Local advisory committees were established on a county basis, and their function was solely advisory. In this way, they were intended to represent local interests to the regional health board. Membership of committees was made up of local elected representatives, the county manager, members of the medical profession and representatives of voluntary social service organisations. The establishment of county advisory committees could be viewed as a further concession to local elected representatives for the loss of influence in the move from county to regional administration. These committees were abolished in 1988.

Reviewing the structures

The necessity of having eight regional health boards for a country with a population of less than four million was raised on occasions. The Department of Health tantalisingly raised this issue in its discussion document *Health: The Wider Dimensions* (1986):

> Given the size of the country and the population, the need for eight separate administrations, each with statutory responsibility for providing the whole range of health and personal social services, has also been questioned.[10]

The department did not, however, indicate how many health boards there should be, nor did it suggest an alternative structure.

The role of health boards was analysed in some depth in the *Report of the Commission on Health Funding*. The commission identified a number of weaknesses in the actual operation of the existing structure, such as a confusion of political and executive functions, a lack of balance between national and local decision-making, inadequate accountability and insufficient integration of services.[11]

One of the main problems cited by the commission was that many voluntary agencies providing health services were funded directly by the Department of Health and not by health boards. These included voluntary hospitals (accounting for over half of acute hospital services) and some of the larger voluntary organisations providing services for people with disabilities. The Department of Health and the Minister for Health were consequently involved in the management of services rather than concentrating exclusively on developing and monitoring policy. This contributed to a situation where communication lines between the Department of Health and health boards were inevitably blurred. The commission made the general point that accountability in the system, as between health boards and the department, lacked clarity. Similarly, the commission also referred to health boards that, by nature of their membership, became unnecessarily involved in the management of services.

In order to overcome these weaknesses, the commission recommended that the Minister for Health and the Department of Health should formulate health policy and should not be involved in the management of individual services; the management of the services should be transferred to a new agency, the Health Services Executive Authority, which would be responsible for the management and delivery of health and personal social services in accordance with policy set by the minister. Under this recommendation, existing health boards would be abolished and a structure of area general managers would be established, covering defined geographical areas in which the manager would be responsible for the delivery of services.[12]

Reaction to the commission's recommendation for a fundamental change in the administrative structure was largely negative. It was argued that the weaknesses identified by the commission could be solved without establishing a Health Services Executive Authority. According to this viewpoint, health management is far more complex than that of other public services, and does not lend itself to a clear split between policy and execution, as recommended by the commission, but requires a political and professional input as is provided by the health board structure.[13]

While the NESC supported the general diagnosis of the difficulties within the existing structure, it did not accept that the commission's proposed structure was entirely consistent with the diagnosis. The NESC, however, did not offer a definite view on any alternative structure.[14]

Not surprisingly, members of health boards were united in their opposition to the administrative changes proposed by the commission, arguing that the existing system had worked satisfactorily.[15]

In the decade or so following publication of the commission's report, deficiencies in the health system as identified by the Commission on Health Funding began to be addressed, although this stopped short of the abolition of health boards and their replacement by a national agency.

The Health (Amendment) (No. 3) Act, 1996, sometimes referred to as the accountability legislation, had three main objectives:

i. to strengthen and improve the arrangements governing financial accountability and expenditure procedures in health boards;
ii. to clarify the respective roles of the members of the health boards and their chief executive officers;
iii. to begin the process of removing the Department of Health from detailed involvement in operational matters.

The process of funding voluntary public hospitals and the main voluntary organisations for people with intellectual disabilities through health boards, rather than directly by the Department of Health, commenced in 1998.

The Eastern Regional Health Authority (2000)

In 1991 Dr Rory O'Hanlon, TD, Minister for Health, referred to failings in the health service structure as identified by the Commission on Health Funding and indicated that the fragmentation of services and the lack of coordination were particularly acute in the Dublin area because of the multiplicity of autonomous agencies involved in the provision of health care. He proposed to establish a single new authority that would be responsible for health and personal social services in the Eastern Health Board area, and that would subsume the functions of the health board as well as some of the functions of the Department of Health. The minister's proposals for the other seven health boards were less clear.[16] In effect, the minister accepted the diagnosis of the Commission on Health Funding but the remedy was different to the one prescribed.

The department's strategy statement *Shaping a Healthier Future* reiterated the policy changes proposed by Dr Rory O'Hanlon and also promised legislation to establish a new authority in the eastern region. In 1996 Michael Noonan, TD, Minister for Health, re-announced the proposals made by his predecessor.

The ERHA was eventually established by legislation in 2000. As part of the restructuring, the former Eastern Health Board (covering the counties of Dublin, Kildare and Wicklow) was replaced by three area health boards – the East Coast Area Health Board, the Northern Area Health Board and the South Western Area Health Board. The ERHA became responsible for the health and personal social services in the eastern region, covering a population of 1.4 million. All of the main voluntary service providers, such as hospitals and agencies for the intellectually disabled, most of them previously funded directly by the Department of Health and Children, now came under the aegis of the ERHA. Rather than be involved in the direct provision of services, the ERHA was charged with the planning, commissioning, monitoring and evaluation of services provided by the three area health boards and thirty-six voluntary providers. The direct funding link between the latter and the Department of Health and Children was thus ended, thereby freeing the department to concentrate on policy and strategic issues.

Establishment of the HSE (2005)

The Deloitte and Touche report associated with the *Health Strategy* noted:

> It is difficult to imagine any demand-led service which has grown at the rate of the Irish health service, which is still operating within a structure devised over thirty years ago. The optimum shape of the system including the role and structure of health boards needs to be re-evaluated.[17]

The *Health Strategy* proposed a review of structures, which was subsequently undertaken by Prospectus and Watson Wyatt Worldwide in consultation with the Department of Health and Children. The report, *Audit of Structures and Functions in the Health System*, usually referred to as the Prospectus report, was published in 2003, and its recommendations for changes to existing structures were resonant of those made by the Commission on Health Funding in 1989. In relation to health boards it noted that individually they had 'evolved at different paces, resulting in a considerable variation in their organisational structures and practices', which hindered 'a standardised approach to the preparation and implementation of national strategies'.[18] Because of this and other considerations, the Prospectus report recommended the abolition of health boards and the establishment of a Health Services Executive to manage the services as a single national entity.

In 2001 the Minister for Finance, Charlie McCreevy, TD, announced the establishment of a commission to consider financial management in the health services. In the context of a substantial annual increase in expenditure since 1997, he expressed concern that the quality and quantity of services that people receive should reflect this investment. The report of the Commission on Financial Management and Control Systems in the Health Services, usually referred to as the Brennan report (after the chairperson, Professor Niamh Brennan), was also published in 2003. One of the main problems it identified was 'the absence of any organisation responsible for managing the health service as a unified national system'.[19] It recommended the establishment of an executive at national level to manage the health services, but it also recommended that the health board structure be retained 'to safeguard the need for local democratic representation'.

The Prospectus and Brennan reports, with different terms of reference, had agreed on the need for a national agency to oversee developments in the health services. These proposals for reform of health structures were endorsed by government and were regarded as 'essential to the creation of a system that is accountable, effective, efficient and capable of responding to the emerging and ongoing needs of the public'.[20] The Health Act, 2004, provided for the establishment of the HSE, which replaced the health boards and some other agencies and assumed responsibility for health services from January 2005.

In a sense, the establishment of the HSE marked the culmination of an inevitable, evolutionary process of rationalisation over several decades that resulted in the number of administrative units being reduced from over ninety to one national agency.

The HSE structure

One of the main changes to arise from the establishment of the HSE was in the composition of the board of management. Effectively, power was taken from local elected representatives, and the Health Act, 2004, provided for a total of twelve members: the chairman and ten ordinary members to be appointed by the Minister for Health and Children, with the chief executive officer acting as an *ex officio* member.

Within the HSE, two principal national service directorates were established: the National Hospitals Office (NHO) and the Primary, Community and Continuing Care (PCCC) Directorate. The NHO would be responsible for resource allocation, service delivery and performance management of the fifty public and voluntary public hospitals in the country through ten hospital network managers, whose geographic areas correspond to that of the former health boards. The PCCC Directorate would be responsible for delivering health and personal social services in a community setting through thirty-two local health offices.

Administrative areas for the NHO and the PCCC Directorate and other functions of the HSE are subsumed into four regions, i.e. Dublin Mid Leinster, Dublin North East, South and West. These regions are an amalgam of the former health board areas. For example, the West region covers the areas of the former North Western, Western and Mid Western Health Boards, stretching from Donegal to Limerick.

In each of these four regions a health forum, comprised of elected representatives from local authorities, was established by regulation under the Health Act, 2004. Each city and county council within the four regions was allocated a number of representatives based on population, e.g. three representatives for a population up to 75,000, and six representatives for a population of 175,000 to 225,000. On this basis, the number of representatives is forty (Dublin Mid Leinster and West), thirty-nine (South) and twenty-nine (Dublin North East). The function of the forums is to make representations on the range and operation of health and personal social services in their region; they do not have any executive functions.

Within a few years of the establishment of the HSE, it became apparent that there was a need for a more effective organisational structure and better integrated patient care. It was recognised that integrated care between primary, community and acute care was more difficult to achieve with separate organisational 'pillars' in the NHO and the PCCC Directorate, each having separate budgets. Arising from a review of structures by McKinsey and Company, proposals aimed at integration were adopted in 2008. The principal change involved the integration of the two national services delivery posts, the NHO and the PCCC Directorate, under a National Director of Integrated Service Delivery. In 2009 the HSE appointed four regional directors of operations to manage all services within the four regions (see above), within nationally determined priorities and parameters.

Some fundamental changes to the HSE are proposed in the Fine Gael/Labour *Programme for Government* (2011) where it is envisaged that the HSE will cease to exist over time and that its functions will return to the Minister for Health or be taken over by the universal health insurance system (see later section in this chapter).

Eligibility for health services

In general terms, access to health care in Ireland is defined by a dual system, with the lowest-income groups having free access, subject to a means test, and the remainder of the population having to pay for services.

Prior to 1991 the system was highly complex, with the population divided into three categories. This situation had evolved over a considerable period of time. From 1851 the low-income group had eligibility for health services under the dispensary system of the Poor Law, and in 1953 the middle-income group obtained limited eligibility for services, leaving the higher-income group without any entitlement. In 1979 further reforms were introduced to simplify the system of eligibility but the three-tiered system remained until 1991.

From 1991 the population has been divided into two categories for eligibility for health services. In Category I, the lowest-income group – i.e. medical card holders and their dependants, accounting for one-third of the population – are entitled to all health services free of charge; the remaining two-thirds are in Category II and are entitled to a more limited range of services.

The main difference between the two categories is that while the medical card population (Category I) is entitled to a free general practitioner (GP) service and hospital service (in public wards of public and voluntary public hospitals), the rest of the population (Category II) are liable for GP fees but are entitled to a 'free' hospital service (subject to a maximum annual charge of €1,200 in 2010) on the same basis as the medical card population.

Medical cards

Persons with full eligibility for health services are defined in the Health Act, 1970, as 'adult persons unable without undue hardship to arrange general practitioner, medical and surgical services for themselves and their dependants and dependants of such persons'.[21] Those with full eligibility receive a General Medical Services card (medical card) that entitles them and their dependants to free health services.

Entitlement to a medical card is based on assessment of means, and community welfare officers of the HSE carry out the means test. In practice, means tests are not carried out on recipients of certain social welfare payments who have already been means-tested. The *Health Strategy* made a commitment to provide a clear statutory framework in relation to eligibility for health and personal social services.[22] Despite this commitment there is still no statutory basis for determining eligibility for a medical card. Qualifying income limits were both determined and updated jointly by health boards annually from 1972, and the HSE has taken over this function since 2005.

In 1972 the dispensary system dating from 1851 was abolished and replaced by a choice-of-doctor scheme, which allowed patients with medical cards to visit a doctor of their choice and at the same surgery as that used by private fee-paying patients. The ending of the stigma associated with the treatment of patients in separate premises and the introduction of greater uniformity through national income guidelines produced by the newly established health boards made the system more acceptable to medical card holders.

The number of persons covered by medical cards – i.e. medical card holders and their dependants – increased up to the late 1980s, declined for several years and began to increase again after 2004 (Table 5.1).

Table 5.1: *Medical card population, selected years, 1972–2009*

	No. of persons	*% of total population*
1972	864,106	29.0
1976	1,193,909	37.0
1980	1,199,599	35.6
1986	1,326,048	37.4
1988	1,324,849	37.4
1990	1,221,284	34.9
1996	1,252,385	34.6
2001	1,199,454	31.2
2004	1,153,283	28.4
2009*	1,478,560	33.1

* Excluding 98,325 GP visit card holders.

Sources: Annual reports of the General Medical Service Payments Board and of Primary Care Reimbursement Service, Health Service Executive.

A number of factors account for the increase throughout the 1970s and early 1980s. Firstly, the take-up of medical cards would have increased as a result of the abolition of the dispensary system, to which a certain stigma was attached. Secondly, the introduction of uniform guidelines to determine eligibility for medical cards would also have led to an increase in take-up. Thirdly, during this period there was an increase in the social welfare population, mainly due to the increase in unemployment, and thus, by definition, there was an increase in the lower-income group. The sharp increase from 2008, after many years of decline, was due to the introduction of the GP visit card and the downturn in the economy.

Extending eligibility for medical cards

In July 2001 eligibility for medical cards was extended to all persons aged seventy and over, irrespective of income. This policy change was to prove highly controversial. It was announced in Budget 2001 by Charlie McCreevy, TD, Minister for Finance, without any health care rationale, and was only communicated to officials in the Department of Health and Children one day prior to the budget. Insufficient time to consider the full implications of this change led to an underestimate of the number of persons aged seventy and over likely to be eligible. The original estimate was 39,000 people at a cost of €19 million, whereas the actual number was 70,000 at an additional cost of €51 million.[23] The cost was added to by the fact that the capitation rate for each new seventy-year-old, negotiated with the Irish Medical Organisation, was much higher than that for existing seventy-year-old medical card holders. In Budget 2009 Brian Lenihan, TD, Minister for Finance, announced that the automatic entitlement to a medical card for those aged seventy and over would no longer apply, i.e. that persons in this age group would have to undergo a means test in order to qualify for the medical card. Such was the level of outrage by those whose medical cards were to be withdrawn, by the public at large, by groups representing older persons such as Age Action Ireland and the Irish Senior Citizens' Parliament, by opposition parties and by some government deputies that within less than a week the government was forced to alter its position, with the result that fewer persons would lose out. The effect of the changes in the aftermath of the budget announcement was that an estimated 95 per cent of people aged over seventy (330,000 out of 350,000 persons) would retain their medical card while an estimated 5 per cent (20,000 persons) would lose their automatic entitlement to the medical card.

The *Health Strategy* had indicated that 'significant improvements will be made in the income guidelines [for medical cards] in order to increase the number of persons on low incomes who are eligible for a medical card and to give priority to families with children and particularly children with a disability'.[24] In its 2002 election manifesto, Fianna Fáil made a commitment to 'extend eligibility to over 200,000 extra people, with a clear priority being given to families with children'.[25] Within a year, however, economic difficulties meant that resources were not available to extend eligibility on the scale envisaged.

In response to representations from some voluntary organisations showing that there was a strong financial deterrent for many families outside the qualifying income limit for medical cards to visit their GP, the government announced the introduction of a special medical card. The GP visit medical card would entitle the holder and dependants to free GP service but not to free prescribed drugs and medicines. When the GP visit card was introduced in 2005, it was estimated that 200,000 would be entitled to it. The income limit for the GP visit card was set at 25 per cent above the income limit for the full medical card. However, the take-up of the GP visit card was disappointing, and in 2006 the income limit was increased to 50 per cent above that for the full medical card. The increase in the qualifying income limit was also accompanied by a national advertising campaign to encourage greater take-up. By the end of 2009 there were 1,478,560 medical card holders and 98,325 GP visit card holders.

As might be expected there is considerable variation between counties in relation to the proportion of the population covered by medical cards. These differences broadly reflect per capita income variation within the country. In general, counties in the border, midland and western areas have higher proportions covered by medical cards than the rest of the country. In 2004 Donegal had the highest proportion of population covered by medical cards (46.1 per cent), and Dublin the lowest (27.1 per cent).[26] Official statistics on medical cards by county have not been published since 2004.

Attempts at rationalisation of the system of eligibility

Reference has already been made to the fact that the system of eligibility was highly complex up to June 1991. An attempt was made in 1974 to rationalise the then three categories into two categories, as was achieved in 1991. Brendan Corish, TD, Minister for Health, announced that from April 1974 everyone would be entitled to free hospital inpatient and outpatient services. However, the minister was obliged to defer the introduction of the scheme because of the opposition of hospital consultants to the possible effects on their conditions of employment and on their remuneration in particular.[27]

The *Report of the Commission on Health Funding* recommended that people should have available to them a certain level of necessary health services, including primary care, hospital care, long-term care and personal social services. It pointed out, however, that this did not necessarily mean that they should all be publicly funded or delivered by public agencies or provided free of charge. The commission recommended that the lowest-income group (medical card holders and their dependants) should remain eligible for all necessary health services free of charge. The rest of the population should be eligible for 'core' services.

The commission's recommendations regarding eligibility basically envisaged a two-tier system, i.e. the abolition of the higher-income category (Category III), thus leaving two categories, as at present: Category I for medical card holders and Category II for all others. A similar proposal was made in the social partnership agreement *Programme for Economic and Social Progress*. As already noted, the present two-tier system of eligibility came into effect in 1991. Unlike in 1974, the opposition by hospital consultants to an extension of entitlement to 'free' hospitalisation was more muted on this occasion.

The commission had also recommended that patients would have to opt for either public or private care, and should not be allowed to combine them, and that those opting for private care should pay the full costs involved.

Private health insurance

Over the past fifty years the number of persons with private health insurance has grown considerably.

The Voluntary Health Insurance Board (VHI) was established under the Voluntary Health Insurance Act, 1957, essentially as a means by which those in the higher-income group, who did not have eligibility to health services at the time, would be able to insure themselves against the cost of medical care.

In 1958, one year after its establishment, 57,000 persons were covered by the VHI scheme. It was clear that, over time, persons in Category II with eligibility for subsidised hospital services had also invested in supplementary cover to enable them to have private or semi-private accommodation and private treatment in hospitals. The rationalisation of the system of eligibility in 1991 did not change this pattern. In fact, the numbers in private insurance continued to grow in line with economic growth and a significant increase in the numbers in employment from the mid 1990s.

The EU Commission forced competition in private health insurance on a reluctant Department of Health in the early 1990s. In accordance with the Health Insurance Act, 1994, the health insurance market in Ireland was opened up to competition, thus ending the virtual monopoly that the VHI had enjoyed for almost four decades. At the beginning of 1997, BUPA (British Union of Private Assurance) commenced operating in the Irish market and thereby introduced an element of competition into a market hitherto dominated by VHI. Within one year BUPA had 55,000 subscribers, and by 2002 had approximately 300,000 subscribers. Its business and customer base was taken over by the Quinn Insurance Group early in 2007. Another company, Vivas, entered the market in 2004 and was taken over by Hibernian Health in 2008, subsequently becoming Hibernian Aviva. By 2009 VHI had the largest share (64 per cent) of the private health insurance market, followed by Quinn Healthcare (22 per cent) and Hibernian Aviva Health (10 per cent).[28]

The White Paper *Private Health Insurance* (1999) set out an ambitious programme for change. This included the transformation of the VHI into a commercial semi-state agency and the retention of a revised system of community-based rating. It also proposed an amendment to the risk-equalisation scheme provided for in the Health Insurance Act, 1994, a highly controversial and complex scheme that would prevent insurers targeting mainly young, healthy and low-risk subscribers. The White Paper acknowledged the 'potential for conflicts of interest to occur' because the Minister for Health and Children is both 'owner' of the VHI and the regulator of the private health insurance market.[29] It therefore proposed the establishment of a Health Insurance Authority to regulate the market. The Health Insurance Authority was established on a statutory basis in 2001.

Health insurance companies operate a community rating system, i.e. all age categories are charged the same premium even though the risk of ill health obviously varies depending on age. While the government remained committed to this principle, the question of risk equalisation inevitably had to be faced once competitors were allowed to enter the market. Risk equalisation, whose introduction was recommended by the Health Insurance Authority, involves transfer of payments between insurers to spread some of the claim costs of high-risk members. In 2006, following an unsuccessful challenge in the High Court to risk equalisation, BUPA decided to withdraw from the Irish market, leading to the acquisition by the Quinn Insurance Group. However, BUPA appealed the High Court decision, and in 2008 the Supreme Court ruled that risk equalisation was invalid because it was based on an incorrect interpretation of the term 'community rating' in a provision of the Health Insurance Act, 1994.

In the context of proposed reforms in the health insurance market, the government announced in 2010 that it hoped to invest about €300 million in VHI prior to it being put on the market for sale by 2013. In effect, this would mean the state divesting itself of ownership of the VHI. The investment is required to bring VHI's reserves up to the level required for authorisation by the Financial Services Regulatory Authority. For some time the VHI's status as an insurer that is not authorised by regulators had been regarded as a clear market distortion because it did not have to operate under the same rules as rival insurers.

The numbers with private health insurance increased from 1.871 million (48.2 per cent of the population) in 2001 to a peak of 2.299 million (51.6 per cent of the population) in 2008. With the economic downturn there was a slight reduction in the insured population to 2.262 million by the end of 2009 (50.7 per cent of the population).[30] Even allowing for a further decline in health insurance coverage, it is clear that a large number of persons in Category II, with an entitlement to subsidised hospital care in public hospitals, have invested in supplementary cover to enable them to have private or semi-private accommodation and private treatment by consultants in hospitals. This highlights the public/private mix in the Irish health system.

The public/private mix

An integral feature of the Irish health care system is the public/private mix at primary care and hospital level. While the introduction of the choice-of-doctor scheme in 1972 ended the differences in access between public and private patients to GPs, the same cannot be said for access to inpatient hospital services. The existence of private and public beds, the operation of private health insurance and the work practices of hospital consultants have led to the emergence of a two-tier system. The result has been that those covered by private insurance have had apparent ease in gaining access to hospital care while others have had to wait somewhat longer for treatment.

In theory, access to hospital services is available to all, especially since 1991 when changes in eligibility categories were introduced. In practice, waiting lists for public patients became the norm throughout the 1990s. One of the acknowledged reasons for the increase in membership of private insurance schemes in the same decade was that private health insurance provides faster access to hospital care and the avoidance of waiting lists.[31]

Proposals by the Commission on Health Funding envisaged a continued mix of public and private care. The fundamental principle of the majority of members of the commission was that it should not be necessary, nor should it be perceived as such, to take out private insurance in order to secure access to treatment. The role of private insurance therefore should be to provide cover for those wishing to avail themselves of private care and to provide cover for costs for which those without medical cards would be liable. The commission was opposed to public subsidisation of private care when the state was already providing a core service to the entire population. It also recommended the introduction of a common waiting list for hospitals, arguing that priority of admission should be determined solely by medical need and not by the public or private status of the patient.

Because of growing concern with waiting lists, or, more particularly, waiting times, for hospital care, a waiting list initiative backed by additional funding commenced in 1993. Despite this, the numbers on waiting lists did not decline appreciably throughout the 1990s, with annual average numbers of around 30,000. This became an important issue and reinforced a public perception that the system was failing public patients.

Despite increased investment in health and in employment of additional staff in the late 1990s, the gap between public and private patients widened. Waiting lists became the order of the day (over 30,000 patients annually), but ironically these applied principally to public patients (medical card holders or others not covered by private insurance) while private patients appeared to gain ready access to hospital. The problem was acknowledged in the White Paper *Private Health Insurance* and was highlighted in a week-long series of articles on the health services in *The Irish Times* in 2000.[32] The implications of inequalities in the public/private system for public patients was also highlighted in a report by the Society of St Vincent de Paul in 2001.[33] Increasingly, the ability to pay appeared to have become the determining factor in access to hospital inpatient services.

The public/private mix and the public waiting lists were central issues in the *Health Strategy*. Inevitably, much of the public focus was on the acute hospital sector where approximately 6,000 beds had been removed due to financial constraints in the late 1980s and early 1990s. The *Health Strategy* indicated that an additional 3,000 beds would be provided by 2011. All the beds would be designated for public patients. It also proposed the employment of additional hospital consultants. The *Health Strategy* also committed that no adult would have to wait longer than three months for hospital treatment (a commitment to reduce the waiting time to a similar time frame had been made in *Shaping a Healthier Future* in 1994). One of the means of meeting this target was by the establishment of a Treatment Purchase Fund to purchase bed capacity from private hospitals in Ireland or abroad. In effect, the *Health Strategy* proposed that the controversial two-tier system of hospital service, leading to waiting lists for public patients, be tackled by a combination of the provision of additional beds, the Treatment Purchase Fund initiative and the appointment of additional consultants, rather than the introduction of a common waiting list as recommended by the Commission on Health Funding.

The National Treatment Purchase Fund

In 2002 the National Treatment Purchase Fund (NTPF) was established as an independent statutory body whose aim is to reduce the length of time public patients wait for surgery. This would be achieved by ensuring that those public patients waiting for treatment for an unacceptable length of time would be treated in private hospitals either in Ireland or abroad. Public patients on a waiting list for an operation or procedure may be referred to the NTPF or may contact the NTPF themselves, and it will then source treatment for these patients, usually in hospitals in Ireland. Initially, the NTPF faced many problems in its efforts to reduce the length of times patients waited. Since then, an increasing number of patients (inpatients, outpatients and radiology patients) have been treated under the NTPF, from 1,920 in 2002 to a peak of 36,268 in 2008, with a total number of 164,449 treated in the period from 2002 to 2009.[34] It is generally acknowledged that the NTPF has made a substantial difference to reducing waiting lists. Waiting time for surgery reduced from 2–5 years in 2002 to a median waiting time of 2.5 months for both medical and surgical patients nationally by 2009.

Hospital consultants' contracts

The hospital consultants' contracts, setting out the terms of remuneration and other matters while also facilitating private practice, have been viewed as a factor in reinforcing the public/private divide in access to hospital services.[35] Under the 1997 contract, hospital consultants were paid a salary for treating public patients (thirty-three hours' unmonitored work per week) while they were paid on a fee basis for each private patient. The White Paper *Private Health Insurance* noted:

> under these circumstances rational economic behaviour would suggest that a stronger incentive exists for those consultants who are significantly involved in private practice to concentrate a disproportionate time on these private patients.[36]

The White Paper also noted that there was a widely held public perception that public patients tended to receive more of their care from medical staff other than consultants.

The Health Services (Inpatient) Regulations, 1991, specified that all public beds must be formally designated by the Minister for Health and Children and that private patients must, except in emergency cases, be accommodated in designated private beds. The purpose of this measure was to ensure equity of access to public hospital facilities. This measure was introduced in the context of reducing the eligibility categories from three to two (see previous section in this chapter). The arrangement was that 80 per cent of beds in public hospitals would be designated as public, with 20 per cent designated private. These ratios were not observed in all cases, with the percentage for private beds being exceeded, and the *Health Strategy* proposed that all extra beds would be designated for public patients.[37]

A special report, the *Medical Consultants' Contract*, by the Comptroller and Auditor General (2007) noted that the 1997 contract allowed consultants to treat private patients while discharging their obligation to the public hospital where there were also private beds. The contract provided that a consultant's overall proportion of private to public patients should reflect the ratio of private to public beds, as designated by the minister at individual hospital level, and noted that, overall, 20 per cent of all beds in public hospitals were designated as private beds. However, the report also noted that, in practice, private patient treatment in public hospitals exceeded 20 per cent in all three categories of clinical activity – elective, emergency inpatient and day case. The report stated:

> to the extent that private patients are accommodated and treated in excess of the designated level, there are implications for equity of access. It also means that less resources than intended are being applied for the treatment of public patients.[38]

A follow up to the report of the Comptroller and Auditor General by the Committee of Public Accounts in 2008 noted among its findings that:

> The 80:20 split for private practice in public hospitals was largely ignored ultimately to the detriment of public patients.[39]

A new hospital consultants' contract, finalised in 2008 after four years of negotiations, should help to ensure equality of access to hospitals. This contract introduced a range of reforms that benefit patients, assist in the development of a consultant-provided service and ensure that maximum value for money is obtained from the investment in existing and additional consultant posts. The key changes include a longer working week, a longer working day, greater equity for public patients through a public-only contract type, limits on private versus public practice and a common waiting list in diagnostic services, including radiology and laboratory services.

The new contract, which involves strict monitoring of private practice, should provide greater equity for public patients by limiting the amount of private practice conducted by consultants who accept the new contract.

The case of Susie Long

Issues concerning the two-tier public/private health system in Ireland were tragically highlighted in 2007 through the case of Susie Long, a mother of two teenage children from Kilkenny. She contacted the RTÉ radio programme *Liveline* and, in a lengthy email, indicated how, as a public patient, she had spent seven months waiting for her cancer to be diagnosed. Had she been a private patient, i.e. with private health insurance cover, she would have had to wait a matter of days rather than months.

From the time of her contact with *Liveline*, Susie Long's predicament and the issues that it raised were highlighted on several occasions in the ensuing months. Her case encapsulated the difference between public and private and the inequalities that this could give rise to. Susie Long died on 12 October 2007, aged 41. Following her death, the Taoiseach, Bertie Ahern, TD, acknowledged in the Dáil that 'very regrettably, the system did not live up to its standards in that case. That has clearly been put forward'.[40]

Co-located hospitals

Another related issue in the public/private debate was the decision by government in 2005 to allow the development of private hospitals, with tax relief provided for the developers, on the sites of some of the major public hospitals in eight locations, as a means of providing additional bed capacity in the system. The Minister for Health and Children, Mary Harney, TD, directed the HSE to implement a policy to encourage the private sector to invest in these new co-located hospitals. The intention was to provide 1,000 private beds and, in so doing, free up private beds in the public hospitals, where 20 per cent are allocated as private.

There was no consultation process with major stakeholders prior to the government decision, not even with the public hospitals involved.

From the time the policy was adopted by government the issue became controversial, with arguments both for and against the proposed development raised, especially during the general election campaign of 2007. Much of the debate was conducted on ideological grounds, with arguments both for and against the further privatisation of health care at its core. From the government's perspective, the move was a practical measure to provide additional beds in a speedy manner. In this it was acknowledging that the public sector could not deliver the same number of beds in a similar timescale. Opponents of co-location saw it as part of a trend towards greater reliance on private care, and were concerned that, as private hospitals do not provide the full integrated care package, public hospitals would inevitably be left with more complex cases involving extended care.

While certain preparatory steps were undertaken by the HSE to advance the projects in most of the locations in the two years following the government's decision, it is highly unlikely that all of the eight proposed co-located hospitals will be completed.[41]

An alternative model?

Issues arising from the public/private mix have been touched on in various official policy documents but, with the exception of a report by the NESF in 2002 (see below), they have not been considered in any depth. While the situation for public patients has improved, mainly by reducing waiting times, there appears to be a broad acceptance of the two-tier system.

As already noted, the Commission on Health Funding accepted the two-tier system but recommended a common waiting list for access to hospital services. The *Health Strategy* focused on reducing waiting times by a combination of measures and even suggested that the inequitable access under the two-tier system was perceived rather than real. It had a brief key message: 'the perceived two-tier aspect of healthcare to be eliminated'.[42]

As an input into the implementation of the *Health Strategy*, the NESF prepared a report on access to hospital care.[43] It provided an analysis of the public/private mix and noted that one of the striking features in recent years had been the accelerated increase in private insurance and that private use of public beds was much greater in Ireland than in other EU countries. The report was critical of the *Health Strategy* for failing to address some of the key issues of the public/private mix, such as the delays experienced by patients waiting for their first appointment with a hospital consultant. It also questioned whether the achievement of the targets on waiting times constituted equity of access and suggested that even then 'public patients might well still have to wait longer for essential treatment than private patients and not necessarily be treated in the same way when in hospital'.[44] The NESF considered that structural change might be necessary to ensure that patients are dealt with on an equal footing and recommended that alternative models in other countries that do not have the same equity problems as Ireland should be independently investigated as a matter of priority. It did not elaborate on the nature of the structural change required.

Proponents of an alternative model seem unable to win sufficient support for reform and, over the years, the issue has been raised sporadically rather than in a sustained manner. This may well reflect the fact that reform has never gained sufficient populist support. In any case, half of the population are covered by private health insurance, and for them it is therefore less of an issue. The introduction of 'a national comprehensive health service for the entire population free at the point of use' covering both hospital services and GP services was an objective of the Irish Congress of Trade Unions in the 1980s.[45] However, no sustained campaign for change emerged from this, and it did not feature in the social partnership agreements as an issue for further consideration. Perhaps this is because the public/private mix has become such an established feature of the health care system that it has gained general acceptance by the most influential sections of society and tacit acceptance by the rest of the population.

In recent years alternatives to the two-tier system have been proposed by political parties. In 2000 the Labour Party produced a discussion document in which it proposed the introduction of a universal health insurance system. It ruled out the possibility of a universal public system along the lines of the National Health Service in Britain on the grounds that it would be 'extremely difficult' to introduce. The document proposed that everyone would be covered by health insurance; the state would pay the full premium for those on low incomes while others would pay for their own cover.[46]

In 2009 Fine Gael produced proposals for a FairCare system, to be introduced in three phases over five years, which would abolish the existing system and replace it by a universal health insurance based on the model in the Netherlands. It would entail free GP services for the entire population, with the state funding the insurance premiums of medical card holders and some other groups. In addition, the co-located hospitals plan would be halted and the NTPF would be abolished.[47]

The Adelaide Hospital Society has also published policy papers that have addressed issues concerned with inequity and unfair access in health services.[48]

In the general election of 2007, the manifestos of Fine Gael and the Labour Party included a commitment to introduce a universal health insurance scheme, but this did not feature as an important issue during the campaign. In the 2011 general election campaign, the two parties again favoured the introduction of a universal health insurance scheme in the context of proposed reforms of the health services. The Fine Gael/Labour *Programme for Government* (2011) contained a commitment to introduce a universal health insurance scheme with equal access to health care for all by 2016.

Health service delivery

The two main service delivery functions in the HSE are the NHO and the PCCC Directorate, and, as already noted, these two functions were more closely integrated as part of a restructuring programme. The two functions cover the majority of health services delivered to the population. In this overview chapter it is not possible to cover all of the services or those for different care groups. Instead, some of the main features of primary care services, mental health services and hospital services are considered.

Primary care

For the majority of people, primary care is the first point of contact they have with health and personal social services. In most cases this means contact with a GP who provides services to both private and public patients, the latter being medical card holders and their dependants.

The GP service is an integral part of what is known as the General Medical Service (GMS) for medical card holders. As already noted, a free service for poor persons was provided from 1851 in local dispensary districts. This system continued until the Health Act, 1970, provided for its abolition. The White Paper of 1966 had referred to the advantages of the dispensary system but indicated that the segregation of the population into fee-paying patients (who attended the doctor's surgery) and public patients (who attended the dispensary) outweighed any of its merits.[49] Consequently, the Health Act, 1970, provided for the introduction of a choice-of-doctor scheme under which eligible persons would not be discriminated against in regard to place of treatment. The choice-of-doctor scheme comes under the GMS, which also subsumes the service provided by pharmacists to those eligible.

The choice-of-doctor scheme, introduced in 1972, gave eligible patients – i.e. medical card holders and their dependants – a choice of doctor to the greatest extent practicable and ended the discrimination and stigma attached to the dispensary system. The introduction of the choice-of-doctor scheme has been described, with considerable justification, as 'a major landmark in the history of social development in Ireland'.[50]

Up to 1989, participating doctors were paid a fee per consultation in accordance with a scale that varied depending on the time when the service was given and, in the case of domiciliary consultation, on the distance travelled. Under the former dispensary system, most of the doctors supplied drugs, medicines and appliances to eligible patients. Under the GMS, retail pharmaceutical chemists, who have entered into agreement with the HSE, are the primary channels of supply of drugs prescribed for eligible persons. Until recently, prescriptions were dispensed without charge to the patient. The pharmacist recoups the cost of the drugs and, in addition, is paid a dispensing fee by the HSE. In some rural areas where the doctor's practice is located at a considerable distance from the nearest retail pharmacist participating in the scheme, the doctor may dispense the medicines and is paid a dispensing fee for each patient.

Since its inception, expenditure on the GMS has been a matter of some concern, especially the cost of providing drugs and medicines, which have accounted for about two-thirds of the total expenditure on the GMS annually. The report of a working party in 1974 noted that a number of doctors overprescribed to a significant extent. This consisted of prescribing too many items, prescribing excessive quantities and constantly prescribing the more expensive drugs without regard to their cost.[51] The report considered but rejected the introduction of a prescription charge for medical card holders. In 2010 a prescription charge of 50 cent per item, subject to a maximum of €10 per month, per person or family, was introduced.

A working party report in 1984 considered different methods by which the GMS might be made more cost-effective, with a special emphasis on the way in which doctors were paid.[52] The Irish College of General Practitioners was critical of the fee-per-item system on the grounds that:

> the GP's income depends solely on the number of face-to-face consultations which can be fitted into each day. It medicalises minor illness and induces unhealthy doctor dependence in the patient.[53]

Under a new system of payment introduced in 1989, participating doctors receive a capitation payment in respect of each panel patient, weighted by reference to demographic characteristics (gender and age) and geographic factors (distance of the doctor's principal place of practice from the patient's home).

In 2007 there were agreements with the HSE for the provision of services by 2,347 doctors, 1,587 pharmacies, 1,243 dentists and 524 optometrists. Most of the doctors care for both private and eligible patients, although the ratio between both categories of patients may vary considerably between parts of the country or within large urban areas, such as Dublin, since there is a divergence in the distribution of medical card holders by geographic area, which reflects differences between socio-economic groups. Table 5.2 indicates the cost per eligible person in 2007 (with comparative figures for 2001) for services by doctors and pharmacists under the GMS.

Table 5.2: *Costs per eligible person with medical cards, 2001 and 2007*

	Doctor (€)	Pharmacist (€)	Total (€)
2001	169.46	371.08	540.54
2007	349.03	856.14	1,205.17

Source: Annual reports of Primary Care Reimbursement Service, Health Service Executive.

With reference to GMS costs per eligible person, the Deloitte and Touche report *Value for Money Audit of the Irish Health System* (2001) indicated:

> This represents real value for money. If this is seen as a premium paid to GPs to cover their registered population, the cost per person per year is relatively low.[54]

While the cost per person may be relatively low, increases in the medical card population may have significant cost consequences for the HSE. In its annual report for 2008 it noted:

> Deteriorating economic circumstances during 2008 resulted in significantly increased demand for many services delivered by the HSE, particularly in the area of primary care and medical card services. More people became eligible for medical and GP Visit cards (6% and 13% respectively). When these types of demands exceed the allocated budgets, the extra cost has to be met by redirecting funds from other areas.[55]

Primary care teams

The *Health Strategy* proposed the introduction of an interdisciplinary, team-based approach to primary care provision. A more detailed account was provided in *Primary Care: A New Direction* (2001), which acknowledged that services were fragmented with little teamwork and limited availability of many professional groups, that liaison between primary and secondary care was often poor and that many services provided in hospitals could be provided more appropriately in the community.[56] It indicated that members of a primary care team (PCT) would include GPs, nurses/midwives, health care assistants, home helps, physiotherapists, occupational therapists, social workers and administrative personnel, all working from the one centre. These teams would effectively offer patients a 'one-stop-shop' to cater for up to 95 per cent of their health needs. It envisaged that teams would serve a population of 8,000 to 10,000, and a commitment was made to the establishment of 600 such teams by 2011.

Ten pilot sites were selected for the development of PCTs, and by 2006 these remained the only teams in existence. The ten-year social partnership agreement *Towards 2016* (2006) contained a commitment to introduce up to 100 PCTs annually.[57]

The Oireachtas Committee on Health and Children reviewed progress in implementing the primary care strategy, and its findings, published in 2010, found that progress had been significantly less than might have been expected at that stage.[58] The report indicated that 222 teams had been established at the end of 2009. However, it noted that many of these did not have a physical base. A breakdown indicated that 112 were described as 'at advanced functioning stage', which it defined as holding clinical team meetings to discuss and plan integrated care for individual clients, and that 31 teams were in place 'without GPs'.

The report made forty recommendations to speed up the implementation process. It listed a range of possible incentives, such as tax reliefs, stamp duty reliefs and rates reliefs, to expedite the provision of primary care centres. It also recommended that the number of GP training places be increased to ensure that a sufficient number of GPs are available to work in PCTs in the future.

Mental health services

With the establishment of the HSE in 2005, responsibility for the management of mental health services fell to the PCCC Directorate.

For many decades the focus of care in relation to psychiatric illness was the psychiatric hospital. In the past few decades, however, there has been a decline in the number of patients in such hospitals, and there is now far greater emphasis on the provision of a range of community services. Inpatient treatment is provided in public psychiatric hospitals, units attached to general hospitals and a small number of private psychiatric hospitals.

The *Report of the Commission of Inquiry on Mental Illness* (1966) indicated that in 1961 there were 7.3 psychiatric beds per 1,000 of the population, which appeared to be the highest in the world.[59] No clear explanation emerged for these exceptional rates of residence in psychiatric hospitals, but the commission suggested a possible combination of reasons – high rate of emigration, low marriage rates, unemployment, social and geographic isolation in rural areas, and unhelpful public attitudes towards mental illness, which do not help discharge.

A census of patients in psychiatric hospitals in 1981 indicated that approximately one-third of patients were over sixty-five years of age, four-fifths were single and one-fifth were resident in hospitals for twenty-five years or more.[60]

The report of a study group, *The Psychiatric Services: Planning for the Future* (1984), summarised the situation in relation to existing services as follows:

> At present, the psychiatric hospital is the focal point of the psychiatric service in most parts of the country. Large numbers of patients reside permanently in these hospitals. Many of them have lived there for years in conditions which in many cases are less than adequate because of overcrowding and capital underfunding. In addition, staff and public attitudes have tended to concentrate effort on hospital care as a result of which community facilities are relatively underdeveloped. The hospitals were designed to isolate the mentally ill from society and this isolation still persists.[61]

Planning for the Future provided a new planning framework for the development of a community-based psychiatric service, and was widely welcomed. In summary, the report set out guidelines for future development as far as possible in community settings, with the emphasis on resources being transferred from large psychiatric hospitals to a range of alternative community-based services and to acute general hospitals.

The report proposed the gradual dismantling of psychiatric institutions and their replacement, as far as possible, by units in general hospitals and the development of community-based services. This approach was in keeping with the general emphasis on community care and the move away from institutional care. It envisaged the provision of high-support hostels for a small number who would require long-term inpatient care and the provision of appropriate housing in the community.

Progress in implementing the recommendations of *Planning for the Future* was slow, and the *Green Paper on Mental Health* (1992) noted:

> In most health boards there are some psychiatric services which are comprehensive and community-oriented as defined in *Planning for the Future*, but such services are still not the norm.[62]

The Green Paper also noted that the psychiatric hospital still played a major role in the psychiatric service but that this role was diminishing and changing.

Almost a decade later, the *Health Strategy* indicated that while considerable progress had been made in many health board areas in implementing the change from institutional to community-based care, as recommended in *Planning for the Future*, few had completed the process.[63]

Implementation of the recommendations in *Planning for the Future* was monitored in a detailed manner by the Inspector of Mental Hospitals, whose annual reports recorded the progress, or lack of it, in different parts of the country. In the 2001 report the ongoing replacement of old institutional mental hospitals with acute psychiatric units attached to general hospitals was noted. However, the report also stated:

> Provision of community-based residential accommodation alternatives to run-down, old-fashioned psychiatric hospital accommodation proceeds somewhat unevenly throughout the country.[64]

The Mental Health Act, 2001, represented the legislative outcome of the Green Paper (1992) and White Paper (1995) on mental health. The act deals mainly with protecting the rights of individuals who may be involuntarily detained in psychiatric hospitals. Under the act, any person detained involuntarily is entitled to a review after twenty-one days by a committee of three, comprising a psychiatrist, a lawyer and one other person. The Mental Health Commission was established in 2002 under the Mental Health Act, 2001, and its main functions are to ensure that the act is fully implemented and to establish modern systems of care, including high quality of services and high standards of clinical practice.

A Vision for Change

Following wide-ranging consultation, *A Vision for Change: Report of the Expert Group on Mental Health Policy* was published in 2006. It made recommendations on how the mental health services should be managed and organised. The vision was 'to create a mental health system that addresses the needs of the population through a focus on the requirements of the individual'.[65]

The expert group recommended that a programme of capital and non-capital investment in health services was required over the next seven to ten years, in parallel with the reorganisation of mental health services. It noted that there has never been a single national management structure for mental health service provision and that this was a major factor in the continuing marked disparity of service provision between areas. It therefore recommended the establishment of a National Mental Service Directorate within the HSE that, inter alia, would establish national service priorities and agree a national service budget. It recommended the development of community mental health teams, consisting of psychiatrists, psychologists, social workers, nurses, occupational therapists, counsellors and support workers, covering catchment areas with populations between 250,000 and 400,000. In addition, there should be one acute inpatient unit with fifty beds and one day-hospital for areas with 300,000 people. The report also recommended the closure and sale of all remaining mental hospitals and the reinvestment of the proceeds of the sales into the mental health services; the closure of large mental hospitals and the expansion of community services has been government policy since *Planning for the Future*. A general welcome for the report from service providers was tinged with a certain amount of scepticism as to whether funds would be made available for its implementation.

An independent monitoring group was established to monitor implementation of the recommendations in *A Vision for Change*. In successive annual reports the monitoring group acknowledged that *A Vision for Change* had been adopted by government and embraced by all parties as the framework for developing services for people with mental health problems. However, it expressed dissatisfaction with the slow rate of progress and the lack of a comprehensive plan, and it considered 'that the recommendations of *A Vision for Change* could not be implemented effectively without a National Mental Health Service Directorate'.[66] The group noted that the absence of a dedicated leader at senior national level in the HSE had impeded progress in the implementation of *A Vision for Change*.

In its annual report for 2008 the Mental Health Commission also expressed disappointment and concern at the lack of progress, and the Inspector of Mental Health Services noted that 'comprehensive community-based services are still lacking in most parts of the country'.[67]

Commenting on the slow progress in relation to services, the Inspector of Mental Health Services recently noted:

> 2009 was a year in which there was limited change of a positive nature on the ground ... Discerning changes in the quality of care and treatment on a national basis is difficult on a year on year comparison. The National Mental Health Services may be compared to a rusty old tanker, the change in direction of which may only be measured over a long period. Changes may only be noticed in decades rather than years.[68]

Much progress has been made in relation to mental health services since the *Report of the Commission of Inquiry on Mental Illness* in 1966. The number of inpatients has declined from 19,801 in 1963 to 3,314 in 2007. Most of the large psychiatric hospitals have closed, and psychiatric units have opened in most general hospitals. Community services and facilities have improved. Yet among mental health services providers there is general agreement that mental health services are not accorded the priority required and that there is not a sufficient commitment to adequate funding by government.

Hospital services

Inpatient and outpatient hospital services are provided either in public hospitals, voluntary public hospitals or private hospitals.

Public hospitals, managed by the HSE, evolved from the infirmaries and the workhouses of the nineteenth-century Poor Law. Following the abolition of the workhouses in the 1920s, a county system of hospitals began to emerge.

Some of the voluntary hospitals date from the early eighteenth century, and some are owned by religious orders. They are mainly located in the larger urban areas, especially Dublin, where the greatest demand for services existed and where financial support for their upkeep was also likely to be more readily available. A number of these hospitals were closed in the late 1980s. The level of state support for these hospitals increased over time and they are now funded by the HSE; hence they are referred to as voluntary public hospitals.

Some private hospitals were established by religious orders and share the same campus with voluntary public hospitals (e.g. Mater Private Hospital and the Mater Hospital). Others that have been established more recently include the Blackrock Clinic and the Beacon Hospital, both in Dublin. These private hospitals do not receive direct state subsidies.

Acute hospital activity

In 2008 the HSE's National Service Plan outlined its objective of shifting the balance of activity in acute hospitals to delivering more day-case procedures while at the same time reducing the activity ratio of inpatient-to-day-case procedures. The throughput of all cases in acute hospitals has increased in recent years (see Table 5.3).

Rationalisation of hospital facilities

Over a period of time the nature of service provision in hospitals has been increasingly influenced by a range of factors or drivers of change.

Table 5.3: *Service activity in acute hospitals, 2005–09*

Activity	2005	2009	% change 2005–2009
Inpatient discharges	575,476	593,359	+3
Day cases	512,034	669,955	+31
Outpatient attendances	2,601,950	3,357,106	+29
Emergency department attendances	1,099,139	1,119,719	+2

Source: Health Service Executive, *Annual Report and Financial Statements 2009* (Health Service Executive, Dublin, 2010), p. 42.

These include developments in medical technology; expansion of health care knowledge and expertise in clinical practice; improvements in the general quality and safety of services; demographic changes, including the optimum population of a hospital catchment area; and ongoing medical staffing and training requirements. As a result, the environment in which acute hospitals now operate differs in many respects from those of several decades ago.

The establishment of the Health Information and Quality Authority (HIQA) under the Health Act, 2007, has provided a further impetus for improvements in acute hospitals. HIQA's statutory role includes setting standards for health and social services and monitoring health care quality. The current clinical model of care being developed by the HSE on a regional basis, in accordance with international best practice, is one where non-acute care is provided in locally accessible centres and where acute care is delivered in a single regional centre for managing the most complex cases. This also has implications for the configuration of hospital services.

It is against this background that a process of rationalisation of hospitals and hospital facilities has been ongoing. A century ago, Ireland had a large number of small hospitals, and various proposals and attempts to rationalise the system have been made with varying degrees of success. Some of the main proposals and developments are considered in this section.

Hospitals Commission's report (1936)
The first report of the Hospitals Commission, covering the period 1933–6, recommended against the development of each county hospital but favoured the grouping of hospitals in suitable geographic centres 'irrespective of county boundaries'. It submitted a scheme for the development of twelve main regional centres, county hospitals in areas

remote from regional centres and a network of district hospitals in the provincial towns. The commission was critical of the situation in Dublin where there were two many small hospitals, and it recommended the development of two general hospitals in south Dublin and two in north Dublin.[69] These proposals were not pursued, partly because the government had already embarked upon the development of county hospitals.

The Fitzgerald report (1968)

In 1967 Sean Flanagan, TD, Minister for Health, appointed a consultative council to review the hospital system. The report, published in 1968, is usually referred to as the Fitzgerald report, after the chairman of the council, Professor Patrick Fitzgerald.[70] In general, the report indicated that the existing hospital system was defective in many ways and suggested that the system could only be improved by a radical reorganisation involving, among other things, a considerable reduction in the number of centres providing acute treatment. It recommended that the hospital system be reorganised into three regions based on the medical teaching centres in Dublin, Cork and Galway. Each region would have a regional hospital of 600–1,000 beds, offering a full range of services, supported by a number of general hospitals of about 300 beds throughout the region. The existing county hospitals would become community health centres providing some inpatient services. There was no official commitment to implement the recommendations of the Fitzgerald report.

General Hospital Development Plan (1975)

Following a process of consultation with the medical profession, health boards and Comhairle na nOspidéal, the *General Hospital Development Plan* (GHDP) was announced by Brendan Corish, TD, Minister for Health, in 1975. It differed fundamentally from the Fitzgerald report in the number of acute care hospitals to be established. The GHDP envisaged the development of general hospitals in twenty-three locations (about twice as many as envisaged in the Fitzgerald report) and speculated on a further number of community hospitals in formats and locations to be decided upon. The plan contained no detail of the future development of hospital services in either Cork or Limerick cities beyond tentative mention of the possibility of a major hospital service in the northeast area of Cork city. In addition, decisions in some other cases were postponed pending further consultation. The main differences between the GHDP and the Fitzgerald report were distance of population from a general hospital (thirty miles versus sixty miles, respectively) and, related to that, the number of centres in which general hospitals should be located (twenty-three versus twelve, respectively).

The GHDP could be viewed as a balance between professional medical opinion and broader political considerations. *The Irish Times* commented that 'it is not so much a national plan of any substance as an interim political statement on the state of play at local level'.[71]

In its pre-election manifesto of 1977, the Fianna Fáil party included an undertaking 'to preserve the role of the county hospital in providing the necessary level of services for the local community'.[72]

Since the GHDP was not comprehensive, and in the absence of a detailed policy statement from the new government, Comhairle na nOspidéal concluded that the country would in the future be served by a limited number of large specialised hospitals in Dublin, Cork and Galway (at least seven and possibly nine), and by a large number of smaller general hospitals (about twenty-four or twenty-six). Comhairle indicated that:

> Inherent in such a situation of many small hospitals is the danger that medical deficiencies, spelled out in the Fitzgerald Report and for which that body proposed medical solutions, will continue to exist.[73]

Rationalisation in the 1980s

It was largely in the context of cutbacks in public expenditure on the health services that a rationalisation of hospitals occurred in the late 1980s. During this period a number of the public voluntary hospitals and the smaller public district hospitals were closed, often amid considerable controversy. The most notable example was that of Barrington's Hospital in Limerick, a public voluntary hospital that had been established under charter in 1830. The proposal by the Department of Health to close this hospital gave rise to vehement public opposition, with an estimated 20,000 persons attending a demonstration in Limerick city in January 1988 to protest against the closure. It also led to the government being defeated on a private members' motion in the Dáil in February 1988. The defeat briefly raised the prospect of a general election, but the motion was not binding on the government and the hospital closed in the following month.

The number of acute care hospitals and, consequently, the number of beds were reduced from the mid 1980s to the early 1990s (Table 5.4). Approximately 4,000 beds were removed from the system between 1984 and 1988, and a further 2,000 were removed between 1991 and 1993. However, this did not occur as a result of any coherent national plan. The closures of some hospitals were brought about either by the

Department of Health reducing budgets to health boards, leaving them with no option but to close the smaller hospitals, or by the department simply informing a number of voluntary public hospitals, which it funded directly, that they would have to close.

Table 5.4: *Acute hospital beds and average length of stay (ALOS), selected years, 1980–2000*

	Beds	ALOS
1980	17,665	9.7
1984	17,633	7.5
1988	13,632	7.0
1991	13,806	6.8
1993	11,809	6.7
2000	11,832	6.6

Source: Department of Health and Children, *Acute Hospital Bed Capacity: A National Review* (Department of Health and Children, Dublin, 2002), Table 1.1, p. 18.

This absence of national planning led the chief executive of the South Eastern Health Board to comment in 1987 that:

> In the absence of an agreed national plan the effect will be to downgrade all our acute hospitals and instead of a limited number of good hospitals we will have a larger number of poor hospitals.[74]

Rationalisation of hospital services in Dublin along the lines proposed by the GHDP has been achieved. The plan allowed for six major general hospitals – the Beaumont, the Mater and the James Connolly memorial hospitals on the north side and St Vincent's, St James's and Tallaght hospitals on the south side. This rationalisation was a protracted affair that took several years to complete, partly because, in some cases, it involved the amalgamation of existing hospitals with different traditions and ethos. This was particularly true of Tallaght hospital, opened in 1998 in the south-west suburbs, which is an amalgam of three former city hospitals – the Adelaide, Meath and National Children's hospitals. While this amalgamation is recognised in the formal name, i.e. the Adelaide and Meath Hospital Dublin Incorporating the National Children's Hospital, it is more commonly referred to simply as Tallaght Hospital.

The Hanly report (2003)
Yet more proposals with implications for the reconfiguration of hospitals were contained in the report of a task force usually referred to as the

Hanly report (after the chairman, David Hanly).[75] The task force was established to consider the implications of the European Working Time Directive under which the working week (an average of over seventy-five hours) for non-consultant hospital doctors (NCHDs) would be introduced in stages by 2009.

Different options were considered by the task force, but the preferred option was to employ a much larger number of consultants working in teams, with revised working patterns and a significantly reduced number of NCHDs. The Hanly report indicated that 'hospitals without sufficient volume of patients and activity cannot sustain large numbers of consultants' and that 'best results in treatment are achieved when patients are treated by staff working as part of a multi-disciplinary specialist team'.[76] In short, the Hanly report recommended a consultant-provided hospital service, as opposed to the existing consultant-led service.

The task force examined two regions – East Coast Area Health Board and Mid Western Health Board – and proposed a reconfiguration of hospital services. For the mid west region (Counties Limerick, Clare and Tipperary North), the report concluded that Limerick Regional Hospital should function as the major hospital for the region while Ennis, Nenagh and St John's (Limerick) should function as local hospitals. The local hospitals would not have 24-hour accident and emergency services. Within a relatively short time, reaction to the proposals at local level became clear. Public protest meetings in Ennis and Nenagh attracted estimated crowds of 20,000 and 10,000, respectively, in November 2003.[77] Opposition to and criticism of the Hanly proposals were also voiced by some hospital consultants.

The Hanly report (2003) was phase I of a national audit and covered the former Mid Western and East Coast Area Health Board regions only. In 2004 a phase II group, also under the chairmanship of David Hanly, was appointed to consider the configuration of hospital services in the rest of the country. For a variety of reasons the phase II group did not meet, and it was formally disbanded in 2005. The HSE was subsequently requested to take the recommendations of the Hanly report on board in consultations with health professionals and local communities in any possible reorganisation and development of acute hospital services.

In 2009 the HSE went ahead, against local opposition, even by some GPs, with an action plan for hospital service reconfiguration in the mid west along the lines recommended in the Hanly report. The action plan had been informed by another review, carried out jointly by two consultancy firms, which made the case for one regional 'centre of excellence' for acute care for the mid west.[78]

Specialist services

Reviews have also been carried out on specialist hospital services. Examples where such reviews have become policy include paediatrics and cancer care.

Children's Health First, a report commissioned by the HSE and compiled by McKinsey and Company consultants, was published in 2006. Having considered best international practice in the provision of paediatric care, the report recommended that, given its population, the Republic could support only one world-class children's hospital. It concluded that this hospital should be in Dublin, that it should have 380 beds (285 inpatient beds, 54 intensive care unit beds and 41 day beds), that it should be adjacent to an adult hospital, that the site should have space for future expansion and that it should be easily accessible by public transport.[79] The report's recommendation, endorsed by the board of the HSE, would have major implications for the three children's hospitals in Dublin – Our Lady's Hospital for Sick Children, Crumlin; the Children's University Hospital, Temple Street; and the National Children's Hospital, which is based in Tallaght Hospital.

A task force, with representatives from the Department of Health and Children and the HSE, was established to advise on the most appropriate location. Its report indicated that both the Mater Hospital and St James's Hospital satisfied the clinical and access criteria for the new hospital but concluded that the project could be delivered more quickly on the Mater site.[80] The boards of two Dublin hospitals, St James's Hospital and Our Lady's Hospital for Sick Children, Crumlin, expressed concerns at the decision, describing the process as 'fatally flawed' and the report as 'extremely short on detail and transparency'. Both boards called for a review of the decision.[81] Despite these concerns, the government approved the decision to locate the hospital at the Mater Hospital site.

In 2000 an expert working group recommended that, in accordance with international best practice, women diagnosed with breast cancer should be treated in thirteen centres on a multidisciplinary model of care.[82] A second national cancer strategy (2006) recommended that cancer centres should be networked together in managed cancer-control networks, and that there should be a broad aim of equipping each of the HSE's four administrative regions with broad self-sufficiency of services in relation to the more common forms of cancer.[83] These recommendations were taken on board in 2007 when it was announced that eight named hospitals would be designated as specialist centres to provide all care for cancer patients. The hospitals designated for providing cancer care were Beaumont and the Mater (serving HSE Dublin North East region); St James's and St Vincent's (serving HSE

Dublin Mid Leinster region); Cork University Hospital and Waterford Regional Hospital (serving HSE South region); University College Hospital Galway and Limerick Regional Hospital (serving HSE West region). The strategy envisaged that each hospital grouping would serve a population of 500,000 people, and that a special outreach cancer care service would be provided for the HSE West region 'on a sole exception basis' at Letterkenny General Hospital, because of its remote location. As part of the strategy, some small hospitals were ordered to cease providing care to breast cancer patients, and cancer services were to be reduced on a phased basis in others. With the exception of Sligo and, to a lesser extent, Castlebar, where public protest meetings were held, there was little opposition to this proposal from the communities affected by the withdrawal of certain cancer services. Concern over the possible misdiagnosis of cancer cases over a four-year period in the Midland General Hospital at Portlaoise may well have been a factor in persuading patients to accept that, despite travel inconvenience, care in a regional centre of excellence was preferable to that in a local hospital.[84]

Hospitals and politics

In the context of hospital rationalisation or reconfiguration, it has been noted that the 'location and type of hospital available to each patient, community and region in Ireland is probably the most contentious issue in Irish health politics'.[85]

The importance of the hospitals issue is reflected in the stand taken on occasions by elected politicians defending the status of a constituency hospital and the emergence of 'hospital candidates' at general or local elections.

One of the most high-profile cases of defiance concerned Michael Smith, TD, Minister for Defence, representing the constituency of Tipperary North. At a public meeting organised by Nenagh Town Council in November 2003 he indicated that he refused to endorse the recommendations of the Hanly report. Within a few days, however, he withdrew his opposition and, in a letter to the Taoiseach, stated that he accepted fully 'the core principles of the Hanly Report'.[86] Another notable objection to government policy came from Dr Jimmy Devins, TD, Minister of State at the Department of Health and representing the constituency of Sligo, who, in 2007, in the context of the cancer strategy, indicated that he was 'absolutely outraged' at the decision to discontinue cancer surgery in Sligo General Hospital.[87] Two years later, when the breast cancer unit was formally closed in Sligo, he and another Fianna Fáil TD for Sligo, Eamon Scanlon, resigned from the Fianna Fáil parliamentary party.[88]

A number of candidates owe their electoral success to their stance of preserving the status of their local hospital. Tom Fox was elected an independent candidate in the general election in 1989 in the Roscommon constituency on the basis of his support for the hospital in Roscommon town, and he retained the seat in the 1992 general election. Paudge Connolly was similarly elected in 2002 for the Cavan/ Monaghan constituency on a platform of maintaining services in Monaghan Hospital.

Financing the health services

The principal source of income for health services is general taxation (Table 5.5); up to 1977, however, local taxation was an important and significant source of income.

Table 5.5: *Sources of finance for statutory non-capital health services, 2004**

	€m	%
Exchequer	8,113	85.2
Health contributions and miscellaneous	1,079	11.3
Receipts under EU regulations	336	3.5
Total	9,528	100.0

* Estimated.

Source: Health statistics (Department of Health and Children).

During the nineteenth century a local rate constituted the primary source of income for health services, and only towards the end of the century was state aid provided. By 1947 state grants accounted for 16 per cent of the total cost of the services. Post-war developments in the health services necessitated increased state expenditure. Under the Health Services (Financial Provisions) Act, 1947, the state agreed to meet any further increase in costs until such time as these costs were shared equally by each health authority and the exchequer, a position that was reached in 1951 and that continued up to the mid 1960s. The White Paper of 1966 indicated that local rates were not a form of taxation suitable for collecting revenue on the scale required for proposed developments in the health services and recommended instead that the cost of further extensions of the services should not be met by the local rates. As a consequence, the exchequer's contribution amounted to 56 per cent of total costs by 1970. The government decided in 1973 to remove health charges from local rates over a four-year period, and by 1977 the transfer had been completed.

Another source of revenue, the health contribution, was introduced under the Health Contributions Act, 1971, at the request of the Department of Finance, which was concerned at the falling contribution from local rates. Payment of the contribution, or levy, did not confer entitlement to any health service. Up to 1991 the health contribution was based on a percentage of earnings subject to an income limit that was usually adjusted upwards on an annual basis. In 1991, however, the income limit was abolished, and the contribution was levied on total income. Some changes to the contribution level were made in recent years, especially in 2009, as a means of boosting exchequer returns. In 2011 the health contribution and the existing income levy were abolished and replaced by a universal social charge (USC), which is separate from income tax. The USC is to be applied to 'the provision of services' but not necessarily health services as was the case with the health levy.

A further source of income since 1973 is derived from receipts under EU regulations. These receipts are mainly in respect of health services provided for people for whom Britain is liable under EU regulations, e.g. recipients of British pensions and dependants of persons employed in Britain. The amount that the Irish government had been receiving under this heading was questioned by the British government in 2008, and there was a consequent reduction in the contribution from that source.[89]

An important source of revenue for hospitals for several decades was the Hospitals Trust Fund. A number of voluntary hospitals joined forces to run a sweepstake from horse racing in 1930. The venture proved successful and, under the Public Hospitals Act, 1933, available surpluses of ensuing sweepstakes were made payable to the Hospitals Trust Fund, appointed by the Minister for Local Government and Public Health to administer the funds. The income from the fund was used mainly for capital expenditure on all hospitals. Up to 1974, voluntary hospitals were financed by capitation grants from the Department of Health and grants from the Hospitals Trust Fund towards revenue deficits. The role of the Hospitals Trust Fund in financing hospital development and services had declined considerably in importance when the sweepstake was wound up in 1987. It had, however, made a substantial contribution to the development of hospitals. Barrington has noted:

> The availability of sweepstake money enabled a level of investment in hospitals, which arguably, could not or would not have been provided otherwise.[90]

Commission on Health Funding (1989)
In considering the question of financing, the Commission on Health Funding concluded that the level of public health funding could not be

determined by reference to a fixed proportion of gross domestic product or by reference to international comparison. The level could only be decided in the context of the available resources and the priorities attached by Irish society to different social objectives.

The commission referred to three main methods of funding health services: general taxation, social insurance and private insurance. It pointed out that no country relies exclusively on any of these approaches. The majority of the commission favoured public funding as the main funding method. It opted for this in preference to private funding on the basis that:

- it would achieve a greater degree of comprehensiveness since the state as central funder is favourably placed to plan and organise the delivery of a unified, integrated service for all categories of patient;
- the implementation of policy shifts, such as the transfer of resources from institutional to community care, can be more easily achieved when there is a single major health funder;
- equity of contribution towards the cost of services can be achieved by way of progressive taxation or social insurance;
- equity of access can be controlled administratively to ensure that necessary services are available to all on the basis of need.

By contrast, the majority felt that a private funding model would not be equitable (there could be discrimination against high-risk groups), comprehensive (arising from problems in enforcing mandatory health insurance) or cost-effective (the international evidence suggests that cost control is not more successful under a private funding model).

Once the commission had opted for a public funding model, the choice was then between general taxation and a compulsory health insurance/earmarked tax system (linking the services provided with their cost). A majority favoured general taxation on the grounds that compulsory health insurance was effectively another tax offering no real advantages over general taxation.

The commission also recommended that the health contribution should be abolished. It pointed out that while local taxation was a major source of funding for health services in the past, it should not be reintroduced for this purpose since it could hinder national planning of facilities.

With the exception of the health contribution, the commission had, in effect, recommended retention of the status quo in relation to financing the health services, and there has not been any alternative proposal since its report was published in 1989.

In 2004 over four-fifths (85.2 per cent) of funds for health services were derived from the exchequer, with the health contribution and hospital outpatient charges accounting for just over 10 per cent, and receipts under EU regulations accounting for the balance (Table 5.5). There has not been any significant change in these proportions over the past few decades. The 2004 statistics by the Department of Health and Children on sources of funding are the most recently published.

Irish health care in a European context

Several aspects of the Irish health care system have been the subject of public criticism in recent years. The emergence of 'crisis points' from time to time have served to undermine public confidence in a system that was expected to improve once the HSE was established as a single national agency with responsibility for the delivery of health services in place of the regional health boards. In this context it is interesting to see how Ireland compares with other European countries on the basis of a number of health indicators.

For several years the Euro Health Consumer Index (EHCI) has been compiled by the Health Consumer Powerhouse from a combination of public statistics, patient polls and independent research. As such, it is a useful barometer of the changing status of the health care systems in various European countries. In the 2006 survey, Ireland ranked twenty-fifth out of twenty-six countries, but in subsequent years its position improved considerably. In the 2009 survey, Ireland ranked thirteenth out of thirty-three European countries, up two positions on the previous year.

The EHCI 2009 grouped thirty-eight indicators of quality into six groups:

i.   patient rights and information;
ii.   e-health;
iii. waiting times for treatment;
iv.   health outcomes;
v.   range and reach of services provided;
vi.   pharmaceuticals.

In the 'health outcomes' group, Ireland scored full marks in four of the seven indicators, while e-health, such as the electronic transfer of data between professionals, was an area where Ireland performed the poorest.

The Netherlands topped the list with a total score of 875 out of a possible 1,000 points, followed by Denmark (819 points) and a smaller group of 'strong performers' in Iceland, Austria and Switzerland.

Ireland's score was 701, behind Belgium and Finland but ahead of the UK and Italy.

Ireland was one of three countries listed in EHCI 2009 as having 'a domestic-marketing problem', where the views of patient organisations differed from official statistics. According to the report, 'this was particularly striking for Ireland, which after HSE reform has been steadily climbing in the EHCI, but where the responses from patient organisations on issues such as waiting times are very negative still in 2009'.[91]

Notes

1. This section draws extensively on B. Hensey, *The Health Services of Ireland*, 4th edn (Institute of Public Administration, Dublin, 1988), Chapter 1.
2. See J. Robins, *Fools and Mad, A History of the Insane in Ireland* (Institute of Public Administration, Dublin, 1986); J. Reynolds, *Grangegorman, Psychiatric Care in Dublin since 1815* (Institute of Public Administration, Dublin, 1992).
3. J. Robins, *The Miasma: Epidemic and Panic in Nineteenth Century Ireland* (Institute of Public Administration, Dublin, 1995), p. 108.
4. Ibid., p. 241.
5. There are various accounts of the controversy surrounding the Mother and Child Scheme. These include relevant sections in R. Barrington, *Health, Medicine and Politics in Ireland, 1900–1970* (Institute of Public Administration, Dublin, 1987); N. Browne, *Against the Tide* (Gill & Macmillan, Dublin, 1986); G. Deeney, *To Cure and to Care: Memoirs of a Chief Medical Officer* (Glendale Press, Dublin, 1989); J.H. Whyte, *Church and State in Modern Ireland, 1923–1979*, 2nd edn (Gill & Macmillan, Dublin, 1980); J. Horgan, *Noel Browne, Passionate Outsider* (Gill & Macmillan, Dublin, 2000).
6. Barrington, op. cit., p. 279.
7. Hensey, op. cit., Chapters 1–4.
8. Government of Ireland, *The Health Services and Their Further Development* (Stationery Office, Dublin, 1966), pp. 63–4.
9. Barrington, op. cit., p. 274.
10. Department of Health, *Health: The Wider Dimensions* (Department of Health, Dublin, 1986), p. 35.
11. Government of Ireland, *Report of the Commission on Health Funding* (Stationery Office, Dublin, 1989), p. 15.
12. Ibid., Chapter 9.
13. L. Joyce and C. Ham, 'Enabling managers to manage: health care reform in Ireland', *Administration*, Vol. 38, No. 3 (1990), p. 227.
14. National Economic and Social Council, *Report No. 89, A Strategy for the Nineties: Economic Stability and Structural Change* (Stationery Office, Dublin, 1990), pp. 285–6.
15. *Health Service News*, Vol. 2, No. 2 (May 1990), pp. 4–5.

16. Address by Dr Rory O'Hanlon, TD, Minister for Health, at the launch of the *Report of the Dublin Hospital Initiative Group* and the announcement of the reorganisation of health services, 18 September 1991.

17. Deloitte and Touche, *Value for Money Audit of the Irish Health System: Executive Summary* (Department of Health and Children, Dublin, 2001), p. 8.

18. Department of Health and Children, *Audit of Structures and Functions in the Health System* (Stationery Office, Dublin, 2003), p. 52.

19. Government of Ireland, *Commission on Financial Management and Control Systems in the Health Service* (Stationery Office, Dublin, 2003), p. 5.

20. Department of Health and Children, *The Health Service Reform Programme* (Department of Health and Children, Dublin, 2003), p. 4.

21. Government of Ireland, *Health Act, 1970* (Stationery Office, Dublin, 1970).

22. Department of Health and Children, *Health Strategy: Quality and Fairness, A Health System for You* (Department of Health and Children, Dublin, 2001), p. 75.

23. Comptroller and Auditor General, *2001 Annual Report of the Comptroller and Auditor General* (Stationery Office, Dublin, 2002), pp. 100–2.

24. Department of Health and Children, *Health Strategy*, op. cit., p. 77.

25. Fianna Fáil, *A lot done. More to do. Fianna Fáil Manifesto 2002–2007* (Fianna Fáil, Dublin, 2002), p. 61.

26. Department of Health and Children, *Health Statistics 2005* (Department of Health and Children, Dublin, 2005), p. 118.

27. See J. Curry, *Irish Social Services*, 1st edn (Institute of Public Administration, Dublin, 1980), pp. 186–7.

28. Health Insurance Authority, *2009 Annual Reports and Accounts* (Health Insurance Authority, Dublin, 2010), p. 45.

29. Department of Health and Children, *White Paper Private Health Insurance* (Stationery Office, Dublin, 1999), p. 73.

30. Health Insurance Authority, op. cit., p. 44.

31. Department of Health and Children, *White Paper Private Health Insurance*, op. cit., p. 8.

32. M.A. Wren, 'An unhealthy state', *The Irish Times*, 2–6 October 2000.

33. Society of St Vincent de Paul, *Health Inequalities and Poverty* (Society of St Vincent de Paul, Dublin, 2001).

34. National Treatment Purchase Fund, *Annual Report 2009* (National Treatment Purchase Fund, Dublin, 2010), p. 9.

35. See M.A. Wren, *Unhealthy State: Anatomy of a Sick Society* (New Island, Dublin, 2003); and S. Burke, *Irish Apartheid: Healthcare Inequality in Ireland* (New Island, Dublin, 2009).

36. Department of Health and Children, *White Paper Private Health Insurance*, op. cit., p. 13.

37. Department of Health and Children, *Health Strategy*, op. cit., pp. 107–8.

38. Comptroller and Auditor General, *Medical Consultants' Contract* (Stationery Office, Dublin, 2007), p. 9.

39. Committee of Public Accounts, *Third Interim Report on the 2006 Report of the Comptroller and Auditor General: Expenditure on Health Services* (Stationery Office, Dublin, 2008), p. 8.

40. See Burke, op. cit., pp. 7–12.

41. The 2007 HSE annual report indicated that site locations and private providers for six private hospitals were identified, and that some progress was made on finalising project arrangements, including the number of beds in each hospital. No reference is made to these projects in either the 2008 or the 2009 annual reports.

42. Department of Health and Children, *Health Strategy*, op. cit., p. 57.

43. National Economic and Social Forum, *Report No. 25, Equity of Access to Hospital Care* (Stationery Office, Dublin, 2002).

44. Ibid., p. 89.

45. P. Cassells, 'Health services', in D. Nevin, *Trade Union Priorities in Social Policy* (Federated Workers Union of Ireland, Dublin, 1981), pp. 82–6.

46. Labour Party, *Curing Our Ills: Irish Healthcare 2000 Delivering Excellence for All. Labour Party Proposals for Hospital and GP Care in a New Century* (Labour Party, Dublin, 2000).

47. Fine Gael, *FairCare: Fine Gael Proposals to Reform the Health Service and Introduce Universal Health Insurance* (Fine Gael, Dublin, 2009).

48. See S. Thomas et al., *Social Health Insurance: Options for Ireland* (The Adelaide Hospital Society, Dublin, 2006).

49. Government of Ireland, *The Health Services and Their Further Development*, op. cit., p. 30.

50. Consultative Council on General Medical Services, *The General Practitioner in Ireland, Report of the Consultative Council on General Medical Services* (Stationery Office, Dublin, 1974), p. 45.

51. Working Party on Prescribing and Dispensing in the General Medical Service, *Report of the Working Party on Prescribing and Dispensing in the General Medical Service* (Stationery Office, Dublin, 1974), p. 45.

52. Working Party on the General Medical Service, *Report of the Working Party on the General Medical Service* (Stationery Office, Dublin, 1984).

53. Irish College of General Practitioners, *The Future Organisation of General Practice in Ireland: A Discussion Document* (Irish College of General Practitioners, Dublin, 1986), p. 34.

54. Deloitte and Touche, op. cit., p. 25.

55. Health Service Executive, *Annual Report and Financial Statements 2008* (Health Service Executive, Dublin, 2009), p. 66.

56. Department of Health and Children, *Primary Care: A New Direction* (Stationery Office, Dublin, 2001).

57. Department of the Taoiseach, *Towards 2016: Ten-Year Framework Social Partnership Agreement 2006–2015* (Stationery Office, Dublin, 2006), p. 52.

58. Joint Committee on Health and Children, *Second Report: Report on Primary Medical Care in the Community* (Houses of the Oireachtas, Dublin, 2010).

59. Commission of Inquiry on Mental Illness, *Report of the Commission of Inquiry on Mental Illness* (Stationery Office, Dublin, 1966), p. xv.

60. Medico-Socio Research Board, *The Irish Psychiatric Hospital Census, 1981* (Medico-Socio Research Board, Dublin, 1983), pp. 11–12.

61. Department of Health, *The Psychiatric Services: Planning for the Future* (Stationery Office, Dublin, 1984), p. xi.

62. Department of Health, *Green Paper on Mental Health* (Stationery Office, Dublin, 1992), p. 14.

63. Department of Health and Children, *Health Strategy*, op. cit., p. 145.

64. Inspector of Mental Hospitals, *Report of the Inspector of Mental Hospitals for the Year Ending 31st December, 2001* (Stationery Office, Dublin, 2001), p. 4.

65. Expert Group on Mental Health Policy, *A Vision for Change: Report of the Expert Group on Mental Health Policy* (Stationery Office, Dublin, 2006), p. 14.

66. Expert Group on Mental Health Policy, *A Vision for Change – the Report of the Expert Group on Mental Health Policy, Third Annual Report on Implementation 2008* (Stationery Office, Dublin, 2009), p. 3.

67. Mental Health Commission, *Annual Report Including the Report of the Inspector of Mental Health Services 2008* (Mental Health Commission, Dublin, 2009), pp. 3, 56.

68. Mental Health Commission, *Annual Report Including the Report of the Inspector of Mental Health Services 2009* (Mental Health Commission, Dublin, 2010), p. 78.

69. Barrington, op. cit., pp. 120–1.

70. Consultative Council on the General Hospital Service, *Outline of the Future Hospital System, Report of the Consultative Council on the General Hospital Service* (Stationery Office, Dublin, 1968).

71. 'One for the grave', *The Irish Times*, 21 October 1975.

72. Fianna Fáil, *Action Plan for National Reconstruction: Fianna Fáil Manifesto for General Election* (Fianna Fáil, Dublin, 1977), p. 25.

73. Comhairle na nOspidéal, *2nd Report January 1975–December 1978* (Comhairle na nOspidéal, Dublin, 1978), p. 24.

74. P. McQuillan, 'What should we provide? Service emphasis to achieve objectives', *Papers Presented at Conference on 'Health in the 1990s', 7–9 May 1987* (Association of Health Boards in Ireland in association with the Institute of Public Administration, 1987), pp. 55–6.

75. Department of Health and Children, *Report of the National Task Force on Medical Staffing* (Department of Health and Children, Dublin, 2003).

76. Ibid., p. 15.

77. T. O'Brien, 'Protesters warn against cuts to A&E in Ennis', *The Irish Times*, 17 November 2003; E. Donnellan, 'Nenagh rally told hospitals could be sued if Hanly plans go ahead', *The Irish Times*, 1 December 2003.

78. Horwarth Consulting Ireland and Teamwork Management Services, *Review of the Acute Hospital Services in HSE Mid West: An Action Plan for Acute and Community Services* (Health Service Executive, Dublin, 2008).

79. McKinsey and Company, *Children's Health First* (Health Service Executive, Dublin, 2006).

80. Health Service Executive, *Report of the Joint Health Service Executive/Department of Health and Children Task Group to Advise on the Optimum Location of the New National Paediatric Hospital* (Health Service Executive, Dublin, 2006).

81. See T. McNamara et al., 'Review of developments, structure and management in the public sector 2006', *Administration*, Vol. 54, No. 4 (2007), pp. 26–7.

82. Sub-Group to the National Cancer Forum, *Development of Services for Symptomatic Breast Disease: Report of the Sub-Group to the National Cancer Forum* (Department of Health and Children, Dublin, 2000).

83. National Cancer Forum, *A Strategy for Cancer Control in Ireland 2006* (Department of Health and Children, Dublin, 2006).

84. For background, see report by J. Fitzgerald, *Management, Governance and Communications Issues Arising from the Review of Breast Radiology Services at Midland Regional Hospital Portlaoise* (Health Service Executive, Dublin, 2008).

85. Burke, op. cit., p. 154.

86. A. Beesley, 'Smith expresses "regret" to Ahern over Hanly comments', *The Irish Times*, 15 November 2003.

87. M. McDonogh, 'Devins criticises cancer strategy', *The Irish Times*, 23 October 2007.

88. H. McGee and M. McDonogh, 'Government majority lost as TDs defect over cancer unit closure', *The Irish Times*, 6 August 2009.

89. M. Wall and M. Hennessy, 'Reduced UK payment to leave HSE short', *The Irish Times*, 24 November 2008.

90. Barrington, op. cit., p. 284.

91. A. Bjornberg et al., *Euro Health Consumer Index 2009* (Health Consumer Powerhouse, Brussels, 2009), p. 7.

6

Welfare of Certain Groups

Introduction

The basic social services – housing, education, health and income maintenance – cater for needs that are common to all members of society. However, certain groups have special needs, and services over and above the basic ones have evolved to cater for these needs. Such groups include older people, children and persons with disabilities (both intellectual and physical/sensory). While these groups are catered for to some extent by the basic services, special provision is also required. Hence services such as residential care for children or sheltered employment for people with disabilities have been developed.

This chapter examines welfare services for older people, children, persons with disabilities and the Travelling community.

Older people

The term 'older people' is now regarded as acceptable terminology, and has replaced terms such as 'elderly' and 'aged'. It is usual to classify those aged sixty-five or over as older people since this is the generally accepted age of retirement from employment. It is also the age used internationally for comparisons of the proportions of total populations of older people.

A demographic feature common to most developed nations is the relatively high proportion of people aged sixty-five and over. This is mainly due to the reduction of mortality rates in infancy and childhood that has led to a considerable increase in life expectancy. The average life expectancy at birth in Ireland during the period 1925–7 was 57.4 years for males and 57.9 years for females; by 2005–07 these figures had increased to 76.8 and 81.6 years, respectively. Older people formed an increasing proportion of the total population up to the 1950s; in 1841 the proportion was approximately 3 per cent, and by 1956 this had increased to 11.2 per cent. While the absolute number of older people has continued to increase, the percentage of such persons in the total population has remained remarkably stable over more than half a century. By 2006 it was 11.0 per cent, marginally lower than fifty years earlier (Table 6.1). This is largely explained by the general population increase over the same period.

Table 6.1: *Persons aged sixty-five and over, selected years, 1926–2006*

Year	Number	% of total population
1926	271,700	9.1
1936	286,684	9.6
1946	314,322	10.6
1956	315,063	11.2
1966	323,007	11.2
1971	329,819	11.1
1981	368,954	10.7
1991	394,830	11.4
1996	413,882	11.5
2002	436,001	11.1
2006	467,926	11.0

Source: Census of population (Central Statistics Office).

A feature of the population of older people is the increasing proportion living alone. In 1966 such persons accounted for one-tenth (10.8 per cent) of all older people. By 2006 this proportion had increased to over a quarter (26.7 per cent). Those living alone are acknowledged to constitute a vulnerable group with potentially high demands on health and welfare services.

While various population projections differ, all indicate a further increase in the number of older people over the next few decades, with implications for the provision of health and welfare services for this group.

Growing concern over the increasing numbers of older people and the inadequacy of existing services was recognised in 1965 with the appointment of an interdepartmental committee whose function was to examine and to report on the general problems of the care of the aged, and to make recommendations regarding the improvement and extension of services. The committee's report, *Care of the Aged*, was published in 1968. The recommendations of the report on improved services were, in the committee's view:

based on the belief that it is better, and probably much cheaper, to help the aged to live in the community than to provide for them in hospitals or other institutions.[1]

The report reflected the prevailing and increasing emphasis on community as opposed to institutional care.

In addition to this report, in 1986 a working party was established to review the existing health and welfare services for older people, and its report, *The Years Ahead – A Policy for the Elderly*, was published in 1988.

Services for older people may be considered under the two broad headings of community care and residential services.

Community care

The *Care of the Aged* report stressed the importance of providing adequate community support services. These would include social welfare payments, housing, and general health and welfare services.

Social welfare

There have been considerable improvements in the social welfare system for older people over the last few decades. The main schemes are the state pension (contributory) and state pension (non-contributory), payable at the age of sixty-six. The former is paid to persons who have been in insurable employment and have made a sufficient number of contributions, while the latter is subject to a means test. The state pension (transition), introduced in 1970, is also an insurance-based scheme and applies to persons who retire from insurable employment at age sixty-five; at age sixty-six they can revert to the state pension (contributory).

In 2006 some significant administrative changes were introduced that resulted in the migration of recipients between scheme types; for example, recipients of widow/widower's pension, deserted wife's allowance, blind pension or one-parent family payments were transferred to state pension (non-contributory) on reaching sixty-six years of age. While these changes make comparisons with previous years more difficult, they do not take from the underlying upward trend in the number of recipients of state pensions.

Even allowing for changes in the definition of schemes in 2006, there has been a substantial increase in the number of recipients of these pensions over a few decades (Table 6.2). This increase is due to a number of factors. In the 1970s the qualifying age for the old-age pension was gradually reduced, over a five-year period, from seventy to sixty-six years, and the means test for the (non-contributory) pension was eased. Increase in life expectancy has also contributed to the rise in numbers. A notable feature of the pension population is the decline in the number of recipients of the state (non-contributory) pension. This is due to the broadening of the social insurance base in 1988 to include self-employed persons, who previously would have had to resort to the state (non-contributory) pension, as well as to changes in the eligibility conditions that made it easier to qualify for the (contributory) pension.

Table 6.2: *Recipients of state pensions, selected years, 1966–2009*

Pension	1966	1996	2001	2009*
State pension (contributory)	49,556	67,988	94,871	265,102
State pension (non-contributory)	112,621	101,624	89,061	97,798
State pension (transition)	–	69,740	80,326	8,378
Total	162,177	239,352	264,258	371,278

* Note changes in 2006, referred to in text, which make comparisons with previous years more difficult.

Source: Annual *Statistical Information on Social Welfare Services* (Department of Social Protection).

Several other improvements in the social welfare system for older people have been introduced, such as the Living Alone Allowance (1977) and the Age Allowance (for those over eighty years). The *Report of the Commission on Social Welfare* indicated that payments to older people were the highest of all social welfare payments and that they were closest to the minimally adequate income recommended by the commission.[2] However, *The Years Ahead* indicated that:

> the general improvement in the income position of the elderly hides wide differences in income among the elderly themselves. The incomes of the elderly span a spectrum from the very wealthy to the very poor.[3]

In 2009 the maximum weekly personal rate of the state (contributory) pension was €230.30 while the state (non-contributory) pension was €219.00. These rates were not altered in the next two years, and state pensions were the only weekly social welfare payments to be exempt from decreases in Budgets 2010 and 2011. In the context of proposed restructuring of the Irish pension system, encompassing public and occupational pension schemes, the government indicated that it would seek to ensure that the level of the state pension is maintained at 35 per cent of average weekly earnings. It also proposed to raise the retirement age for state pensions gradually to sixty-eight years by 2028.[4]

Housing

Older people have benefited from a general improvement in housing over several decades. One of the features of the older population is that the majority own their dwellings. In the 1970s local authorities normally allocated 10 per cent of new dwellings to older people and people with disabilities. More recently, the role of providing special housing for older people has been largely taken over by a growing number of voluntary housing associations (see Chapter 3). These associations have provided housing schemes, mainly for older people, in urban areas and villages throughout the country.

While there are few older people in the private rented sector, most of those in the former rent-controlled dwellings were older people.[5] Following the abolition of rent control in 1982, their interests, such as security of tenure, have been provided for in legislation. A special rent allowance scheme was introduced to ensure that they would not experience financial hardship because of the abolition of rent control and the subsequent increase in rents (see Chapter 3). The number of recipients of this allowance has declined from 1,348 in 1986 to 192 in 2009.

Despite improvements in housing, however, it is still likely that some of the worst living conditions exist in dwellings occupied by older people.

Health and welfare services

A number of developments and improvements have occurred in the health and welfare services since the *Care of the Aged* report was published. These include the introduction of the choice-of-doctor scheme under the GMS. It was estimated that a high proportion of older people (approximately 70 per cent) were in receipt of a medical card, which gives an entitlement to all basic health services free of charge, following the introduction of the choice-of-doctor scheme in 1972.

In 2001 a major change in the medical card scheme was introduced when all persons aged seventy and over became entitled to a medical card, irrespective of income. In Budget 2009, however, it was announced that the universal entitlement to a medical card for the over-seventies would be ended and a means test reintroduced. As a result of opposition to this move, the government altered, but did not completely reverse, its decision, and an estimated 20,000 persons on relatively high incomes lost automatic entitlement to the medical card (for further details on this issue see relevant section in Chapter 5).

There has been an expansion in domiciliary services for older people in recent decades. The public health nursing service, a key service involving domiciliary visiting, was extended in the 1970s, and this was accompanied by the development of the home help service, meals on wheels and day care services for older people by health boards and voluntary organisations. The main beneficiaries of the home help service are older people living alone. Despite improvements in the community health and welfare services, *The Years Ahead* indicated that less progress had been made in relation to the expansion of dental services, the provision of physiotherapy and chiropody, the development of a social work service for older people and the boarding out of older people. In recommending that the home help service be improved, the report indicated that just over 9,400 of older people were in receipt of this service and that, despite its importance in maintaining older people at home in a cost-effective way, the evidence suggested that the service was in fact contracting.

A more recent development has been the provision of home care packages for older persons. These were introduced in 2006 and were mainly intended for those at risk of admission to long-term care, inappropriate admission to acute hospitals or discharge from acute hospitals to home. The package may include nursing care, home help and/or various therapies such as physiotherapy and occupational therapy. In 2009 a total of 8,959 clients were in receipt of a home care package, as compared with 5,283 in 2006. A review of the scheme by the NESF in 2009 indicated inconsistencies and inequalities in the operation of the scheme. It noted that eligibility for the scheme varied between different HSE areas, as did the amounts of funding that may be provided to successful applicants. It noted that Dublin North Central had a much higher proportion of home care package funding per person aged over sixty-five years than other areas. Average amounts paid out per week under the packages varied from €71 to €400. The report noted that 'this provides at best inconsistencies and at worst inequities in the amount of care which people can access through a home care package'. The report also noted different means tests and different medical assessments for the scheme in different areas.[6] The reason for these different approaches was that national guidelines were not implemented. In response to the criticisms in the NESF report, the HSE established guidelines in 2010 to ensure implementation of the home care package scheme uniformly across the country.

Residential services
When the *Care of the Aged* report was published in 1968 a substantial number of older people were in long-term care in county homes, some of which originated as Poor Law workhouses and catered for all categories of persons with very little assessment of their needs. In effect, they were catch-all institutions catering for a wide variety of older people.

Extended care of older people is now provided in long-stay hospitals and in voluntary and private nursing homes. Since the early 1980s there has been a substantial increase in voluntary and private nursing home beds. The growth in nursing homes has been most apparent in the Dublin area, where about half of all patients in private nursing homes are concentrated.

The Years Ahead expressed concern about the general level of standards in private and voluntary nursing homes, the relationship between health boards and these homes, and the manner in which the homes were subvented. Notwithstanding existing legislative safeguards, it recommended that further measures should be adopted, such as the introduction of a licensing system and the establishment of an independent inspectorate. The Health (Nursing Homes) Act, 1990, was introduced in response to these needs, and it provided for the registration and inspection of homes, the introduction of regulations relating to the standards of care, and the reform of the existing system of subvention to these homes.

A special *Prime Time Investigates* programme was screened on RTÉ in 2005, highlighting various problems in a private nursing home, Leas Cross, in north County Dublin. The programme led to considerable controversy and ultimately raised concerns about standards in all nursing homes.[7] A review of practices and standards at Leas Cross nursing home highlighted, among other things, a conflict of interest arising from the fact that the health boards were responsible for carrying out inspections on the same nursing homes that they were funding through subventions and payment for contract beds. Under a new system, introduced from July 2009, HIQA has assumed responsibility for the independent inspections of all nursing homes, public and private. HIQA also published the *National Quality Standards for Residential Care Settings for Older People in Ireland* in 2008, and these standards now apply to all nursing homes.

Apart from standards, another matter of concern for some time had been the cost of care in nursing homes. The Nursing Home Subvention Scheme was introduced in 1993 under the Health (Nursing Homes) Act, 1990. The scheme facilitated the expansion of long-stay facilities for older persons; between 1994 and 2002 expenditure on the scheme increased four-fold, and there were 6,200 in receipt of the subvention in 2002. A review of the scheme in 2002 highlighted the fact that 'applicants and residents with the same level of need and resources are being treated differently in different health boards', and it stated that 'the absence of consistency and standardisation in the application of the regulations has also led to horizontal and vertical inequity across the country'.[8]

In 2006 the Minister for Health and Children, Mary Harney, TD, announced her intention of introducing a new financial arrangement for residents of nursing homes – the Fair Deal Scheme. Under this scheme, the state would claim a proportion of all disposable income of an older person and up to 15 per cent of the estate following their death. Delay in introducing the scheme was caused by legal difficulties that hindered the drafting of the necessary legislation. The scheme came into operation in October 2009 under the Nursing Home Support Act, 2009. The Fair Deal Scheme, which replaces the Nursing Home Subvention Scheme, is intended to equalise state support for public and private long-term care recipients, to ensure that care is affordable and that no older person has to sell their home during their lifetime to pay for that care.

The National Council on Ageing and Older People, established by government (as the National Council for the Aged) in 1981, was an advisory body to the Minister for Health on all aspects of ageing and the welfare of older people until it was dissolved in 2009 under the Health (Miscellaneous Provisions) Act, 2009. It has produced a number of excellent reports on these issues. In 1997, in a review of the implementation of recommendations in *The Years Ahead*, the council was highly critical of the lack of progress.[9] It noted that no legislative framework had been established for the development of services, that no agency had taken a lead role in ensuring that recommendations were implemented, that there was considerable regional variation in the implementation status of recommendations and that a new blueprint for the future development of policy was required. Ironically, the review pointed out that the only piece of legislation introduced since *The Years Ahead* – i.e. the Health (Nursing Homes) Act of 1990 – had led to a growth in institutional rather than community-based care. By contrast, it noted that the discretionary but essential community services such as the home help service lack a legislative base.

While there have been important developments since the comments of the council in 1997, the core issues identified remain. The introduction of the Fair Deal Scheme ensures that the balance of funding remains with residential care, an area where improvements in standards and inspection levels have been provided for in legislation. By contrast, despite the introduction of home care packages in 2006, some community services remain discretionary, characterised by a lack of uniformity throughout the country in the assessment of means, the assessment of need, the application of schemes and the level of funding provided.

The Years Ahead report contained a review of developments since the *Care of the Aged* report. It concluded that there had been 'substantial improvements' in services for older persons, which had reinforced their independence and ability to live at home. It also noted many positive features about being elderly in Ireland:

> While much remains to be done it cannot be said that as a nation we have failed our elderly citizens. The majority have an adequate income, own their own homes, are active and independent and express considerable satisfaction with their lives. While it is often claimed that families are no longer willing to care for their elderly relatives when they become dependent, the evidence before us does not support this claim.[10]

Twenty-five years on from *The Years Ahead* it is reasonable to claim that, in general, services for older persons have improved further.

Child welfare

This section is concerned with those children who, for whatever reason, are not receiving adequate care and protection in a home environment and are consequently taken into the care of the HSE.

Up to the early 1970s the main statutory means of dealing with children in care was to place them in residential care, i.e. in industrial schools or reformatories. Industrial schools dated from 1858 and were designed to cater for young children, while the reformatories, which originated in 1868, were for older, delinquent children. These institutions were generally run by religious orders.

In 1970 a report on industrial and reformatory schools, usually referred to as the Kennedy report (after the chairman, District Justice Eileen Kennedy), was published. The key recommendation of this report was that:

> The whole aim of the child care system should be geared towards the prevention of family breakdown and the problems consequent on it. The committal or admission of children to residential care should be considered only when there is no satisfactory alternative.[11]

In 1980 the *Final Report of the Task Force on Child Care Services* was published. This report has its origins in 1974, following a government decision to allocate the main responsibility in relation to child care to the Minister for Health. The minister established the task force to make recommendations on the extension and improvement of services for deprived children and to draw up a Child Care Bill. The task force report also recognised that, as far as possible, deprived children should be catered for in a family or community setting rather than residential care.

There have been a number of important developments in relation to child welfare over the past few decades. It could be argued that the impetus for some of these developments lay with the Kennedy report and the task force report.

The philosophy underlying the Kennedy and task force reports has been reflected in policy. Following the Kennedy report, the numbers of children in care fell for several years, and this was accompanied by an increased emphasis on family support services. In 1968–9 there were 4,834 children in care. Of these, three-quarters were in residential care and one-quarter in foster care. Within a decade or so these proportions were reversed. Having fallen below 3,000 in 1989, the number of children in care began to increase thereafter, reaching 5,517 in 2001. By 2008 there were 5,357 children in care, with the majority (88.5 per cent) in foster care.

With the establishment of health boards in 1971, social workers were employed under the Community Care Programme. A particular focus in social work is child care and child-centred family case work, with an emphasis on keeping families together in their own homes as far as possible, rather than resorting to alternative care. Where this is not possible, one of the preferred options is placement with foster parents, with residential care as a last resort.

Many of the industrial and reformatory schools were closed in the early 1970s, partly in response to the development of community services and, in some instances, because the religious orders involved in their management decided, sometimes because of their own declining numbers, to opt out of providing this type of service. The residential centres are now based on group homes rather than the traditional large institutions. The terms 'residential home' and 'special school' have replaced those of industrial and reformatory schools, respectively, since the early 1970s. The funding of these homes is on a budget basis since 1984, as compared with the capitation system of the past. Furthermore, special courses have been provided for child care workers since the early 1970s. These residential centres are now subject to inspection by the Social Services Inspectorate of HIQA (see later section in this chapter).

The Kennedy report had recommended that the Department of Health, rather than the Department of Education, should be responsible for all residential care facilities. This did not happen until 1982. The Kennedy report and the task force report also referred to the fact that administrative responsibility for child care services was divided between three government departments – Health, Justice and Education. Thus, for example, the Department of Health was responsible for personal and social services, the Department of Justice administered the adoption service and juvenile justice system, and the Department of Education was responsible for the industrial and reformatory schools. The Department of Health was recommended to take overall responsibility for all child services. The Department of Health assumed responsibility for developing child care services in 1974. To further emphasise its role, the title of the department was changed to the Department of Health and Children in 1997. In 2011 the department's functions were divided, and child welfare functions became the responsibility of a new department, the Department of Children. It is intended that the Department of Children will be responsible for all child-related functions.

The Office of the Minister for Children and Youth Affairs (OMCYA) was established in 2005 as part of the Department of Health and Children to bring greater coherence to policymaking and to coordinate the work of a number of areas, such as child welfare and protection. The functions of the office were integrated into the Department of Children in 2011.

For over eighty years the main legislation governing the child care system was the Children Act, 1908. The Kennedy report had recommended the introduction of a composite children's act, and, as previously mentioned, the terms of reference of the task force included the preparation of a new Child Care Bill; however,the task force did not prepare this bill. Various pieces of legislation concerned with child welfare have been enacted in the past few decades.

In 1988 a Child Care Bill was introduced in the Dáil and, following many amendments, was eventually enacted three years later. The Child Care Act, 1991, has been described as 'a watershed in child care policy in Ireland'.[12] Its purpose was to update the law in relation to the care of children, particularly children who have been assaulted, ill-treated, neglected or sexually abused, or who are at risk. Among the main provisions of the act were the following:

- the placing of a statutory duty on health boards (now the HSE) to promote the welfare of children (up to age eighteen) who are not receiving adequate care and protection;
- strengthening the power of health boards (now the HSE) to provide child care and family support services.

The provisions of the Child Care Act, 1991, were implemented on a phased basis over several years. Some high-profile cases of child abuse (see later section in this chapter) hastened implementation:

The Act was not fully implemented until December 1996. The delay was not only due to lack of staff but also had its roots in political inertia. It took three child sexual abuse cases, the 'X' case in 1992, the Kilkenny Incest case in 1993 and the Kelly Fitzgerald case in 1994 to raise public awareness and to finally motivate the government to fully implement the Act.[13]

In addition, the Adoption Act, 1988, introduced some limited reforms in the adoption area, and the Status of Children Act, 1987, abolished the legal concept of illegitimacy.

Today, the main legislation covering children and the juvenile justice system is the Children Act, 2001, which replaced the Children Act, 1908, and is based on the principle that detention of children should only be used as a last resort. The act was the result of cooperation between three government departments – Justice, Equality and Law Reform; Health and Children; and Education and Science.

Arising from recommendations in the *Report of the Youth Justice System* (2006), a programme to implement youth justice reforms, including changes to legislation and the setting up of the Irish Youth Justice Service (IYJS), was initiated. The IYJS was established in 2005, and its role includes the development of a unified youth justice policy, the management and development of children detention facilities and the implementation of provisions of the Children Act, 2001. The IYJS is co-located with the OMCYA but continues to report to its parent department, the Department of Justice, Equality and Defence.

The low age of criminal responsibility in Ireland, established under the Children Act, 1908, was frequently highlighted over several decades, and this was accompanied by recommendations to increase it. In 2006, under the Children Act, 2001, the age of criminal responsibility was effectively raised from seven to twelve years. With a few exceptions, no child under the age of twelve years can now be charged with an offence.

There has been considerable improvement in the quality and level of services provided for children since the Kennedy report. There has been a primary emphasis in child care services since the early 1990s on the protection and care of children who are at risk, and there is a particular focus on a preventive approach to child welfare, involving support to families and individual children in order to avoid more serious intervention at a later stage. There is now a strong emphasis on preventive measures and early intervention programmes.

Child abuse

Since the early 1990s there has been concern about the increased incidence of reported child abuse cases, and this has been heightened by a number of high-profile cases, such as the *Kilkenny Incest Investigation*

(1993). Following this case, a number of other instances of sexual or physical abuse of children came to light.

Many of the reported abuses took place in former residential care centres, such as industrial schools, while others occurred in ordinary day schools, in the community or in the home. This led to the drawing up of guidelines for staff in residential centres, and there was a protracted debate on whether reporting of child sex abuse should be mandatory or not. Mandatory reporting has not yet been introduced.

In 1999 the Department of Health and Children published *Children First: National Guidelines for the Protection and Welfare of Children*. The guidelines were intended to support and guide health professionals, teachers, members of the Garda Síochána and people involved in sporting, cultural, community and voluntary organisations who come in regular contact with children.

The three-part documentary series *States of Fear*, which aired on RTÉ in April/May 1999, highlighted the abuse of children in former industrial and reformatory schools.[14] The series generated considerable controversy and public concern, and had a significant impact on subsequent policy. The Taoiseach, Bertie Ahern, TD, made a public apology on 11 May 1999, the date of the transmission of the third part of the series, to those who had suffered abuse in institutions:

> On behalf of the State and all its citizens, the government wishes to make a sincere and long overdue apology to the victims of childhood abuse for our collective failure to intervene, to detect their pain, to come to their rescue ... I want to say to them that they were gravely wronged, and that we must do all we can now to overcome the lasting effects of their ordeal.

A Commission to Inquire into Child Abuse was established by legislation in 2000, and it held its first public sitting in June 2000. The principal functions of the commission were to listen to persons who had suffered abuse in childhood in institutions, to conduct an inquiry into abuse of children in institutions and to find out why it occurred and who was responsible. Certain legal and other issues delayed the work of the commission, whose report was eventually published in 2009. The *Report of the Commission to Inquire into Child Abuse*, usually referred to as the Ryan report (after the chairman of the Commission, Justice Sean Ryan), consists of five volumes.[15]

The Ryan report contains harrowing accounts of the lives of children in the institutions and details incidences of abuse of all kinds – physical, sexual, neglect and emotional. While physical abuse was severe and pervasive, sexual abuse was particularly endemic in boys' institutions.

The report noted that some religious congregations admitted that abuse took place but did not accept responsibility for it. It also found that the Department of Education, responsible for financing the institutions, had a deferential and submissive attitude towards the religious congregations, and that this compromised its statutory duty to carry out inspection and monitoring of institutions.

The Ryan report made twenty recommendations. Among these were the building of a memorial to the victims of abuse, bearing the words of apology issued by the Taoiseach in 1999, and the regular review of national child care policy and provision of services.

Considerable anger and outrage at the findings of the report were expressed by groups representing victims of abuse, by the President of Ireland, by the Catholic hierarchy, by politicians and by the public at large. In a special debate in Dáil Éireann the Taoiseach, Brian Cowen, TD, said the report had 'shone a light into probably the darkest corner of the history of the state and what is has revealed must be a source of the deepest shame to all of us'.[16]

Within two months of publication of the Ryan report, the OMCYA published a 99-point plan for implementing its recommendations. The plan not only accepted the twenty recommendations in the report but also went further and made commitments to putting the *Children First* guidelines on a statutory basis, to fill 270 social work vacancies and to ensure that every child in care was allocated a social worker.

In response to a request from government, most of the eighteen religious congregations agreed to make further financial contributions to be used to support the survivors of abuse in institutions. (In 2002 the religious orders had agreed with government on a financial contribution to a compensation fund for victims of abuse; see under Residential Institutions Redress Board below.)

Apart from the Ryan report on abuse in state-financed educational institutions, other investigations have been carried out by the state in relation to clerical abuse of children in the Catholic Diocese of Ferns, Wexford, and the Dublin Archdiocese. These two reports were concerned with how allegations of sexual abuse by priests were handled by church and state authorities over several decades.[17] They were critical of the failure of church authorities to report all allegations to the Garda Síochána. Only in recent decades did allegations begin to be taken seriously and to be dealt with in an appropriate manner. There appeared to be far more concern with protecting the perpetrators than helping the victims of abuse. The reports highlighted the pre-eminent position of the Catholic Church in Irish society, which seemed to set its members apart from the laws of the state.

Residential Institutions Redress Board

Arising from the work of the Commission to Inquire into Child Abuse and related issues, the Residential Institutions Redress Board was established by the government under the Residential Institutions Redress Act, 2002, to provide a mechanism for financial compensation for victims of abuse. The work of this board was separate from that of the Commission to Inquire into Child Abuse. As part of an agreement with government in 2002, religious orders agreed to contribute €128 million (in the form of cash and property) to the compensation fund, with the state having to make up the balance. It soon became clear that the state's contribution would be far more substantial than the original estimate of total costs of €400 million. The Comptroller and Auditor General estimated that the potential number of claimants could be 8,900 and that the scheme could cost €828 million.[18]

The board received a total of 14,935 applications. By the end of 2010 it had completed the process for 14,386 cases, and 900 of these cases had been withdrawn or refused, or had resulted in no award. The fact that the application did not relate to a residential institution was the main reason for the majority of refusals. The average value of the awards was €62,845, with the largest award being €300,500.[19]

Registration and inspection of residential centres

The Child Care Act, 1991, provided for the registration and inspection of children's residential centres in the voluntary sector. In 1999 the Department of Health and Children established the Social Services Inspectorate as an independent body to inspect the social service functions of health boards. During the first phase of its work, the inspectorate focused on residential child care provided by health boards.

The inspectorate was integrated into HIQA on its establishment in 2005, under the Health Act, 2007, as an independent body to help drive continuous improvement in health and social care services (see Chapter 5). HIQA's role is to set national standards for the provision of health and social care services, except mental health services, in Ireland.

National Children's Strategy

In 2000 a National Children's Strategy, *Our Children – Their Lives*, was launched. The main components of the strategy included the establishment of an independent statutory body – a National Office for Children – and the appointment of an Ombudsman for Children. The National Office for Children was established in 2001 and subsumed into the OMCYA on its establishment in 2005.

Ombudsman for Children

The Ombudsman for Children Act, 2002, provided for the establishment of the Ombudsman for Children's Office. The ombudsman's role is to promote and safeguard the rights and welfare of children and to examine and investigate complaints against public bodies, schools and voluntary hospitals. Since its establishment, the Ombudsman for Children's Office has highlighted issues of concern to child welfare.

The office has made submissions to government on various legislative proposals, has commented on government policies and has carried out reviews of services relevant to the welfare of children. An example is the review of the implementation of the *Children First* guidelines that were published in 1999. The office's report recognised that 'substantial efforts have been made at various times since 1999 to implement *Children First*'. However, it indicated that both the Office of the Minister for Children and the HSE had failed to properly implement the guidelines over the past decade, leaving children at risk of abuse. It identified critical weaknesses in the child-protection system that should have been addressed through proper implementation of the guidelines. The report made findings of 'unsound administration' on the part of the Office of the Minister for Children and noted that it had failed to put in place proper mechanisms to implement the guidelines between 2003 and 2008, which had led to a lack of collaboration between different state agencies. It also made findings of 'unsound administration' on the part of the HSE, which did not make child protection a priority during a period of fundamental reform in the health services.[20] In response to the report, the HSE acknowledged that many of its child care services were not being delivered 'in a standardised or consistent manner'.[21]

The Fine Gael/Labour *Programme for Government* (2011) has proposed to reform the delivery of child protection services by removing child welfare and protection from the HSE and establishing a dedicated Child Welfare and Protection Agency. It has also proposed to put the *Children First* guidelines on a statutory basis.

Proposed amendment to the Constitution

The *Kilkenny Incest Investigation* report recommended that a constitutional referendum be held to protect the interests of the child in the family. The investigation team indicated that:

> We feel that the very high emphasis on the rights of the family in the Constitution may consciously or unconsciously be intrepreted as giving a higher value to the rights of parents than to the rights of children. We believe that the Constitution should contain a specific and overt declaration of the rights of born children.[22]

The report recommended that consideration be given to the amendment of Articles 41 and 42 of the Constitution so as to include a statement of the constitutional rights of children. Subsequently, this recommendation gained widespread acceptance and support from various groups with the aim of ensuring that, where a child's family has failed them, any decisions about care should give priority consideration to the child.

In 2006 the government announced its intention to hold a constitutional referendum, and a process of consultation and discussion with relevant groups was initiated with the aim of achieving consensus on the wording of an appropriate amendment. In 2007 the government published a bill containing its proposals to amend the constitution, but the wording of the proposed amendment was widely criticised. The matter was subsequently referred to a special joint Oireachtas committee, which published its final report with an agreed alternative wording in 2010.[23] However, concern over the wording continued and a decision to hold a referendum was delayed. A further amended wording was agreed by the outgoing government in 2011, several weeks prior to the general election. In the subsequent general election campaign all the established political parties indicated their willingness to hold a referendum on this issue.

The National Children's Alliance

The National Children's Alliance, representing over ninety non-governmental organisations, was established in 1995. It aims to secure the rights and needs of children by campaigning for full implementation in Ireland of the UN Convention on the Rights of the Child (1990). Commencing in 2009, the alliance began publishing an annual 'report card', graded by an external assessment panel, in which it awarded an overall grade based on the government's record on meeting its own policy commitments to children in areas such as health, education and well-being. In 2009 it awarded an overall D because government action had been 'barely acceptable'. Its 2010 report card gave an overall D⁻, based on analysis of twenty-nine key commitments by government, which indicated that the grades were either the same as or worse than 2009. The 2011 report card awarded another overall D⁻. The best grades were awarded for work undertaken in early childhood education and in care and social work provision, while the lowest grades were in the areas of alcohol, financial support for families and implementation of *Children First* guidelines. The 2011 report also outlined actions that the government must take if it is to deliver on its own promises.[24]

People with disabilities

Within the past few decades there has been greater awareness of and concern with the rights of persons with disabilities. Increasingly, the thrust of policy has been on inclusion, i.e. providing the means for persons with disabilities to participate to the greatest extent possible in all aspects of life. This has been accompanied by an increasing emphasis on the rights of such persons and an emphasis on mainstreaming services. The *Health Strategy* (2001) stated:

> The principle which underpins policy is to enable each individual with a disability to achieve his or her full potential and maximum independence, including living within the community as independently as possible.[25]

Definition and terminology

Section 2 of the Disability Act, 2005, defines disability as:

> a substantial restriction in the capacity of the person to carry on a profession, business or occupation in the State or to participate in social or cultural life in the State by reason of an enduring physical, sensory, mental health or intellectual impairment.[26]

This definition covers a wide range of disabilities.

Until the early 1990s the term 'handicap' was widely used to cover both physical and mental disabilities. The report *Needs and Abilities* (1990), by the Review Group on Mental Handicap Services, recommended that the term 'mental handicap' should no longer be used.[27] It suggested 'intellectual disability' as a more appropriate term. It took some time for this change in terminology to gain widespread acceptance and usage, even among statutory agencies. At the 1998 annual general meeting of the National Association for the Mentally Handicapped of Ireland, an umbrella organisation with over 160 affiliated organisations, a motion to alter its name was defeated; the name was changed to Inclusion Ireland in 2006.

Two broad categories of disabilities are now distinguished:

i.   intellectual disability (formerly mental handicap);
ii.   physical and sensory disability (covering a wide variety of disabilities such as visual or hearing impairment and physical disabilities arising from congenital causes, accidents or chronic or long-term illness).

While there are issues common to the two categories, each also has particular concerns. In this chapter only the more salient services are considered for each of the two main categories, together with trends in the provision of services and some specific issues such as legislation.

Numbers of people with disabilities

A NESC report (1980) stressed the need for a register of people with disabilities as a prerequisite to the planning of services, while a 1984 Green Paper indicated that there was no comprehensive source of information on the number of persons with disabilities.[28]

The *Needs and Abilities* report highlighted the need for good-quality information on persons with intellectual disabilities. This provided the impetus for the establishment of an intellectual disability database in 1995. The need for reliable information on the health service needs of persons with physical and/or sensory disability was also referred to in policy documents.[29] Arising from this, a committee was established in 1998 to prepare detailed proposals for the development of a national database, which commenced in 2001.

The publication *A Strategy for Equality: Report of the Commission on the Status of People with Disabilities* (1996) indicated that accurate figures were not available, but it estimated the total number of people with disabilities to be 360,000. The census of population of 2002 included a question on disabilities for the first time. The results indicated that there were 323,707 persons with disabilities (physical, mental or emotional conditions); the census of 2006 indicated that 393,800 persons, or 9.3 per cent of the population, had a disability. The extent to which these people require services could vary considerably.

It is generally recognised that, despite the progress made in recent decades, there are substantial unmet needs among the population with disabilities, i.e. a large proportion will require new or enhanced services.

Services and service providers

A range of services exists for people with disabilities. These are provided either directly by statutory agencies or in partnership with voluntary service providers. A number of government departments provide services directly, set standards, have oversight functions or provide funding for services. These include the Department of Health and the Department of Social Protection. In addition, there are a number of statutory agencies with different functions; these agencies include the HSE, the National Disability Authority and the National Council for Special Education (NCSE).

In relation to intellectual disability, voluntary organisations at national and local level have played a pioneering role in providing services since the nineteenth century and have been to the forefront in both service delivery and service development. Religious orders providing services include the Brothers of Charity, the Daughters of Charity and the St John of God Brothers. Other organisations include St Michael's House and Stewarts Hospital in Dublin and Western Care Association in Mayo.

An estimated 150 organisations, whether at national or local level, provide services for persons with physical or sensory disabilities.

Despite advances in medical care and community support services, it is recognised that a significant number of persons with disabilities, especially the intellectually disabled, will require long-term care. During the 1970s the main emphasis in the intellectual disability services was on the development of residential facilities. These have been provided largely by voluntary organisations, especially religious orders, and much of the capital for this development came from the Department of Health and the health boards.[30] Since the 1980s, however, the emphasis has been on providing a comprehensive network of services with a continuum of care. This includes sheltered housing, hostel accommodation, short-term residential care, respite care and a range of community support services.

Services for the physical and sensory disabled

The main thrust of the report of the Review Group on Health and Personal Social Services for People with Physical and Sensory Disabilities, *Towards an Independent Future* (1996), was the development of services to enable people with a physical or sensory disability to live as independently as possible in the community. It recommended that priority be given to the provision of more day care, respite care, nursing and therapy services, personal assistants and residential accommodation to achieve this goal.[31]

Services for the intellectually disabled

The main initiative for the provision of services for the intellectually disabled has come from voluntary organisations, including religious orders and parents' and friends' associations. These provide a range of services, such as residential care, training and day care centres, and specialist services.

The current emphasis in policy on intellectual disability is the development of community-based alternatives to institutional care. Persons with intellectual disabilities are catered for in different settings – i.e. psychiatric hospitals (where a diminishing number are catered for), special residential centres, hostels and supervised lodgings, and there is an increasing emphasis on day care provision.

Since the first intellectual disability database report in 1996, 'there has been a significant growth in the level of provision of full-time residential services, residential support services, and day services'.[32]

While the number of places in residential care and day centres has grown considerably over the past two decades or so, the demand for such places continues. This is due to a number of factors, such as developments in treatment, personal care plans and longer life expectancy. Increased longevity is an area of special concern for ageing parents of adult children with intellectual disability.

In 2009 there were 26,066 persons registered with the National Intellectual Disability Database, and 98 per cent were in receipt of services, the highest number since the database was established in 1995.[33] About 84 per cent of those in receipt of services availed of one or more multidisciplinary supports. The services most commonly availed of by adults were social work, medical services and psychiatry, while for children the most common were speech and language therapy, social work and occupational therapy. Almost two-thirds of those registered lived at home with parents, siblings, relatives or foster parents. The 2009 report of the database also recorded a continuing decline in the numbers of people with intellectual disability accommodated in psychiatric hospitals.

In 2009 there were 29,749 persons under sixty-six years of age registered with the National Physical and Sensory Disability Database Committee, and 83.7 per cent were in receipt of therapeutic intervention and rehabilitation services.[34] The most commonly availed of services included at least one technical aid or appliance, day services and activities, personal assistance and support services, and planned respite services, while a relatively small proportion availed of residential services.

In the context of the growth in and continuing need for residential centres, the issue of independent standards for, and inspections of, these centres is important, just as in the case of those for older persons. In 2009 HIQA published *National Quality Standards for Residential Services for People with Disabilities*. However, due to the state of public finances, the government decided not to move to full implementation of the standards, including regulation and inspection. Instead, it hoped to commence progressive implementation on a non-statutory basis.

Commission on the Status of People with Disabilities

In 1993 a Commission on the Status of People with Disabilities was established 'to advise the government on practical measures to ensure that people with a disability can exercise their rights to participate, to the fullest extent of their potential, in economic, social and cultural life'. Throughout the commission's report *A Strategy for Equality* is a strong emphasis on the rights of people with disabilities, and it noted that:

People with disabilities are the neglected citizens of Ireland. On the eve of the 21st century, many of them suffer intolerable conditions because of outdated social and economic policies and unthinking public attitudes ... Public attitudes towards disability are still based on charity rather than on rights, and the odds are stacked against people with disabilities at every turn. Whether their status is looked at in terms of economics, information, education, mobility, or housing they are seen to be treated as second-class citizens.[35]

The commission estimated that there were 360,000 people with a disability and contended that the problems encountered by them did not centre on physical pain or discomfort. Instead, frustration arose from the sense that people with disabilities were being put in a position of having to deal with a myriad of social barriers in addition to their disabling conditions. The commission proposed a range of legislative and other changes to improve and promote the rights of people with disabilities. In particular, it recommended an amendment to the Constitution to guarantee the right of equality and prohibit discrimination. The commission, while acknowledging that the report was ambitious, made over 400 recommendations, which when implemented 'should change the world for many people with disabilities, including their families and carers'. The commission also recommended the introduction of a Disability Act.

Disability legislation
The 1984 Green Paper noted that while other countries had legislation to safeguard the rights of disabled persons it would need to be demonstrated clearly here that such measures would contribute in a practical way to an improvement in their conditions. It further stated:

The most important thing which any disadvantaged minority needs is goodwill and understanding. The government are convinced that the promotion of the rights of disabled people can be best achieved by general agreement rather than by measures of compulsion.[36]

This conclusion was rejected by some organisations. For example, the Union of Voluntary Organisations for the Handicapped (later renamed Disability Federation of Ireland), in its response to the Green Paper, argued that a basic framework of rights should be set out in a Rights of Persons with Disabilities Act.[37] Subsequently, the case for legislation gathered momentum. As already noted, the Commission on the Status of People with Disabilities recommended the introduction of a Disability Act, which would set out the rights of people with disabilities together with a means of redress for those whose rights are denied.

Disability is one of the nine grounds under which discrimination is prohibited under the Employment Equality Act, 1998, and the Equal Status Act, 2000 (see Chapter 9).

In 2002 a Disabilities Bill, designed to provide a framework for the assessment of need and provision of services for people with disabilities, was withdrawn by government in the face of mounting criticism of various provisions of the bill by voluntary organisations and opposition political parties. For example, the bill envisaged a timescale ranging from five to thirteen years in seeking to make transport, buildings and services accessible, a timescale that was considered unacceptable. Above all, the proposed legislation did not guarantee rights and also prohibited persons with disabilities from taking civil actions against the state. Even the statutorily established National Disability Authority had called for changes to the bill. Subsequent to the withdrawal of the bill, a consultative process was initiated in order to arrive at a consensus on the provisions of legislation. The culmination of this process was the National Disability Strategy (see below).

The Disability Act, 2005, was the outcome of a long period of campaigning, mainly by voluntary groups. However, some of these organisations were not completely satisfied with the outcome. While many provisions in the act were welcomed, the fact that it was not rights based was considered a fundamental flaw. The government had argued that the country could not afford rights-based legislation. On the issue of rights, the act provides for an individual right to an independent assessment of need and to a related service statement. It does not guarantee the provision of services.

National Disability Strategy

In 2004 the government launched the National Disability Strategy to advance the disability agenda and promote the inclusion of people with disabilities in the mainstream of Irish society. The principal elements of the strategy are:

- The Disability Act, 2005;
- The Education for Persons with Special Education Needs Act, 2004;
- A personal advocacy service for people with disabilities, as provided for in the Citizens Information Act, 2007;
- Six statutory sectoral plans on disability for six key government departments;
- A multi-annual investment programme in priority disability services, primarily HSE-funded care services, 2004–09.

The Disability Act

The Disability Act, 2005, the background to which has been outlined, was designed as a positive action measure to support the provision of disability-specific services and to improve access to mainstream services for people with disabilities. In addition to providing an individual right to an independent assessment of need and to a related service statement, the act also provides a statutory basis for accessible buildings and services, six sectoral plans and positive action for employment in the public service. The nature of this legislation is unusual in that it seeks to make provision for services that come within the ambit of a number of government departments and agencies.

The Education for Persons with Special Education Needs Act

The 1980 NESC report recommended that, as far as possible, children with disabilities should be educated with other children.[38] The *Report of the Primary Education Review Body* (1990) had commented that there were limits to the degree of integration possible and that, in many instances, partial integration might be the only feasible option.[39] There are special classes attached to ordinary schools, as well as a number of special schools especially for children with intellectual disability. The current policy is the integration of special needs education into mainstream education, where this is possible, while retaining the option of special provision where necessary.

Section 9 of the Education Act, 1998, provides that recognised schools shall provide an education to students that is appropriate to their abilities and needs, and that they should use available resources to ensure that the educational needs of all students, including those with a disability or other special educational needs, are identified and provided for.

The provisions of the Education for Persons with Special Education Needs Act, 2004, are designed to ensure that, to the greatest extent practicable, people with disabilities 'shall have the same right to avail of, and benefit from, appropriate education, as do their peers who do not have disabilities'.[40] It makes provision for children up to eighteen years of age, and a child is entitled to an assessment to determine if a special educational need exists. The act also provided for the establishment of the NCSE, an independent body that would assume responsibility for special education in place of the Department of Education and Science. The NCSE's functions include providing a range of services at local and national level in order to meet the educational needs of children with disabilities and planning for the integration of children with special needs in a mainstream setting. As part of its local service provision it has responsibility to improve the coordination between the education and health sectors in supporting children with special needs. A main function of the NCSE is the sanctioning of teaching and special needs assistant resources to support individual children with special educational needs.

This legislation was a response, in part, to various challenges concerned with the legal right of children with a disability to education. In one highly publicised case in 2000 the rights of a young adult, Jamie Sinnott (then aged twenty-three), to an education were upheld by the High Court. However, the government appealed the decision in 2001 to the Supreme Court, which ruled that the state was only obliged to provide education up to age eighteen.

Advocacy service

Under the Citizens Information Act, 2007, the organisation Comhairle was replaced by the Citizens Information Board (CIB), and its functions were amended and extended to include the function of the provision of an advocacy service for certain persons with disabilities. One of the ways in which the CIB supports advocacy services to the general public is through the network of Citizens Information Services, where information providers advocate at different levels in relation to difficulties with access to social welfare, housing, health and employment. This includes supports such as negotiating complex information to help people through the appeals process.

Following the success of over forty pilot projects, the CIB established a national advocacy service in 2011 to provide independent, representative advocacy services for people with disabilities.

Sectoral plans

When the National Disability Strategy was launched in 2004, outline sectoral plans were published by six government departments – Health and Children; Social and Family Affairs; Transport; Environment, Heritage and Local Government; Marine and Natural Resources; and Enterprise, Trade and Employment. These plans were developed in 2006, and in each plan the government departments have indicated their role in the progression of the national strategy. For example, the sectoral plan of the Department of Health and Children sets out, in detail, arrangements for the phased implementation of Part 2 of the Disability Act, 2005, which provides, inter alia, for an independent assessment of health needs.

Multi-annual investment

The strategy also involved a multi-annual investment programme for a number of priority disability-specific services. In Budget 2005, provision was made for a €900 million disability package to provide more residential, day and respite places over a five-year period.

Some implementation issues

In 2007 implementation of the first phase of Part 2 of the Disability Act, 2005, concerning assessment of persons, commenced for children under five years of age, and was scheduled to commence for children aged from five to eighteen years in tandem with the implementation of the Education for Persons with Special Educational Needs Act, 2004. In 2009, due to the state of the public finances, the government decided to defer further implementation of Part 2 of the Disability Act and the Education for Persons with Special Education Needs Act.[41]

National Disability Authority

The *Strategy for Equality* report recommended the establishment of a National Disability Authority to 'monitor the impact of public policy and services on people with a disability'.[42] The National Disability Authority was established in 2000 as a statutory body by the National Disability Authority Act, 1999. It subsumed some of the functions of the former National Rehabilitation Board and came under the aegis of the Department of Justice, Equality and Law Reform.[43] The authority's aim is to ensure that the rights and entitlements of people with disabilities are protected.

Within its broad remit, the authority acts as a central national body to assist in the coordination and development of disability policy, to undertake research and to develop statistical information for the planning, delivery and monitoring of disability programmes and services.

One of the functions of the authority is to monitor compliance with Part 5 of the Disability Act, 2005, which sets out the obligations of public service bodies with regard to the employment of people with disabilities. Unless there are good reasons to the contrary for doing so, these bodies must ensure that at least 3 per cent of their employees are people with disabilities. In its third statutory report for 2008 on this issue, the authority noted that 55 per cent of public sector bodies had achieved or exceeded the statutory minimum 3 per cent target for employing staff with a disability in 2008.[44] It also noted that for the first time since the target became a statutory requirement in December 2005 all fifteen government departments had achieved or exceeded the target, with an average of 3.9 per cent, and that 3.5 per cent of staff of local authorities were people with disabilities.

Previous to this, in 1977, the government had introduced a quota scheme for the public service with a staff target of 3 per cent for disabled persons to be reached at the end of 1982. Two decades later it was acknowledged that the target had been reached in the civil service but that 'progress towards meeting the target is much slower in the broader public service'.[45] *A Strategy for Equality* recommended that the 3 per cent quota be fully attained within three years (i.e. by 1999), but the subsequent lack of commitment and progress was exemplified by the fact that there was not an annual publication of compliance with the quota.[46] Unlike the current scheme, there was no statutory basis for the 1977 scheme.

Role of voluntary organisations

While the state's involvement in the provision of services is considerable, and has been growing in recent decades, voluntary organisations have made, and continue to make, substantial contributions in the area of disability services. It is generally recognised that voluntary organisations have played a prominent role in the development of these services, pioneering services in many instances. Many of these organisations have emerged because of concern among parents of children with disabilities about the lack of adequate services.

Voluntary organisations operate at local, regional or national level, and some are large providers of services, including St Michael's House and the religious order the Daughters of Charity, both of which provide specialised day and residential care and a range of support services for people with intellectual disabilities and their families. Particular forms of disability tend to have their own organisation, such as Down Syndrome Ireland, Headway, Enable Ireland, the Irish Society for Autism, the Multiple Sclerosis Society of Ireland and the National Council for the Blind of Ireland.

At a level above the individual organisations are some umbrella or representative organisations. Inclusion Ireland, the National Association for People with an Intellectual Disability, represents approximately 160 affiliated organisations, mainly for people with intellectual disability. It aims to represent and champion the interests of all people with an intellectual disability and their families and to ensure that their voices are heard. The Disability Federation of Ireland has over 120 member organisations, mainly in the physical/sensory disability areas, and it acts as an advocate for the voluntary disability sector and represents the disability area in social partnership. The National Federation of Voluntary Bodies Providing Services to People with Intellectual Disability is also a national umbrella organisation for the main service providers.

These representative organisations are centrally involved in campaigning for improvements in the disability area. Other organisations also have a campaigning role.

A special value-for-money review conducted by the Comptroller and Auditor General of the provision of disability services by non-profit organisations found that in 2004 the state provided €877 million to such organisations, with the amount of grant varying according to the size of the organisation. In general, the report indicated a lack of proper audit of monies spent or services provided, or measurement of outcomes achieved. It noted that the state's relationships with non-profit organisations regarding the delivery of services 'result from a historical pattern of provision and are largely negotiated rather than the result of contested procurement'.[47] Many of the service-level agreements, where they existed, tended to be high-level frameworks, and some had not been signed for a considerable period after the funding had been provided and the service provision had commenced. It recommended greater evaluation, monitoring and formality of arrangements based on the nature and the scale of services.

The Travelling community

A report on Travelling people by the ERSI in 1986 commented:

> The central conclusion of this study is an inescapable one: the circumstances of the Irish travelling people are intolerable. No humane and decent society, once made aware of such circumstances, could permit them to persist.[48]

In the quarter century since that report was published much has changed, yet much has remained unchanged. Over the past half century the number of Traveller families has increased and there have been some fundamental changes to their general lifestyle.

The census of 2006 indicated that there were 22,435 Travellers, accounting for 0.5 per cent of the total population. An annual count of Traveller families has been undertaken by local authorities for some time. In 1960 there were 1,198 Traveller families, and by 2008 this had increased to 8,398 families. Up to the 1950s Travellers were essentially rural based, but since then there has been a gradual shift to urban areas as the basis of their activities in rural areas, mainly tinsmithing and horse trading, was undermined. There was also a gradual move from temporary, transit roadside accommodation in horse-drawn and other types of caravans to permanent housing. This in turn had implications for the provision of education.

There have been four main official reports on Travellers in the past fifty years, and they record the evolving nature of issues over that time: *Report of the Commission on Itinerancy* (1963), *Report of the Travelling People Review Body* (1983), *Report of the Task Force on the Travelling Community* (1995), *Report of the High Level Group on Traveller Issues* (2006).

These reports dealt with a range of issues affecting Travellers, e.g. health, housing, education and economic aspects of their way of life. Providing support services for this minority group, which is frequently the subject of popular criticism, prejudice and discrimination, has proved challenging at times. Some of the issues highlighted in these reports and subsequent developments are considered in this section. The reports will be referred simply as those of the commission, the review body, the task force and the high-level group in the context of issues and developments.

Definition and terminology

The commission stated that the existence of Travellers in Ireland could be ascribed to many causes, e.g. dispossession in various plantations, descendants of journeying craftsman, eviction and famine. Some could be descendants of early poets, bards and craftsman such as smiths and tanners. Others are likely to have originated in the period from the sixteenth to the nineteenth century when large numbers of peasants were unable to either meet their own subsistence needs or pay the rents demanded by landlords, and were subsequently forced from the land. In addition, there could be other reasons why people adopted a nomadic lifestyle, e.g. as a result of personal social deviancy, such as alcoholism.[49]

The commission defined an itinerant as:

> A person who had no fixed place of abode and habitually wandered from place to place but excluding travelling show people and travelling entertainers.[50]

The review body pointed out that such a definition was inadequate because so many Travellers had a permanent place to live. It used the term 'Traveller' to designate membership of an identifiable group, pointing out that abandonment of the nomadic way of life did not automatically mean renunciation of the Traveller ethic or integration with the settled community.[51] The task force took the view that Travellers were a group with a distinct culture and identity.[52] Since the early 1960s the terminology has changed in official reports from 'itinerant' to 'Traveller'. The terms 'Traveller' or 'Travelling community' have long been accepted among Travellers themselves.

The Equal Status Act, 2000, defined Travellers for the purpose of that act as:

> The community of people who are commonly called Travellers and who are identified (both by themselves and others) as people with a shared history, culture and traditions including historically a nomadic way of life on the island of Ireland.[53]

Travellers are recognised as having distinct grounds for protection under the equality legislation. For some time the main Traveller representative organisations, such as the Irish Traveller Movement, have claimed that Travellers should be recognised as a separate ethnic group. This claim has been supported by other organisations such as the Equality Authority and the Irish Human Rights Commission.[54] In Northern Ireland and Great Britain, Travellers are officially recognised as a minority ethnic group.

Health status

Both the commission and the review body indicated that Travellers have a much lower life expectancy than the population in general and that the proportion of infant and child deaths to all Traveller deaths was very high. Some of this was accounted for by the type of accommodation used by Travellers and the health hazards associated with living on the roadside.

A study of the health status of Travellers carried out by the Health Research Board and published in 1987 indicated some marked differences between them and the population in general. These included the following:

- Life expectancy for male and female Travellers was sixty-two and sixty-five years, respectively, compared with seventy-two and seventy-seven years for males and females, respectively, in the total population.
- Only 2 per cent of Travellers were aged sixty-five or over as compared with 10.7 per cent of the total population.
- The birth rate among Travellers was over double the national rate, i.e. 34.9 as compared with 16.6 per thousand.

The study concluded that:

> The picture which emerges of the travelling people in 1987 from this report is of a group who marry at a very young age and have many children. From before birth to old age they have high mortality rates, particularly from accidents, metabolic and congenital problems, but also from the other major

causes of death. Female travellers have especially high mortality compared to settled women. Those members of the travelling community who do not live in houses, approximately 50 per cent, have even higher mortality ratios than housed travellers, especially females and particularly from accidents.[55]

The review body recommended that health authorities should provide special care and advice for Travellers in relation to the care of mothers and children and the availability of immunisation and family planning services, and that they should educate them on the health dangers associated with caravans as permanent accommodation for a large family.[56]

A number of specific services were subsequently introduced, such as Traveller health units and primary health care projects. The establishment of a Traveller Health Advisory Committee in 1998 led to the adoption of a National Traveller Health Strategy (2002). The strategy acknowledged that in the past the health service responded in a fragmented and often inappropriate manner to the special needs of Travellers, that this was compounded by a lack of awareness among Travellers of the value of preventative services and that discrimination was also a factor in the lack of an effective response to Traveller health needs.[57] One of the key targets set in the revised *National Anti-Poverty Strategy* (see Chapter 8) was to reduce the gap in life expectancy between the Traveller community and the general population by at least 10 per cent by 2007.[58] The strategy recognised that implementation of its recommended actions was crucial in meeting that target.

An *All-Ireland Traveller Health Study* was initiated in 2008, arising from a recommendation in the National Traveller Health Strategy that a needs assessment and health status study be carried out. The results were published in 2010.[59] Among the key findings were:

- Life expectancy for Traveller men was 61.7 years, the same as life expectancy for Irish men in the 1940s. The life expectancy for Traveller men was the same as in 1987, but the gap between them and men in the general population had increased by 5 years, and they now lived on average 15 years less.
- Life expectancy for Traveller women had increased to 70.0 years, an increase of 5 years since 1987. However, Traveller women now lived on average 11.5 years less than women in the general population.
- Deaths from respiratory diseases, cardiovascular diseases and suicides were more markedly increased in Travellers as compared with the general population.

Despite considerable investment in the area of Traveller health, the study indicated that life expectancy for Travellers has not shown the improvement hoped for, especially in Traveller men. Among the positive results from the study were evidence of good access to health services and improvements in women's health. In particular, the uptake of cervical screening among women is higher than that in the general population, and the uptake of breast screening is similar to that in the general population. It is intended that this study will provide a framework for policy development and practice in relation to Traveller health.

Education and training

The commission stated tersely that 'almost all itinerants are completely illiterate'.[60] In 1960 only 160 Traveller children out of a total of 1,640 between the ages of six and fourteen years were attending school. The commission indicated that illiteracy accentuated the Travellers' isolation from the settled population and, in itself, made all the more difficult any attempt to change over to the settled way of life. By 1980 much progress had been made, with about 3,500 Traveller children attending school (about half the total) in special classes or special schools that had been established. The review body noted, however, that progress to second-level education was rare and that there was little improvement in the educational standards of adults, of whom about 90 per cent were illiterate.[61]

By the mid 1990s much progress had been made, with about 4,200 children attending school in special classes or special schools. However, the task force noted that only a small minority had transferred successfully to second level and that very few of these had completed a full second-level education. Almost half the recommendations of the task force were concerned with education. It noted that, despite the significant improvement, lack of regular attendance was a problem within the Traveller community.

Full participation at first level has been achieved and participation at second level has improved. Current policy is to end segregated education at primary and post-primary levels to ensure that Travellers are integrated into mainstream schools. By the end of 2008 work had commenced to end segregated provision in the one remaining Traveller primary school and in the one remaining special school for Travellers.[62]

A report in 2010 on the progression of Travellers through the education system found that, despite a high rate of enrolment in primary school and a high transfer rate to second-level schools, more than 80 per cent of Travellers do not complete their second-level education.[63] The report, commissioned by the National Association of Traveller Centres, indicated that Travellers face a cultural clash with their settled counterparts between the ages of fifteen and nineteen years. While the settled community begins to prioritise career at this point, the Traveller community prioritises marriage, with the result that many leave school.

There are thirty-three senior Traveller training centres throughout the country under the aegis of local VECs that cater for Travellers aged eighteen and upwards who left school with little or no educational qualifications. These provide about 1,000 places, but a value-for-money report by the Department of Education found that the progression rate was relatively low, at 37 per cent. The McCarthy report (2009) recommended the phasing out of these centres within two to three years, with participants being integrated into mainstream adult and education programmes.[64]

Settlement and accommodation

One of the contentious issues concerning Travellers has been the nature of their accommodation. The commission recommended that:

> The immediate objective should be to provide dwellings as soon as possible for all families who desire to settle.[65]

The commission also noted that an overwhelming majority was in favour of settling. The review body noted that no developments since 1963 had lessened the correctness of the commission's assessment. The review body also noted that, while progress had been made, there had also been failures and that 'the greatest failure has resulted from the relative inaction of some local authorities who are slow in implementing government policy'.[66] By 2001 there were almost as many Traveller families on the roadside as forty years earlier. However, this was against a background of a substantial increase in the number of Traveller families over this period.

The Housing (Traveller Accommodation) Act, 1998, provided a legislative framework within which the accommodation needs of Travellers would be met in a reasonable period of time. It also provided for the establishment of the National Traveller Accommodation Consultative Committee (NTACC) on a statutory basis to advise the minister on general matters concerning the accommodation of Travellers and to oversee the implementation of Traveller accommodation programmes.

The act requires that local authorities prepare five-year Traveller accommodation programmes and establish local Traveller accommodation consultative committees. In its first annual report, for 1999, the NTACC expressed disappointment with the slow progress in the provision of new accommodation. In subsequent annual reports it recorded progress in the reduction of families living on the roadside.

A review of the operation of the 1998 act by the NTACC in 2004 noted that the provision of accommodation under the Traveller accommodation programmes varied between local authorities. It recommended that local authorities should be required to set realistic and achievable annual targets for the number of units of accommodation to be provided in each year of the programme.

The NTACC'S 2008 annual report indicated that there were 8,398 Traveller families in different forms of accommodation.[67] These included:

- 3,330 families in standard houses;
- 1,516 families in private rented accommodation;
- 691 families in group housing;
- 574 families in permanent halting-site bays;
- 345 families sharing housing with other families;
- 524 families on unauthorised sites.

The report noted that the number of families living on unauthorised sites and the number of families sharing housing had continued to decline, and that the type of accommodation showing the greatest rate of increase is private rented accommodation. The number of families accommodated by local authorities in 2008 was 5,500, or 65 per cent of the total number of families.

Relationships with settled community

Relationships between Travellers and the settled population have been characterised by prejudice and discrimination on the one hand, and isolation on the other. The review body noted that:

> The general population of the country has very little detailed knowledge of travellers and the problems they face … fear of travellers is in large measure groundless, where there is irrefutable evidence that those who settle in houses usually create no special problems.[68]

The review body even considered the possibility of having special legislation enacted to outlaw discrimination against Travellers but concluded, for various reasons, that this was not feasible.[69] What was not considered feasible in the early 1980s, however, was considered necessary over a decade later. As noted, discrimination against members of the

Travelling community is prohibited under the Employment Equality Act, 1998, and the Equal Status Act, 2000.

On the relationship between Travellers and the rest of the population, a number of non-Traveller members stated in an addendum to the task force report:

> Part of the conflict is also due to the failure of Travellers and Traveller organisations to recognise that today's society finds it difficult to accept a lower standard of conduct from a section of the community who consciously pursue a way of life which sets its members apart from ordinary citizens, appear to expect that their way of life takes precedence over that of settled persons, and which carries no responsibility towards the area in which they happen to reside.[70]

Traveller participation in policy

In the 1960s a number of voluntary organisations, usually settlement committees, were established. For example, in 1969 the first Council of Itinerant Settlement was set up, and in 1973 this became the National Council for Travelling People. Some of these organisations also started to focus on educational projects. There has been a significant change in the past few decades in that Travellers have organised themselves and become politically active, and they now lobby for their rights.[71] Travellers' participation on a variety of committees concerned with Traveller issues is now an established principle.

There are a large number of Traveller organisations operating at a local level. In addition, there are a few main representative organisations. The Irish Traveller Movement was established as a national representative organisation and now has a membership of over ninety Traveller organisations throughout the country. The National Traveller Women's Forum is a national network of Traveller women and Traveller women's organisations. Pavee Point is a resource centre that aims to improve the quality of life and living circumstances of Travellers through working for social justice.

Membership of the Task Force on the Travelling Community included Traveller representatives. The task force's report recommended Traveller participation in the new structures necessary to implement its recommendations:

- Traveller Accommodation Agency;
- Traveller Education Service;
- Traveller Health Advisory Committee.

Two of these bodies were established. Membership of the NTACC, established on a statutory basis in 1999, includes Traveller representatives. Similarly, there has been Traveller representation on the Traveller Health Advisory Committee, established in 1998, which was involved in the preparation of the National Traveller Health Strategy.

While structures were established, with Traveller participation, in relation to accommodation and health, no similar structure was established in education. The Department of Education and Science decided not to establish a Traveller Education Service because it considered that services for Travellers were already being delivered in an integrated manner by sections within the department.[72] While the department did produce *Report and Recommendations for a Traveller Education Strategy* (2006), an education strategy has not been published.

High-Level Group on Traveller Issues

The first progress report on the task force report, published in 2000 by a monitoring committee that also included representatives of Traveller organisations, was an indictment of the lack of progress:

> About one-quarter of all Traveller families continue to live their day to day lives in very poor conditions. Five years after the publication of the Task Force Report, there is a lack of real improvement on the ground ... It raises very serious questions both at home and abroad of our society and why we have been unable to make significant improvements in the quality of life for the Traveller community.[73]

The second and final progress report on the task force report, published in 2005, recorded advances made in many areas since the first progress report. However, the gap between the standard of living of Travelling and settled communities remained apparent:

> The bottom line is that despite the allocation of considerable financial and staff resources and some progress being achieved, Travellers continue to have lower life expectancy, lower education qualifications and, in many cases, unacceptable accommodation.[74]

A high-level group was established in 2003, under the aegis of the Cabinet Committee on Social Inclusion, with a remit to ensure that all agencies, national and local, involved in delivering services would 'focus on improving the integrated practical delivery of such services'. The group also reviewed local pilot projects operated in South Dublin County Council and Clare County Council. The objective of these projects was to bring all of the agencies working with Travellers together in partnership to tackle local issues at a local level.

The group's report, published in 2006, considered that in order to achieve successful outcomes for Travellers there was a need for 'institutionalised inter-agency coordination at national and local level'. The positive experience of the two pilot projects would serve as a useful template for replication on a wider scale. The report identified three priorities for the effective implementation of policy to support the fullest possible participation of Travellers in Irish society:

* coherent inter-agency cooperation;
* meaningful consultation with Travellers and their representatives;
* incorporation of law-enforcement measures in the inter-agency approach.[75]

The social partnership agreement *Towards 2016* (2006) contained a commitment to develop an integrated approach to providing services and supports to Travellers, in line with the recommendations of the high-level group's report.[76] In 2007 the National Traveller Monitoring and Advisory Committee was established, comprising representatives of government departments and other public bodies, members of Traveller organisations and a number of individual Traveller representatives, as well as other social partners. The establishment of the committee was in line with a commitment in *Towards 2016* to pursue improved outcomes for the Traveller community, including access to employment and development of communications between Traveller and settled communities. It was intended that the committee would serve, inter alia, as a forum for consultation on current issues of national importance affecting the Travelling community.

Notes

1. Department of Health, *Care of the Aged* (Stationery Office, Dublin, 1968), p. 13.
2. Commission on Social Welfare, *Report of the Commission on Social Welfare* (Stationery Office, Dublin, 1986), p. 191.
3. Working Party on Services for the Elderly, *The Years Ahead – A Policy for the Elderly* (Stationery Office, Dublin, 1988), p. 19.
4. Department of Social and Family Affairs, *National Pensions Framework* (Stationery Office, Dublin, 2010), pp. 14–16.
5. See, for example, Rent Tribunal, *Annual Report and Accounts, 1985* (Stationery Office, Dublin, 1985), p. 8.
6. National Economic and Social Forum, *Report No. 38, Implementation of the Home Care Package Scheme* (Stationery Office, Dublin, 2009).

7. See T. McNamara et al., 'Review of developments, structure and management in the public sector 2006', *Administration*, Vol. 54, No. 4 (2007), pp. 24–5.

8. E. O'Shea, *Review of the Nursing Home Subvention Scheme* (Stationery Office, Dublin, 2002), p. 119.

9. National Council on Ageing and Older People, *The Years Ahead Report: A Review of the Implementation of its Recommendations* (National Council on Ageing and Older People, Dublin, 1997), pp. 3–32.

10. Working Party on Services for the Elderly, op. cit., p. 26.

11. Department of Health, *Report on the Industrial and Reformatory Schools System* (Stationery Office, Dublin, 1970), p. 6.

12. V. Richardson, 'Children and social policy', in S. Quin et al., *Contemporary Irish Social Policy* (University College Dublin Press, Dublin, 1999), p. 182.

13. Ibid., p. 183.

14. See also M. Raftery and E. O'Sullivan, *Suffer Little Children, The Inside Story of Ireland's Industrial Schools* (New Island Books, Dublin, 1999). This book elaborates on many areas dealt with by the *States of Fear* series.

15. Commission to Inquire into Child Abuse, *Report of the Commission to Inquire into Child Abuse* (Stationery Office, Dublin, 2009).

16. Dáil Éireann, 'Ryan report on the Commission to Inquire into Child Abuse: motion', 11 June 2009, *Dáil Debates*, Vol. 684, No. 3.

17. Government of Ireland, *The Ferns Report* (Stationery Office, Dublin, 2005); Commission of Investigation, *Report into the Catholic Archdiocese of Dublin* (Stationery Office, Dublin, 2009).

18. Comptroller and Auditor General, *2003 Annual Report of the Comptroller and Auditor General* (Stationery Office, Dublin, 2004), p. 77.

19. Residential Institutions Redress Board, *Newsletter*, December 2010.

20. Ombudsman for Children's Office, *A Report based on an Investigation into the Implementation of Children First: National Guidelines for the Protection and Welfare of Children* (Ombudsman for Children's Office, Dublin, 2010).

21. Health Service Executive, *HSE Response to Ombudsman for Children's Investigation into the Implementation of Children First* (11 May 2010), available at http://www.hse.ie/eng/services/newscentre/2010archive/may2010/child renfirst.html [accessed 26 April 2011].

22. South Eastern Health Board, *Kilkenny Incest Investigation* (Stationery Office, Dublin, 1993), p. 96.

23. Joint Committee on the Constitutional Amendment on Children, *Proposal for a Constitutional Amendment to Strengthen Children's Rights: Final Report* (Houses of the Oireachtas, Dublin, 2010).

24. Children's Rights Alliance, *Report Card 2009, Report Card 2010, Report Card 2011* (Children's Rights Alliance, Dublin).

25. Department of Health and Children, *Health Strategy: Quality and Fairness, A Health System for You* (Department of Health and Children, Dublin, 2001), p. 141.

26. Government of Ireland, *Disability Act, 2005* (Stationery Office, Dublin, 2005).

27. Review Group on Mental Handicap Services, *Needs and Abilities, A Policy for the Intellectually Disabled: Report of the Review Group on Mental Handicap Services* (Stationery Office, Dublin, 1990), pp. 13–14.

28. National Economic and Social Council, *Report No. 50, Major Issues in Planning Services for Mentally and Physically Handicapped Persons* (Stationery Office, Dublin, 1980), p. 12; Government of Ireland, *Towards a Full Life: Green Paper on Services for Disabled People* (Stationery Office, Dublin, 1984), p. 22.

29. See Department of Health, *Shaping a Healthier Future* (Stationery Office, Dublin, 1994), pp. 70–1; Department of Health, *Enhancing the Partnership: Report of the Working Group on the Implementation of the Health Strategy in Relation to Persons with a Mental Handicap* (Department of Health, Dublin, 1996), p. 5.

30. For an account of the evolution of issues concerned with statutory and voluntary residential services for persons with mental illness and intellectual disability, see A. Ryan, *Walls of Silence* (Red Lion Press, Kilkenny, 1999).

31. Review Group on Health and Personal Social Services for People with Physical and Sensory Disabilities, *Towards an Independent Future, Report of the Review Group on Health and Personal Social Services for People with Physical and Sensory Disabilities* (Stationery Office, Dublin, 1996), pp. 6–13.

32. C. Kelly et al., *Annual Report of the National Intellectual Disability Database Committee 2009* (The Health Research Board, Dublin, 2010), p. 16.

33. Ibid., pp. 15–16.

34. M.A. O'Donovan et al., *Annual Report of the National Physical and Sensory Disability Database Committee 2009* (The Health Research Board, Dublin, 2010), pp. 17–18.

35. Commission on the Status of People with Disabilities, *A Strategy for Equality: Report of the Commission on the Status of People with Disabilities* (Stationery Office, Dublin, 1996), p. 5.

36. Government of Ireland, *Towards a Full Life*, op. cit., p. 112.

37. Union of Voluntary Organisations for the Handicapped, *Response to the Green Paper on Services for Disabled People* (Union of Voluntary Organisations for the Handicapped, Dublin, 1985), pp. 31–2.

38. National Economic and Social Council, op. cit., p. 12.

39. Department of Education, *Report of the Primary Education Review Body* (Stationery Office, Dublin, 1990), p. 60.

40. Government of Ireland, *Education for Persons with Special Educational Needs Act, 2004* (Stationery Office, Dublin, 2004).

41. Department of Health and Children, *Health Sectoral Plan – 2009 Progress Report* (Department of Health and Children, Dublin, 2009).

42. Commission on the Status of People with Disabilities, op. cit., p. 85.

43. In June 2010 equality and related functions, including disability, were transferred from the Department of Justice, Equality and Law Reform to the Department of Community, Rural and Gaeltacht Affairs. In March 2011 these same functions were transferred to the Department of Justice, Equality and Defence.

44. National Disability Authority, *2008 Report: Compliance with Part 5 of the Disability Act 2005* (National Disability Authority, Dublin, 2009).

45. Government of Ireland, *Partnership 2000 for Inclusion, Employment and Competitiveness* (Stationery Office, Dublin, 1996), p. 32.

46. Government of Ireland, *Towards Equal Citizenship, Progress Report on the Implementation of the Recommendations of the Commission on the Status of People with Disabilities* (Stationery Office, Dublin, 1999), pp. 81–2.

47. Comptroller and Auditor General, *Provision of Disability Services by Nonprofit Organisations, Report on Value for Money Examination No. 52* (Comptroller and Auditor General, Dublin, 2005), pp. 8–10.

48. D.B. Rottman et al., *The Population Structure and Living Circumstances of Irish Travellers: Results from the 1981 Census of Traveller Families* (Economic and Social Research Institute, Dublin, 1986), p. 73.

49. Commission on Itinerancy, *Report of the Commission on Itinerancy* (Stationery Office, Dublin, 1963), pp. 34–5.

50. Ibid., pp. 12–13.

51. Travelling People Review Body, *Report of the Travelling People Review Body* (Stationery Office, Dublin, 1983), pp. 5–6.

52. Task Force on the Travelling Community, *Report of the Task Force on the Travelling Community* (Stationery Office, Dublin, 1995), p. 76.

53. Government of Ireland, *Equal Status Act, 2000* (Stationery Office, Dublin, 2000).

54. See Equality Authority, *Traveller Ethnicity* (Equality Authority, Dublin, 2006); Irish Human Rights Commission, *Submission to the UN CERD Committee on the Examination of Ireland's Combined Third and Fourth Periodic Reports* (Irish Human Rights Commission, Dublin, 2010).

55. Health Research Board, *The Travellers' Health Status Study: Vital Statistics of Travelling People, 1987* (Health Research Board, Dublin, 1989), p. 24.

56. Travelling People Review Body, op. cit., p. 94.

57. Department of Health and Children, *Traveller Health: A National Strategy 2002–2005* (Department of Health and Children, Dublin, 2002), p. 5.

58. Department of Social, Community and Family Affairs, *Building an Inclusive Society: Review of the National Anti-Poverty Strategy under the Programme for Prosperity and Fairness* (Department of Social, Community and Family Affairs, Dublin, 2002), p. 16.

59. Department of Health and Children, *All-Ireland Traveller Health Study* (Department of Health and Children, Dublin, 2010).

60. Commission on Itinerancy, op. cit., p. 64.

61. Travelling People Review Body, op. cit., pp. 59–60.

62. Social Inclusion Division, Department of Social and Family Affairs, *National Action Plan for Social Inclusion 2007–2016, Annual Report 2008* (Social Inclusion Division, Department of Social and Family Affairs, Dublin, 2009), p. 46.

63. N. Hourigan and M. Campbell, *The Teach Report: Traveller Education and Adults, Crisis, Challenge and Change* (National Association of Traveller Centres, Athlone, 2010).

64. Government of Ireland, *Report of the Special Group on Public Service Numbers and Expenditure Programmes* (Stationery Office, Dublin, 2009), p. 63.

65. Commission on Itinerancy, op. cit., p. 61.

66. Travelling People Review Body, op. cit., p. 38.

67. National Traveller Accommodation Consultative Committee, *Annual Report 2008* (National Traveller Accommodation Consultative Committee, Dublin, 2009).

68. Travelling People Review Body, op. cit., p. 35.

69. Under the Prohibition of Incitement to Racial, Religious or National Hatred Act, 1989, the Travelling people are cited as a group about whom offensive material cannot be published.

70. Task Force on the Travelling Community, op. cit., p. 289.

71. S.B. Gmelch, 'From poverty sub-culture to political lobby: the Traveller rights movement in Ireland', in C. Curtin and T.M. Wilson, *Ireland from Below: Social Change and Rural Communities* (Galway University Press, Galway, 1990).

72. Committee to Monitor and Co-ordinate the Implementation of the Recommendations of the Task Force on the Travelling Community, *First Progress Report of the Committee to Monitor and Co-ordinate the Implementation of the Recommendations of the Task Force on the Travelling Community* (Stationery Office, Dublin, 2000), p. 53.

73. Ibid., p. 8.

74. Committee to Monitor and Co-ordinate the Implementation of the Recommendations of the Task Force on the Travelling Community, *Second Progress Report of the Committee to Monitor and Co-ordinate the Implementation of the Recommendations of the Task Force on the Travelling Community* (Stationery Office, Dublin, 2005), p. 6.

75. Department of Justice, Equality and Law Reform, *Report of the High Level Group on Traveller Issues* (Department of Justice, Equality and Law Reform, Dublin, 2006), p. 4.

76. Department of the Taoiseach, *Towards 2016: Ten-Year Framework Social Partnership Agreement 2006–2015* (Stationery Office, Dublin, 2006), p. 58.

7

Voluntary Social Service
Organisations

Introduction

This chapter considers the important role played by the voluntary sector in the provision of social services and the development of social policy.

Up to very recently the voluntary, or charities, sector in Ireland was unregulated, with no statutory definition of what could be classified as a 'charity'. The Revenue Commissioners determined whether an organisation was entitled to charitable tax exemption under the Taxes Consolidation Act, 1997, and in turn they issued a charity reference number (CHY) to those granted charitable tax exemption. However, this did not constitute a register of charities.

Section 3 of the Charities Act, 2009, defines 'charitable purposes' for the first time in primary Irish legislation. A purpose is regarded as charitable if its aim is:

• the prevention or relief of poverty or economic hardship;
• the advancement of education;
• the advancement of religion;
• any other purpose that is of benefit to the community.

'Purpose that is of benefit to the community' includes a range of activities such as the promotion of civic responsibility or voluntary work in the community (see Appendix 1 at end of chapter).[1]

The statutory definition of 'charitable purposes' covers a wide range of voluntary activity. It includes areas that would not have been traditionally regarded as being of a voluntary nature. The Charities Act, 2009, also provides for a formal system of registration for charitable organisations (see later section in this chapter).

The role of voluntary social service organisations is considerable in Ireland, especially if religious orders are included, as their influence on the development of the education and health services has been significant. Information on the number of voluntary organisations will remain imprecise until sections of the Charities Act, 2009, come into force.

Until recently, the extent of voluntary activity has also been a matter of conjecture. A report by the Central Statistics Office established that just under a quarter of the population take part in informal, unpaid charitable work.[2] It also indicated that about two-thirds of people regularly take part in voluntary or community activities, with sport being the most popular activity.

In most cases, voluntary organisations complement the work of statutory agencies. Despite the growth in statutory services over time, the voluntary sector still flourishes and many new organisations have been established within the past few decades.

There is great diversity within the voluntary sector in relation to aims, resources, scope of activity and status of personnel employed. Some employ full-time, paid staff, others rely on unpaid volunteers and some have a combination of both full-time staff and volunteers. Some rely solely on voluntary contributions from the public but the majority receive some statutory grants, mainly from the HSE. Some focus on particular client groups, such as older persons, while others cater for a variety of groups. Some are national organisations with branches throughout the country while others have a narrower geographic base.

Categories of voluntary organisations

Faughnan's classification framework for voluntary organisations, outlined below, reflects diversity in relation to dominant functions.[3]

Mutual support and self-help organisations
These are based on a common interest or need. An example is GROW, the community health movement, which has a network of groups that meet on a regular basis.

Local development associations
These associations operate within a particular geographic locality and are concerned with promoting the development of that area by collective action.

Resource and service-providing organisations
These organisations represent the largest category of voluntary activity in Ireland, as judged by most criteria, e.g. the largest arena for volunteer

involvement. It is also the category with the greatest diversity, and organisations operate at either local or national level. The largest organisation of this kind is the Society of St Vincent de Paul, whose first conference was established in Ireland in the mid-nineteenth century. The society has approximately 1,100 conferences (branches) throughout the country and 9,500 volunteers, supported by some professional staff, and it had a budget in 2009 of approximately €74 million. While the main focus of the society is on support for low-income families, it provides a wide range of services, including sheltered housing for older persons and holiday homes for children.

Representative and coordinating organisations

These organisations act, in some cases, as coordinating bodies or, more commonly, as resource agents for affiliated members of a particular category of voluntary activity. They also act as a focal point for liaising with government or government agencies in order to bring about policy changes. Even with these organisations there is also diversity in relation to the functions and mode of operation. An example of such a representative body is the Disability Federation of Ireland, which has over 120 voluntary disability organisations affiliated to it (see Chapter 6).

Campaigning bodies

Many of the representatives of service organisations are also involved in campaigning for improvement in services. In practice, there are few organisations whose sole functions are to lobby for change. The National Campaign for the Homeless, representing a variety of voluntary organisations, was established to influence and monitor policy in relation to homelessness in the 1980s. More recently, the alliance Older & Bolder, established in 2006, with eight member organisations, champions the rights of all older people and has campaigned for a national positive ageing strategy.

Funding organisations

By comparison with Britain, there are few independent trusts or funding organisations in Ireland that support the activities and projects of voluntary organisations. One of the few is the Irish Youth Foundation. Grants given by such organisations are usually small and of a once-off nature, and supplement the financial assistance provided by statutory bodies. The Atlantic Philanthropies, an American foundation, supports some voluntary groups and projects in various countries, including Ireland.

Evolution of voluntary activity

It is possible to identify some main stages in the evolution of the voluntary sector in Ireland.

Firstly, as already noted, the contribution of religious orders, commencing in the nineteenth century following Catholic emancipation, has been significant, especially in the health services and education. In addition, some philanthropic individuals were responsible for the establishment of voluntary hospitals in the nineteenth century.[4] Apart from establishing voluntary hospitals, religious orders were also pre-eminent in the field of residential care for persons with intellectual disability and deprived children.

Secondly, a strong community self-help tradition with a base in rural Ireland emerged in the twentieth century. The Irish Countrywomen's Association was founded in 1910 and was originally called the Society of the United Irishwomen, whose aim was 'to improve the standard of life in rural Ireland through education and co-operative effort'.[5] Another notable example is Muintir na Tíre, a community-based movement established in 1937 to seek improvement in all aspects of community life.

Thirdly, the development of statutory services, especially those of health boards in the 1970s, provided a focal point for voluntary activity. The establishment of community care programmes under health boards provided the impetus to a greater focus for local voluntary organisations operating in the general welfare area, especially organisations providing services for older persons.

Another factor accounting for the development of voluntary organisations arose from the 1960s onwards as some members of the clergy, but especially some members of religious orders, began to become more involved in social service activity and to branch out from what would have been regarded as the traditional areas of education and nursing care in hospitals associated with these orders. Some members became involved in existing organisations while others were instrumental in establishing new organisations. Some were involved in the establishment of organisations that subsequently attained a high profile nationally. These include Cuan Mhuire, founded by Sr Consilio in 1966 to provide residential treatment for addiction problems; Threshold, representing the interests of tenants in the private rented sector, founded by a Capuchin priest, Fr Donal O'Mahony, in 1978; Focus Ireland, an organisation for homeless persons, founded by Sr Stanislaus Kennedy in 1985; and a support service for young homeless people, now known as the Peter McVerry Trust, established by Fr Peter McVerry in 1985.

Many other members of religious orders, especially female orders, became involved in a variety of local social services.

In 1971 Erskine Childers, TD, Minister for Health, established the National Social Service Council (NSSC) with a broad remit as the focal point for voluntary social services. The NSSC helped to promote the establishment of social service councils (local coordinating bodies) throughout the country. Having been restructured in 1981 as the National Social Service Board and given a statutory basis in 1984, the board's functions were limited to the development of information services in 1988 following an abortive attempt by the government to disband it.

Continued relevance of voluntary organisations

Paradoxically, as the role of state services has increased, that of the voluntary sector has not diminished; it has, in fact, also increased. Among the reasons for this are the following:

- The general pattern has been that voluntary organisations have pioneered the provision of services, with the state becoming involved in a supportive role at a later stage.
- The pioneering role remains relevant as new social problems emerge and as others are redefined.
- Even if it were desirable, it is highly unlikely that the state could afford to completely replace the work of voluntary organisations. In many instances voluntary organisations supplement the basic services provided by the state.
- Voluntary activity provides an outlet for the altruism of many people.
- It is generally recognised that voluntary organisations can respond to social need in a more flexible manner than the way in which statutory agencies can.

While the voluntary sector has obvious strengths, one of the inherent weaknesses of the system is that there may be an uneven geographic spread of organisations. While some areas may be relatively well served by voluntary groups, others may be less so. This applies in particular to services for persons with disabilities, where the voluntary sector has played a pre-eminent role.

Funding of voluntary organisations

Depending on the type of activity engaged in, there are different sources of statutory funding for voluntary organisations. The main source of recurrent funds for the majority of voluntary organisations providing health and welfare services is the HSE. Section 65 of the Health Act, 1953, provides that health authorities may support organisations providing services 'similar or ancillary' to those of the health authority.[6] In the case of larger organisations, the HSE may have a service-level agreement with providers of services, especially those in the disability sector (see Chapter 6).

Different government departments provide funding for a range of schemes operated by the community and voluntary sector at either national or local level. Some of the funding from government departments is derived from the proceeds of the National Lottery.

The balance of funding required by many voluntary organisations is raised in a variety of ways from the public.

Statutory/voluntary relationships

Despite its significant, if unquantifiable, role in the provision of services, it is surprising that there has not been a clear policy framework in which the voluntary sector can develop. The need for a broad plan outlining the role of voluntary services in the total provision of welfare services became more obvious as the voluntary sector grew in importance.

In 1976 Brendan Corish, TD, Minister for Health, indicated that a policy document would be prepared on the scope and structure of welfare services and the respective roles and relationships of the statutory and voluntary organisations in the planning and provision of these services.[7] No such document emerged.

The short-lived Fine Gael/Labour Coalition Government of June 1981 to March 1982 had in its programme a commitment to introduce a charter for voluntary services that would provide a framework for the relationship between the statutory and voluntary agencies.[8] This charter was not pursued following the change of government in March 1982 or the return of the Fine Gael/Labour government in December 1982.

It was against this background that the National Social Service Board produced a discussion document on voluntary social services in Ireland.[9] This recommended an integrated approach to the development of welfare services, with statutory and voluntary bodies working together. It referred to the need for greater consultation and planning between both types of agencies and to the unsatisfactory nature of funding under Section 65 grants, under the Health Act, 1953, and recommended that guidelines be established in relation to the type of activity that would be funded, the duration of funding and the conditions the funding would be subject to.

The *Programme for Economic and Social Progress* (1991) stated that, having regard to the contribution that voluntary organisations make in the delivery of services and in combating poverty, the government would draw up a charter for voluntary social services, which would set out a clear framework for partnership between the state and voluntary activity and develop a cohesive strategy for supporting voluntary activity. It also indicated that a White Paper outlining the government's proposals in this area would be prepared.[10] In 1991, Michael Woods, TD, Minister for Social Welfare, initiated a process of consultation with voluntary organisations in relation to the proposed charter.

Because of the changing context, the government subsequently decided that it would be more appropriate to publish a Green Paper rather than a White Paper. The Green Paper, published in 1997, outlined the diversity of the community and voluntary sector, as well as the range of state funding and support available to the sector.[11] It suggested two sets of guidelines that are of relevance to the relationship between the statutory sector and the voluntary/community sector. The first set were guidelines to inform statutory agencies in their relationship with the voluntary/community sector; for example, each government department and agency should identify and outline its role in relation to the voluntary and community sector and its future plans. The second set were guidelines to inform the voluntary and community sector; for example, there should be openness, accountability and transparency in the work of the various organisations.

The Green Paper also suggested that principles should apply to the funding of the voluntary and community sector. For example, all grants by statutory agencies should be advertised and eligibility criteria should be published.

When the Green Paper was launched in 1997, the intention was to have a year-long consultation process leading to a White Paper. In the event, the White Paper was not published until 2000.[12] Some of the main features of the White Paper were:

- formal recognition of the role of the community and voluntary sector in contributing to the creation of a vibrant, participative democracy and civil society;
- introduction of mechanisms in all relevant public service areas for consultation with the community and voluntary sector groups and for allowing the communities they represent to have an input to policy-making;
- multi-annual funding to become the norm for agreed priority services and community development activities, meaning a major move away

from the existing unsatisfactory and ad hoc funding schemes experienced by many voluntary groups;
• designation of voluntary activity units in relevant government departments to support the relationship with the community and voluntary sector.

An implementation and advisory group, drawn from relevant government departments, statutory agencies and the community and voluntary sector, was established to oversee the implementation of the White Paper decisions and to pursue other issues that arose.

Up to 2002, responsibility for the grants to many voluntary organisations rested with the Department of Social, Community and Family Affairs. In that year, in the context of departmental reorganisations following the general election, the 'community' function, including responsibility for implementation of the White Paper proposals, was transferred to the Department of Community, Rural and Gaeltacht Affairs.

An Agreed Programme for Government between Fianna Fáil and the Progressive Democrats (2002) made a commitment to reform the existing legislation to ensure accountability and to protect against abuse of charitable status and fraud. In keeping with this commitment, the Department of Community, Rural and Gaeltacht Affairs published a consultation paper in 2003, entitled *Establishing a Modern Statutory Framework for Charities*. The consultation paper indicated that the overall policy aim of new legislation would be to introduce an integrated system of registration and regulation for charities. The purpose of legislation would be to:

• give clear statutory guidance regarding the definition of charity;
• require a register of charities to be established;
• put in place an appropriate regulatory framework for registered charities, thereby securing accountability and protecting against fraud.

In the context of a regulatory framework, the consultation paper indicated that there were two main options: either an existing body or bodies would take on regulatory functions in relation to charities, or a new regulatory body (for which the name Caradas was proposed) would be set up to manage the regulation and accountability of charities in the public interest.

The initial expectations of the early 1980s concerning a comprehensive national framework had narrowed down to something different over twenty years later, with an emphasis on a regulatory framework for the voluntary sector. Other aspects of the relationship between the statutory and voluntary sectors would remain to be worked out at agency level.

The Charities Act, 2009

The Charities Bill was not published until 2007, four years after the consultation paper. During its long passage through the Oireachtas, some concerns were raised about various sections of the bill, which was eventually passed in 2009. Like many other pieces of legislation, the Charities Act does not come into force automatically. It will be implemented in stages over time by ministerial order.

The purpose of the Charities Act is to reform the law relating to charities in order to ensure greater accountability and to protect against abuse of charitable status and fraud. Under the act, a new independent regulatory body for the charities sector, the Charities Regulatory Authority (An tÚdarás Rialála Carthanas), is to be established. The authority's role will be to:

- increase public confidence in the charities sector through effective oversight of charitable organisations in Ireland;
- promote compliance by charitable organisations with their legal obligations;
- encourage better administration of charitable trusts;
- provide guidance to charitable organisations, including through the development of codes of practice.

Since there is no central public register of charities in Ireland, a key function of the new Charities Regulatory Authority will be the establishment and maintenance of a register of charitable organisations that will be accessible to the general public. Registration will be mandatory for all charities operating within the state, and any organisation with charitable tax exemptions from the Revenue Commissioners will be automatically entered in the register on the day it is established.

The act makes provision for the keeping of proper accounts and annual statements of accounts by charitable organisations. In recognition of the fact that many of the organisations are small, the reporting and auditing requirements will vary depending on the income of the organisation.

Certain types of organisations, such as political parties, trade unions or representative bodies of employers, will be excluded from being defined as charitable organisations. The act is principally concerned with regulation of the voluntary sector and, from the public's perspective, should lead to greater transparency and accountability.

Consultation and partnership

The Charities Act, 2009, does not cover key elements of the relationship between the state and the voluntary sector as set out in the White Paper of 2000. However, it should be noted that some of those elements, such as multi-annual funding, were put in place in the voluntary disability sector under the National Disability Strategy (see Chapter 6). It must also be acknowledged that, over a period, the voluntary sector has become more involved in the policy process through consultation and partnership with the statutory sector. In general, few major government social policy initiatives now take place without some consultation with representatives of the voluntary sector.

At national level, social partnership agreements have played an important role in the development of the economy. Commencing in 1987, these agreements between government, employers, trade unions and farmers were made every three years up to 2006. Representatives of community and voluntary groups were involved in these agreements for the first time in *Partnership 2000* (1996), and this process was continued in subsequent agreements. In the most recent agreement, *Towards 2016*, agreed in 2006, the groups representing the community and voluntary sector were the Irish National Organisation of the Unemployed, the Congress Centres Network, the CORI Justice Commission, the National Youth Council of Ireland, the National Association of Building Co-Operatives, the Irish Council for Social Housing, the Society of St Vincent de Paul, Age Action Ireland, The Carers Association, The Wheel, the Disability Federation of Ireland, Irish Rural Link, the Irish Senior Citizens' Parliament, the Children's Rights Alliance and Protestant Aid.

Active citizenship

It was partly in the context of a possible decline in voluntary activity that the Taoiseach, Bertie Ahern, TD, established the Taskforce on Active Citizenship in 2006. As part of its terms of reference, the taskforce had to review the evidence regarding trends in citizen participation across the main areas of civic, community, cultural, occupational and recreational life in Ireland. The taskforce's report, published in 2007, referred to active citizenship as being about engagement, participation in society and valuing contributions made by individuals, whether they are employed or outside the traditional workforce. In its view:

being an active citizen means being aware of, and caring about, the welfare of fellow citizens, recognising that we live as members of communities and therefore depend on others in our daily lives.[13]

The taskforce also stated that 'the state of Active Citizenship should be a national priority'. The main recommendations of the taskforce related to increasing participation in the democratic process; improving the interaction between the citizen and state institutions at local and national level; measures to promote a greater sense of community and community engagement; further education on the issues around active citizenship; and measures that provide increased opportunities for the inclusion of ethnic and cultural minorities in an increasingly diverse society. It also set some 'ambitious but realisable targets' in certain areas, e.g. to increase the pool of people active in the community by 60,000 each year for the following three years.[14]

An Active Citizenship Office was established under the aegis of the Department of the Taoiseach, and an implementation group was established to oversee the work of the office. However, with the economic downturn commencing in 2008, the agenda for active citizenship was accorded a low priority and the office was disbanded.

Notes

1. Government of Ireland, *Charities Act, 2009* (Stationery Office, Dublin, 2009).
2. Central Statistics Office, *Community Involvement and Social Networks in Ireland* (Central Statistics Office, Dublin, 2009), p. 7.
3. P. Faughnan, *Partners in Progress: Voluntary Organisations in the Social Service Field* (Social Science Research Centre, University College Dublin, Dublin, 1990), pp. 3–19.
4. An example of a philanthropic individual was Dr Richard Steevens, who, prior to his death in 1710, stipulated in his will that his sister, Grizel, would have the benefit of his property during her lifetime and that after her death the proceeds would be used to establish a hospital. Dr Steevens' Hospital, Dublin, was opened in 1833 and remained a voluntary hospital until its closure in 1987. See D. Coakley, *Doctor Steevens' Hospital: A Brief History* (Dr Steevens' Hospital Historical Centre, Dublin, 1992). Dr Steevens' Hospital is now the head office of the HSE.
5. Irish Countrywomen's Association, *History*, available at http://www.ica.ie/About-us/History.43.1.aspx [accessed 18 April 2011].
6. Government of Ireland, *Health Act, 1953* (Stationery Office, Dublin, 1953).
7. Dáil Éireann, 'Vote 50: health', 29 April 1976, *Dáil Debates*, Vol. 290, No. 374.
8. Government of Ireland, *Fine Gael–Labour, Programme for Government, 1981–86* (Stationery Office, Dublin, 1981).

9.   National Social Service Board, *The Development of Voluntary Social Services in Ireland: A Discussion Document* (National Social Service Board, Dublin, 1982).

10. Government of Ireland, *Programme for Economic and Social Progress* (Stationery Office, Dublin, 1991), p. 24.

11. Government of Ireland, *Green Paper: Supporting Voluntary Activity* (Stationery Office, Dublin, 1997).

12. Government of Ireland, *White Paper, A Framework for Supporting Voluntary Activity and for Delivering the Relationship between the State and the Community and Voluntary Sector* (Stationery Office, Dublin, 2000).

13. Taskforce on Active Citizenship, *Report of the Taskforce on Active Citizenship* (Department of the Taoiseach, Dublin, 2007), p. 2.

14. Ibid., p. 28.

Appendix 1: Extract from Section 3, Charities Act, 2009

'Purpose that is of benefit to the community' includes:

- the advancement of community welfare, including the relief of those in need by reason of youth, age, ill-health, or disability;
- the advancement of community development, including rural or urban regeneration;
- the promotion of civic responsibility or voluntary work;
- the promotion of health, including the prevention or relief of sickness, disease or human suffering;
- the advancement of conflict resolution or reconciliation;
- the promotion of religious or racial harmony and harmonious community relations;
- the protection of the natural environment;
- the advancement of environmental sustainability;
- the advancement of the efficient and effective use of the property of charitable organisations;
- the prevention or relief of suffering of animals;
- the advancement of the arts, culture, heritage or sciences; and
- the integration of those who are disadvantaged, and the promotion of their full participation in society.

These purposes broadly reflect those used by the Revenue Commissioners in determining eligibility for certain tax exemptions and relief for charities.

8

Poverty and Exclusion

Introduction

While there is no universally accepted definition of poverty it is most popularly regarded as lack of sufficient income. But what might be regarded as poverty in developed countries could be quite different to that in, for example, an under-developed Third World country.

It is now accepted in various research reports that poverty is viewed as exclusion, through lack of resources, from the generally approved standards and styles of living in society as a whole. This approach is based on the fact that perceptions of acceptable and minimum standards change over time and between countries with various levels of per capita incomes. Townsend, one of the foremost early writers on the subject, defined poverty in relative terms, the poor being:

> Individuals and families whose resources, over time, fall seriously short of the resources commanded by the average individual or family in the community in which they live.[1]

The official definition adopted in Ireland is broadly similar to Townsend's and emphasises the relative nature of poverty related to living standards in Ireland:

> People are living in poverty if their income and resources (material, cultural and social) are so inadequate as to preclude them from having a standard of living which is regarded as acceptable by Irish society generally. As a result of inadequate income and resources, people may be excluded from participating in activities which are considered the norm for other people in society.[2]

During the 1990s the terms 'social exclusion' and 'social inclusion' began to be used in official policy documents, with 'social exclusion' being used either interchangeably with the term 'poverty' or to encompass something broader. The national partnership agreement *Partnership 2000 for Inclusion, Employment and Competitiveness* (1996) was the first government policy document to both describe and use the terms 'social exclusion' and 'social inclusion'. It is perhaps no coincidence that this agreement was the first since the triennial process started in 1987 to include representatives of voluntary organisations, known as the community platform (in later agreements the community and voluntary pillar), in addition to the already established groups representing employers, trade unions and farmers. *Partnership 2000* referred to social exclusion as follows:

> Social exclusion can be succinctly described as cumulative marginalisation: from production (unemployment), from consumption (income poverty), from social networks (community, family and neighbours), from decision making and from an adequate quality of life. Social exclusion is one of the major challenges currently facing Irish society. To minimise or ignore this challenge would not only result in an increase in social polarisation, which is in itself unacceptable, but also an increase in all the attendant problems such as poor health, crime, drug abuse and alienation, which impose huge social and economic costs on our society.[3]

Partnership 2000 went on to state that:

> Social inclusion will therefore be pursued not in any residual way, but rather as an integral part of this Partnership and a strategic objective in its own right. The primary objective of a social inclusion strategy is to ensure that the benefits of economic growth, and related social improvements, are shared by all sections of the Irish population. Access to jobs is a key to this.[4]

Measurement of poverty

Since poverty is defined in relative terms, it follows that the measurement of the extent of poverty is usually formulated in relation to average incomes in society. Many countries estimate the extent of poverty as the proportion of households/families whose incomes fall below 50 per cent or 60 per cent of either mean income or median disposable income in the population in general. In the context of measuring poverty, a distinction is made between households or groups 'at risk of poverty' and those experiencing 'consistent poverty'.

Various studies were carried out in Ireland in the 1970s and 1980s to estimate the proportion of the population living in poverty, but these varied depending on the criteria used to measure poverty.

Since the late 1980s, however, there appears to be consensus on methods of estimating the extent of poverty, and these have been developed by the ESRI. 'At risk of poverty' is measured by an income poverty line, i.e. persons or households with less than 60 per cent of median disposable income. 'Consistent poverty' is measured by a combination of income poverty line (60 per cent of median disposable income) and basic deprivation indicators. These indicators include a lack of at least one of a number of items, e.g. lack of adequate heating, lack of a warm overcoat. In 1987 the ESRI devised a list of eight items as basic deprivation indicators, and these were used in the measurement of poverty in the government's *National Anti-Poverty Strategy* (NAPS) of 1997. In 2006 the ESRI revised the list of items to more closely reflect changed standards of living in Ireland, resulting in a list of eleven items. At least two of the revised items would now be required, together with the 60 per cent income poverty threshold, to qualify for consistent poverty. This revised definition was also adopted by government in its revised national action plans on poverty (see Appendix 1 at end of chapter for revised and former list of items in the deprivation index).

Changes in the extent of poverty based on the above criteria are considered in the context of the government's national strategies in a later section in this chapter.

Poverty as an issue

In the 1950s and 1960s several studies in the US indicated that, despite increasing affluence following World War II, poverty and inequalities persisted. This 'rediscovery', as Sinfield described it, led to poverty becoming a socially accepted subject for debate and research, to the establishment of pressure groups and eventually to attempts by governments to find a solution to the problem.[5] In Ireland, poverty may be said to have been 'rediscovered' at a conference on poverty organised by the Catholic Bishops' Council for Social Welfare in Kilkenny in 1971.

The Kilkenny conference sparked off what was to be a growing national debate on how the plight of the poor in society could be resolved. Perhaps the most important paper read at the conference was 'The extent of poverty in Ireland' by Seamus O'Cinneide, in which the author estimated that at least one-quarter of the population was living below the poverty line, based on income maintenance rates of payment in Ireland (the Republic and Northern Ireland) in 1971.[6] The social, cultural and educational deprivation associated with poverty was described in other conference papers.[7] It was felt that the causes and effects of poverty in Ireland were not clearly understood and that there was need for further research.

Afterwards, the poverty issue became politicised and was taken up especially by the Labour Party, which, with Fine Gael, formed the coalition government of 1973–7.[8] In the pre-election joint policy statement of the two parties, one of the fourteen points referred to the elimination of poverty and the ending of social injustice as major priorities. At that government's instigation, the Social Action Programme of the then EEC was expanded to include an anti-poverty programme, with pilot schemes in member states. In 1974 Frank Cluskey, TD, Parliamentary Secretary to the Minister for Social Welfare, and a member of the Labour Party, established an advisory committee, the National Committee on Pilot Schemes to Combat Poverty, on a non-statutory basis to initiate and coordinate pilot schemes to combat poverty. The committee was known popularly as Combat Poverty and within a short time became, in effect, an executive body that planned and administered projects and employed the necessary staff. The objectives of Combat Poverty were:

• to bring about practical intervention in areas of deprivation or among groups in need;
• to increase public awareness of the problems of poverty;
• to contribute to the evolution of effective, long-term policies against poverty.

Of the various projects initiated by Combat Poverty, O'Cinneide concluded that 'one is left with an impression of real but unspecifiable gains for a few'.[9] He also pointed out that the greatest failure of Combat Poverty was that it did not increase public awareness of poverty.

At the end of 1980 the work of Combat Poverty was terminated, partly because EEC funds for further projects were no longer available. The committee's final report called for the establishment of a national agency to further develop and expand the work of the pilot schemes.

In 1986 the Combat Poverty Agency (CPA) was established on a statutory basis, reporting to the Minister for Social Welfare. Under the Combat Poverty Agency Act, 1986, the agency had four general functions:

i. advice and recommendations to the Minister (for Social Welfare) on all aspects of economic and social planning in relation to poverty;
ii. initiation and evaluation of measures aimed at overcoming poverty;
iii. promotion, commission and interpretation of research into poverty;
iv. promotion of greater public understanding of poverty.

The CPA recognised that, because of limited resources available, it could not be a major funding source for measures designed to tackle the problem of poverty. Instead, it viewed its role as clarifying the causes and effects of poverty and pointing towards solutions.[10] From its establishment, the agency commissioned various studies on aspects of poverty, and has been to the forefront in highlighting poverty issues. An analysis of the impact of the government's budget on low-income households was a key publication each year. The fact that it was an agency of government did not prevent the CPA from being critical of government policy.

In 2008 the government made a decision to integrate the CPA into the Social Inclusion Unit of the Department of Social and Family Affairs. Effectively, the CPA was abolished as a separate entity, and its full-time staff were transferred in 2009.[11] The move was opposed by some voluntary agencies which felt that an important independent voice would now be lost. The Chairman of the CPA, Brian Duncan, stated:

> I very much regret this decision. It will end Combat Poverty's independence and our ability to speak out publicly on the issues that cause and perpetuate poverty in Ireland.[12]

Helen Johnston, former Director of the CPA, outlined how the nature of poverty had changed over the lifetime of the CPA:

> Poverty was undoubtedly more widespread in the late 1980s than in the late 2000s ... In 1986, poverty was characterised by high and long-term unemployment, low levels of social welfare and large inner-city areas ravaged by disadvantage and drugs. Much has changed in the interim. During the celtic tiger years of the late 1990s and into the early 2000s, poverty concerns related to people who had difficulty accessing the labour market, such as lone parents, people with disabilities and people with low education levels and skills. With net immigration, the Irish population became more diverse. Poverty among non-Irish nationals and inequality and discrimination issues were a further concern. Child poverty remains a key poverty issue.[13]

Reference has already been made in this chapter to Ireland's role in the development of the EU's first anti-poverty programme from 1975 to 1985. This was followed by two further anti-poverty programmes: the second from 1985 to 1989 and the third from 1989 to 1994. The third programme was focused on social exclusion and marginalisation. Pilot schemes in member states were the cornerstone of each programme, and these were designed to demonstrate good practice that could subsequently be mainstreamed. Each programme was evaluated and lessons were learned. Ireland participated in and benefited from each of the EU anti-poverty programmes.[14] The importance of these programmes has been emphasised:

> The EU Anti-Poverty Programmes were highly significant for social policy in that they shifted the focus away from a simplistic concept of poverty to the more complex one of social exclusion. They led to an acceptance that exclusion processes go beyond unemployment and/or low incomes.[15]

National Anti-Poverty Strategy

Poverty as an issue assumed greater significance with the publication of *Sharing in Progress: National Anti-Poverty Strategy* by government in 1997. This followed from Ireland's participation in the United Nations World Summit meeting in Copenhagen in 1995, at which the government agreed to implement a national anti-poverty strategy. The NAPS was signed by the three leaders of the coalition parties in government, i.e. John Bruton of Fine Gael, Dick Spring of the Labour Party and Proinsias De Rossa of Democratic Left. The strategy was based on research, mostly commissioned by the CPA, and widespread consultation with all interest groups. Part of its significance lay in the fact that it was the first comprehensive document by government on the issue of poverty.

Research by the ESRI, based on the 1994 *Living in Ireland Survey* and using relative income poverty lines, indicated that between 21 and 34 per cent of the population were living on incomes below the 50 to 60 per cent of average disposable income (£64 to £77 per week, respectively, for a single adult in 1994).[16] For the same year, however, the study indicated, by using a combination of income poverty lines and basic deprivation indicators, that 9 to 15 per cent of the population could be said to be living in poverty. This section of the population, according to NAPS, 'can be identified as consistently poor, whose income is low and whose ability to draw on accumulated resources is extremely limited'.[17] These were used as benchmark statistics in NAPS, which set a global target as follows:

> Over the period, 1997 to 2007, the National Anti-Poverty Strategy will aim at considerably reducing the numbers of those who are 'consistently poor' from 9 to 15% to less than 5 to 10%, as measured by the ESRI.[18]

As already noted, the method of measurement of poverty adopted by the ESRI was to take 50 per cent and 60 per cent of disposable income together with one of eight indicators, such as lack of a warm overcoat or lack of a good meal in the day.

NAPS also identified five key areas in each of which an overall goal, targets and policy actions were outlined. The areas were:

i.   educational disadvantage;
ii.   unemployment, particularly long-term unemployment;
iii. income adequacy;
iv.   disadvantaged urban areas;
v.   rural poverty.

An overall goal in education, for example, was to eliminate early school leaving so that 90 per cent of children would complete the senior cycle by the year 2000, rising to 98 per cent by 2007. A further objective was that, within a period of five years, no student would have serious literacy or numeracy problems.

The strategy was underpinned by a cabinet subcommittee chaired by the Taoiseach, an interdepartmental policy committee comprised of senior officers, and a NAPS unit in the Department of Social and Family Affairs.

Reviews on the progress of NAPS were carried out. The report of the interdepartmental policy committee for 1999–2000 indicated that some targets had been easily met, especially those related to unemployment. This reduction in unemployment was largely due to the upturn in the economy, which led to increased employment. Other targets proved more difficult to meet. For example, in education, there had been little progress in meeting the target for senior-cycle completion; ironically, one of the reasons for this was the 'pull factor' of increased employment opportunities arising from the growth in the economy. As part of the review, further targets were set and new areas were brought under NAPS. These included housing and homelessness, child poverty, women living in poverty, older people and Travellers' life expectancy.

In 2002 a revised NAPS was published. It indicated that over the period 1994–2000 the proportion of the population in consistent poverty fell from 15.1 per cent to 6.2 per cent.[19] It set new targets to reduce, and if possible to eliminate, consistent poverty. One of the key commitments of the revised NAPS was to achieve a rate of €150 per week for the lowest rates of social welfare, to be met by 2007.

National Action Plan against Poverty and Social Exclusion
Parallel to the development of the first and second NAPS was a European-wide drive to meet the EU objective set by the European Council at Lisbon in 2000 'to make a decisive impact on the eradication of poverty and social exclusion by 2010'.

In line with this, the first national action plan, *National Action Plan against Poverty and Social Exclusion 2001–2003*, was published in 2001. The second plan, *National Action Plan against Poverty and Social Exclusion 2003–2005*, was published in 2003. NAPS has evolved into the national action plan. The most recent plan is the *National Action Plan for Social Inclusion 2007–2016* (2007). It sets out a wide-ranging and comprehensive programme with targets in different areas. In the introduction it is noted that:

> The National Action Plan for Social Inclusion (NAPinclusion) has been prepared in a different context to the original 1997 National Anti-Poverty Strategy. Income support targets (social welfare rates and pensions) have now been achieved and, in line with the National Economic and Social Council (NESC) report on the *Developmental Welfare State*, there is greater emphasis on services and activation as a means of tackling social exclusion.[20]

The plan is based on the life cycle approach as outlined by the NESC, which was adopted in the national partnership agreement *Towards 2016* (2006), and is complemented by the social-inclusion elements of the *National Development Plan 2007–2013* (2007). The life cycle approach or framework was set out in the NESC report *The Developmental Welfare State* as follows:

> A quite fundamental standpoint from which to judge the adequacy and effectiveness of overall social protection is to assess the risks and hazards which the individual person in Irish society faces and the supports available to them at different stages in the life cycle. It provides a simple but comprehensive framework to ensure no population group is overlooked, and facilitates a more reasoned adjudication between competing priorities.[21]

The key life cycle groups are children, people of working age, older people and people with disabilities.

During the period of the Celtic Tiger much progress was made on reducing poverty. The definition of 'consistent poverty' was changed in 2007. The targets set in NAPS on reducing consistent poverty were achieved and further targets set. The *National Action Plan for Social Inclusion 2007–2016* set a poverty-reduction target as follows:

> to reduce the number of those experiencing consistent poverty to between 2% and 4% by 2012 with the aim of eliminating consistent poverty by 2016, under the revised definition.[22]

A report by the ESRI in 2010 noted that the reduction in poverty levels between 2004 and 2007 did not meet the targets set by government in

Building an Inclusive Society (2002), which had set a target of reducing consistent poverty to 2 per cent by 2007.[23] The report indicated that:

- the proportion at risk of poverty fell during the economic boom from 19 per cent in 2004 to 16 per cent in 2007;
- the proportion of people living in consistent poverty also declined during the boom, from 7 per cent in 2004 to 5 per cent in 2007.

For 2009 the Central Statistics Office (CSO) recorded that consistent poverty was 5.5 per cent, up from 4.2 per cent in 2008.[24]

Both the ESRI and CSO reports noted that real increases in social welfare payments, especially improvements in the levels of state pensions, contributed significantly to the reduction in poverty.

The economic downturn and the consequent impact on the public finances, resulting in cuts to some social welfare payments and other social programmes, may mean that the targets set in 2007 will not be achieved by 2016. The ESRI has noted that Ireland faced a 'very challenging situation', with the most vulnerable groups likely to face 'a greater risk of consistent poverty and social exclusion'.[25] It singled out the long-term unemployed and those unable to work due to disability or illness as the groups most at risk of becoming caught in a deepening poverty trap.

The former NAPS unit in the Department of Social and Family Affairs was renamed the Office for Social Exclusion in 2002, and is now responsible for developing, coordinating and driving the National Action Plan against Poverty and Social Exclusion process.

NAPS was arguably the most significant social policy document ever published by government. Since its publication in 1997, high levels of economic growth in Ireland during the Celtic Tiger period have led to considerable success in tackling poverty and social exclusion. With the downturn in the economy since 2008 and the subsequent measures either introduced or planned to stabilise the national finances, prospects for further advancement in the near future appear to be far more limited.

Notes

1. P. Townsend, 'Poverty as relative deprivation: resources and style of living', in D. Wedderburn (ed.), *Poverty, Inequality and Class Structure* (Cambridge University Press, Cambridge, 1974), p. 15; see also P. Townsend, *Poverty in the United Kingdom: A Survey of Household Resources and Standards of Living* (Penguin Books, Harmondsworth, 1979), p. 31.
2. Government of Ireland, *Sharing in Progress: National Anti-Poverty Strategy* (Stationery Office, Dublin, 1997), p. 3.

3. Government of Ireland, *Partnership 2000 for Inclusion, Employment and Competitiveness* (Stationery Office, Dublin, 1996), p. 17.
4. Ibid.
5. A. Sinfield, 'We the people and they the poor, comparative view of poverty research', *Social Studies*, Vol. 4, No. 1 (1975), pp. 3–9.
6. S. O'Cinneide, 'The extent of poverty in Ireland', *Social Studies*, Vol. 1, No. 4 (1972), pp. 281–400.
7. All the conference papers were published in *Social Studies*, Vol. 1, No. 4 (1972). A second conference on poverty was held in Kilkenny in 1974 and the papers are published in *Social Studies*, Vol. 4, No. 1 (1975). A third conference was also organised by the Council for Social Welfare, and held in Kilkenny in 1981, and the papers were published in *Conference on Poverty, 1981* (Council for Social Welfare, Dublin, 1982).
8. See S. O'Cinneide, 'Poverty and policy: north and south', *Administration*, Vol. 33, No. 3 (1985), pp. 378–412.
9. Ibid., p. 393.
10. Combat Poverty Agency, *Strategic Plan* (Combat Poverty Agency, Dublin, 1987), p. 2.
11. For an assessment, by different authors, of the contribution made by the Combat Poverty Agency since its foundation, see J. O'Flynn (ed.), *Poverty, Policy and Practice: Combat Poverty 1986–2009* (Institute of Public Administration and Combat Poverty Agency, Dublin, 2009).
12. B. Duncan, 'Viewpoint: A message from the chairman', *Action On Poverty Today*, No. 23 (Spring 2009), p. 3.
13. H. Johnston, 'Old poverty; new poverty. Both need determination to tackle them', *Action On Poverty Today*, No. 24 (Summer 2009), p. 6.
14. For an assessment of Ireland's participation in the EU Anti-Poverty Programmes, see S. Langford, 'The impact of the European Union on Irish social policy development in relation to social exclusion', in G. Kiely et al., *Irish Social Policy in Context* (University College Dublin Press, Dublin, 1999).
15. Kiely et al., op. cit., p. 96.
16. Government of Ireland, *Sharing in Progress*, op. cit., Appendix 2, p. 33.
17. Ibid., p. 33.
18. Ibid., p. 9.
19. Department of Social, Community and Family Affairs, *Building an Inclusive Society: Review of the National Anti-Poverty Strategy under the Programme for Prosperity and Fairness* (Department of Social, Community and Family Affairs, Dublin, 2002), p. 8.
20. Department of Social and Family Affairs, *National Action Plan for Social Inclusion 2007–2016* (Stationery Office, Dublin, 2007), p. 13.
21. National Economic and Social Council, *Report No. 113, The Developmental Welfare State* (Stationery Office, Dublin, 2005), p. 226.
22. Department of Social and Family Affairs, *National Action Plan for Social Inclusion 2007–2016*, op. cit., p. 13.

23. H. Russell et al., *Monitoring Poverty Trends in Ireland 2004–2007: Key Issues for Children, People of Working Age and Older People, ESRI Research Series 17* (Economic and Social Research Institute, Dublin, 2010), p. 94.

24. Central Statistics Office, *Survey on Income and Living Conditions 2009* (Stationery Office, Dublin, 2010), p. 7.

25. Russell et al., op. cit., p. xix.

Appendix 1: Consistent poverty deprivation index

Persons are regarded as being in consistent poverty if (i) their income is below 60 per cent of median income and (ii) they experience deprivation in relation to the list of deprivation items.

Revised index
Persons lacking two or more items from this index are regarded as being in consistent poverty:

- two pairs of strong shoes;
- a warm waterproof overcoat;
- buy new not second-hand clothes;
- eat meals with meat, chicken, fish (or vegetarian equivalent) every second day;
- have a roast joint or its equivalent once a week;
- had to go without heating during the last year through lack of money;
- keep the home adequately warm;
- buy presents for family or friends at least once a year;
- replace any worn-out furniture;
- have family or friends for a drink or meal once a month;
- have a morning, afternoon or evening out in the last fortnight, for entertainment.

Former index
Persons lacking at least one item from this index were regarded as being in consistent poverty:

- two pairs of strong shoes;
- a warm waterproof overcoat;
- buy new not second-hand clothes;
- eat meals with meat, chicken, fish (or vegetarian equivalent) every second day;
- have a roast joint or its equivalent once a week;
- had to go without heating during the last year through lack of money;
- had a day in the last two weeks without a substantial meal due to lack of money;
- experienced debt problems arising from ordinary living expenses.

Source: Department of Social and Family Affairs, *National Action Plan for Social Inclusion 2007–2016* (Stationery Office, Dublin, 2007), Annex 3, p. 93.

9

Equality Issues

Introduction

Over the past few decades attention has been focused on equality issues. Initially, the focus was on equality of opportunity for women and the ending of all forms of discrimination against them. More recently, the equality agenda has broadened considerably to include other groups and other forms of discrimination. Increasingly, issues of equality and rights have become intertwined.

The first public acknowledgement that a problem existed was the setting up of the Commission on the Status of Women in 1970. The terms of reference were:

> To examine and report on the status of women in Irish society, to make recommendations on the steps necessary to ensure the participation of women on equal terms and conditions with men in the political, social, cultural and economic life of the country.[1]

The commission was established against a background of growing awareness of areas of discrimination against women, as highlighted by the burgeoning Irish Women's Liberation Movement, founded in 1970.[2] The commission's report was published in 1972.

In 1990 a second Commission on the Status of Women was established. Its terms of reference were similar to those of the first commission, and it was expected to review the implementation of the first commission's recommendations. It was also charged with paying special attention to the needs of women in the home. The second commission's report was published in 1993.

The growing political importance of women's issues in the 1980s was emphasised by the creation of a separate function in government, Women's Affairs, which was the responsibility of a minister of state under different governments between 1982 and 1993.

The focus in this chapter is on some of the main areas in which women were discriminated against, the progress made in these areas and the more recent measures to ensure equality in other areas.

First commission's report

The report of the Commission on the Status of Women contained forty-nine recommendations and seventeen suggestions designed to eliminate all forms of discrimination against women in such areas as employment, social welfare, education and the taxation system.

Employment

A number of key recommendations in the commission's report dealt with employment issues.

One of the most significant developments in this area was the introduction of equal pay under the Anti-Discrimination (Pay) Act, 1974. The EEC Directive on Equal Pay for Women and Men (1975) provided that all discrimination regarding pay for 'the same work' or 'work of equal value' in the member states was to be eliminated. In anticipation of this directive, the Anti-Discrimination (Pay) Act, 1974, was introduced in Ireland. The act provided for the full implementation of equal pay by the beginning of 1976. Because of the deteriorating economic situation in Ireland, some employers sought to defer implementation and the government indicated that it would seek derogation from the European Commission. This was refused and the 1974 act came into force on 1 January 1976.[3]

Another development was the Employment Equality Act, 1977, which made it unlawful to discriminate on grounds of sex or marriage in recruitment for employment, conditions of employment, training or work experience, promotion or the classification of jobs. The Employment Equality Act also provided for the setting up of an Employment Equality Agency (EEA). The functions of the EEA, which came into operation in October 1977, were to work towards the elimination of discrimination in employment, to promote equality of opportunity in employment between men and women, and to keep under review the working of the Anti-Discrimination (Pay) Act and the Employment Equality Act.

The annual reports of the EEA contain interesting information on equality of opportunity, or the lack of it, in employment. In the first few reports the EEA referred to the large number of discriminatory advertisements by employers. The EEA carried out formal investigations in certain cases; for example, in the national public transport company

Córas Iompar Éireann (CIÉ), which eventually led to the employment of women as bus conductors.

Social welfare

The first commission's report contained sixteen recommendations relating to social welfare entitlements and payments. The majority of these, including the introduction of schemes of social assistance for wives of prisoners and unmarried mothers, were implemented. The remaining forms of discrimination were largely removed with the implementation of the EC (EU) directive on equal treatment of men and women in relation to matters of social security in 1986. Up to then, married women received less employment benefit and for a shorter period than men did. In general, the other social welfare recommendations were implemented fairly quickly, but this one, which related to one of the most obvious forms of discrimination, had to await an EC (EU) directive. Ironically, member states of the EC were given six years to implement this, i.e. by the end of 1984, but Ireland did not begin to comply until 1986.

Women and the law

A number of recommendations were made to safeguard the rights of women in relation to family and property. Thus, for example, the Family Law (Maintenance of Spouses and Children) Act, 1976, placed a joint obligation on both spouses to support the family. In addition, the Family Home Protection Act, 1976, prevented the sale of the family home by one spouse without the consent of the other spouse.

The commission, in its report, recommended that women should be qualified and liable for jury service on the same terms as men. It also endorsed the recommendation of the Committee on Court Practice and Procedure that the property qualification for jurors should be abolished and that inclusion in the electoral register should be the only qualification test for jury service.

Under the Juries Act, 1975, which came into operation in 1976, all citizens, with a few special exceptions, are now eligible for jury service without discrimination based on sex or property qualifications.

The taxation code

Up to 1980, married couples, when both were working, were effectively discriminated against, as compared with two single persons, under the income taxation code. In practice, married couples paid more tax because the couple's earnings were lumped together, treated as one income and thereby liable to the highest rate of tax.

As a result of the Supreme Court judgment in the Murphy case of 1979, sections of the Income Tax Act dealing with the taxation of married couples were deemed to be unconstitutional. From the tax year 1980/1, married couples were treated on the same basis as two single persons. This was one area where discrimination was only grudgingly removed, mainly because of the cost implications to the exchequer.

Health

There were few recommendations on health services made by the commission. One of them, relating to family planning, would subsequently arouse considerable debate and controversy, though this was not due solely to the commission's recommendation; it merely reflected a growing demand for the legalising of the sale of contraceptives. The commission recommended that:

> information and expert advice on family planning should be available through medical and other appropriate channels to families throughout the country. Such advice should respect the moral and personal attitudes of each married couple, and medical requirements [contraceptives], arising out of the married couple's decision on family planning, should be available under control and through channels to be determined by the Department of Health.[4]

Following considerable controversy, the Health (Family Planning) Act, 1979, came into effect in 1980. This act was restrictive in relation to the channels through which contraceptives were made available, e.g. all contraceptive devices could only be made available on a doctor's prescription. The act was amended, against much opposition, in 1985 to make contraceptives more freely available. It was also amended in 1992, without any opposition, to liberalise the law even further.

Education

As in health, there were few recommendations made by the commission in relation to education. It had recommended that co-education should be introduced wherever possible at primary level. It also recommended that the joint training of male and female teachers should be introduced where possible. Subsequently, the teacher training colleges, hitherto confined to single sexes, became co-educational. Ironically, the vast majority of entrants to teacher-training colleges in subsequent years were female.

Implementation overview

In general, considerable progress was made within a decade in implementing recommendations made in the first report of the

Commission on the Status of Women, and overt forms of discrimination were largely eliminated. By comparison with other commission reports, the Commission on the Status of Women achieved considerable success in terms of recommendations implemented. This was due to a number of key factors, including the roles of the women's movement and a monitoring committee.

The Council for the Status of Women was established in 1973 to campaign for implementation of the recommendations, and it played a key role in maintaining pressure on governments. The council, later renamed the National Women's Council of Ireland, is the representative body for over 150 women's organisations, and its principal function is to promote equality for women.

The Women's Representative Committee, established by the Minister for Labour to monitor progress on implementation of the recommendations, published two progress reports, and its existence was undoubtedly influential in ensuring progress. This was the first time that a monitoring group had been established to oversee progress on the implementation of recommendations of a major policy report. In effect, the committee held the relevant government departments to account for each of the main recommendations. Its published reports, recounting progress or lack of it on each recommendation, together with commentary, proved a vital impetus and stimulus to publicly tracking implementation. Its second and final report was published in 1978.[5]

Some of the recommendations of the commission did not so much involve additional public expenditure as changes in practices. Ireland's entry into the EEC, with its emphasis on equality for women, was an additional factor in the implementation of recommendations.

Second commission's report

The *Second Report of the Commission on the Status of Women*, published in 1993, contained 210 recommendations. The following were five of the key recommendations:

- Article 41.2.2 of the Constitution (stipulating that the state should ensure that mothers are not obliged through economic necessity to work outside the home to the neglect of their duties in the home) should be deleted;
- the introduction of an Equal Status Act;
- a second referendum on divorce;
- a comprehensive childcare service without which there can be no equality of opportunity in the workplace;

- quota systems and reserved seats should be introduced by the political parties to secure a minimum 40 per cent representation of any one sex.

In a reservation to the report, three of the nineteen members of the commission believed the report was unbalanced in favour of helping and validating the woman who is in the paid workforce.

Progress in relation to the five key recommendations has been somewhat mixed.

In relation to Article 41.2.2 of the Constitution, the All-Party Oireachtas Committee on the Constitution recommended that this article and its subsections be recast to include various elements reflecting current thinking and practice in relation to the family. It recommended that Article 41.2.2 be revised in gender-neutral form, which might provide that:

> The State recognises that home and family life give society a support without which the common good cannot be achieved. The State shall endeavour to support persons caring for others within the home.[6]

There has not been a referendum on this issue.

In 1986 a referendum was carried out to amend the Constitution in order to provide for divorce in certain circumstances. The measure was defeated by 63.5 per cent to 36.5 per cent. A further referendum was held almost ten years later, in 1995. On this occasion the measure was passed narrowly by the electorate, with 50.28 per cent for and 49.72 per cent against. The ensuing legislation, the Family Law (Divorce) Act, 1996, provided for divorce where a couple had effectively been separated for five years or more. On the eve of the passing of this legislation *The Irish Times* commented:

> The Dáil moved a step closer to the creation of a pluralist, tolerant and caring society yesterday when it approved the final stages of the Family Law (Divorce) Bill, 1996. After 16 years of political agitation by pro-divorce groups, a succession of court actions and two ill-natured referendums spread over 9 years, one of the most divisive social issues was quietly and firmly determined.[7]

The increase in participation by women in the workforce stimulated by growth in the economy in the late 1990s led to a demand for affordable childcare for working parents. The *Report of the Partnership 2000 Expert Working Group on Childcare* (1999) recommended tax allowances for parents and tax breaks for employers. However, the government, in 1999 and

2000, sought instead to support an increase in the supply of child care places. This mainly took the form of capital grants for the provision of places. Some groups continued to press for direct financial support to families to enable them to meet the costs of childcare. This was acceded to in a limited way by substantial increases in the monthly child benefit in 2001 and 2002, a proposal that the expert working group had ruled out on grounds of cost.

The recommendation to introduce a gender quota system has not met with any success. The issue was raised on occasions in the years following publication of the second commission's report, but it did not appear to command support from the main political parties. Women account for half of the population, yet the proportion of women elected to the Dáil did not exceed 14 per cent until 2011. In the 2007 general election women constituted less than 20 per cent of candidates overall; 22 out of 166 TDs (13.3 per cent) elected were women and 3 of them were subsequently appointed to the cabinet. The results of the 2011 general election showed an improvement, with 25 women elected (15.1 per cent) and 2 being appointed to the cabinet.

A report for the Oireachtas Committee on Justice, Equality, Defence and Women's Rights established that Ireland's record on women's political representation at local, national and European level was very poor and was getting worse.[8] The report noted the following:

- In 1990 Ireland was in thirty-seventh position in the world classification of women's representation in the lower or single house of national parliaments, and by 2009 Ireland had fallen to eighty-fourth position.
- At local level, women's representation on councils has been consistently low over many decades, reaching only 16 per cent of councillors elected in 2009.

The report recommended the introduction of temporary legislation to require political parties to adopt quotas or gender targets in their candidate-selection process. This did not meet with any great enthusiasm from the political parties.

Revised equality legislation

While the focus in the 1970s and 1980s was on forms of discrimination against women, the demand for measures to deal with discrimination in other areas increased during the 1990s. The *Fianna Fáil/Labour Coalition Programme for Government* of 1992 contained a commitment to eliminate inequality for all groups in society that experienced discrimination.

Following considerable debate, two important pieces of legislation were introduced that not only replaced existing legislation but also broadened the focus of discrimination. These were the Employment Equality Act, 1998, and the Equal Status Act, 2000.

An Employment Equality Bill was published in 1996 but, prior to being passed into law, was referred by the President, Mary Robinson, to the Supreme Court in 1997 to decide whether the bill or any of its provisions were repugnant to the Constitution. A number of sections in the bill had given rise to concerns, especially a section that would allow schools to appoint only teachers who conformed to the religious ethos of the school. In the event, the Supreme Court ruled that sections of the bill were repugnant to the Constitution. Interestingly, the principal section which concerned the Supreme Court was that relating to the employment of persons with disabilities rather than, as widely expected, the section dealing with the employment of teachers; the court ruled that the employment of a person with a disability could impose an unreasonable cost burden on an employer.[9] A revised Employment Equality Bill was passed in 1998. The Employment Equality Act, 1998, effectively repealed and replaced the Anti-Discrimination (Pay) Act, 1974, and the Employment Equality Act, 1977.

The Employment Equality Act outlaws direct and indirect discrimination at work and in employment conditions on nine distinct grounds:

i.   gender;
ii.   marital status;
iii. family status;
iv.   age;
v.   disability;
vi.   race;
vii. sexual orientation;
viii. religious belief;
ix.   membership of the Travelling community.

The act provides for a number of exceptions to the principle of equal treatment. For example, an employer is not prevented from discriminating on age or disability grounds where there is clear actuarial and other evidence of significantly increased costs for the employer. Similarly, there is an exemption for religious, educational and medical institutions run by religious bodies where the discrimination is essential for the maintenance of the religious ethos of the institution.

The Equal Status Bill of 1997 was also held to be unconstitutional for broadly similar reasons as to those relating to the Employment Equality Bill. A revised Equal Status Bill was passed in 2000. The Equal Status Act, 2000, deals with discrimination in areas other than employment and covers advertising, collective agreements, the provision of goods and services, education, property and other opportunities to which the public have access. Discrimination is also outlawed on the same nine distinct grounds as those covered by the Employment Equality Act.

Discrimination in the Employment Equality Act and the Equal Status Act is defined as the treatment of one person in a less favourable way than another person is, has been or would be treated on any of the nine grounds. The legislation also prohibits sexual harassment and/or harassment.

Both the Employment Equality Act and the Equal Status Act were subsequently amended in 2004 and are now known as the Employment Equality Acts, 1998 and 2004, and the Equal Status Acts, 2000 to 2004.

Equality agencies

Two important statutory bodies were established under the equality legislation: the Equality Authority and the Equality Tribunal. The Irish Human Rights Commission (IHRC) also has an important function in the promotion of equality issues.

The Equality Authority

The Equality Authority (which subsumes the work of the former EEA) was established in 1999, and its mandate is to combat discrimination and to promote equality of opportunity in the areas covered by the legislation.

The second annual report of the Equality Authority, for 2001, and the first to cover a full calendar year, recorded 300 cases under the Employment Equality Act and 661 under the Equal Status Act, with the largest groups of cases concerning gender (34.6 per cent) and the Traveller community (72.5 per cent), respectively. The report noted that in relation to cases under the Equal Status Act:

> The overwhelming volume of cases arising was unexpected and unprecedented particularly in the area of refusal of service by publicans to members of the Traveller community.[10]

The annual report of the Equality Authority for 2009 indicated that there were over 8,000 enquiries from the public concerning equality legislation. Apart from general information queries, the key grounds of discrimination covered by the enquiries under the Employment Equality Acts were age, disability and gender, while those under the Equal Status Acts were disability, age and race.[11]

Since its establishment, the authority has played a valuable role in raising issues of equality and discrimination in Irish society. As part of its function of bringing about positive change by eliminating discrimination, the Equality Authority published an equality strategy for older people in 2002. It noted that the work of the authority had 'highlighted a widespread ageism in Irish society in particular experienced by older people. Strong negative stereotypes of older people persist'.[12]

The Equality Tribunal

The Equality Tribunal was established in 1999 as an independent statutory body to decide or mediate on claims of unlawful discrimination. It deals with cases arising under the equality legislation, and its decisions and mediated agreements are legally binding. The work of the tribunal has increased considerably since its establishment. In 2000 it dealt with about 100 claims, virtually all of them concerned with gender and work; in 2009 there were almost 1,000 claims, 'touching every corner of daily life' and covering all of the nine grounds set out in the legislation.[13]

The Irish Human Rights Commission

Another important agency which deals, inter alia, with equality issues is the IHRC. This was established in 2000 in line with the Good Friday Agreement (sometimes referred to as the Belfast Agreement) of 1998, which established the Northern Ireland Assembly with devolved legislative powers. The role of the IHRC is to promote and protect human rights in the Republic of Ireland. The human rights that the IHRC is mandated to promote and protect are the rights, liberties and freedoms guaranteed under the Irish Constitution and under international agreements, treaties and conventions to which Ireland is a party. Its functions include reviewing proposed legislation, making recommendations to government and promoting awareness of human rights. The Good Friday Agreement also provided for the establishment of a similar type of body in Northern Ireland.

Since its establishment, the IHRC has played a prominent role in highlighting awareness of human rights issues. As part of its work, the IHRC reports periodically to the United Nations on Ireland's record on racial discrimination. Ireland is a signatory to the UN Convention on the Elimination of all Forms of Racial Discrimination. In its detailed report submitted in 2010 the IHRC recommended, inter alia, that the Irish Government should improve its protection of asylum seekers, Travellers, migrant workers and their families, and victims of human trafficking.[14]

Other landmark equality measures

Apart from the legislative and other measures that stemmed from the equality agenda established by the reports of the two commissions on the status of women, and the changes under the more recent equality legislation, there have been a number of other highly significant developments over the past few decades. These include, in the context of Irish society, what might be termed landmark legislative provision on issues related to illegitimacy, homosexuality and civil partnership.

The Status of Children Act, 1987
The concept of illegitimacy and the associated overt forms of discrimination against illegitimate children, especially in relation to succession rights, had given rise to some debate from the 1970s, with social reformers arguing for change. A report by the Law Reform Commission in 1982 indicated that illegitimacy was 'a negative concept' and recommended that legislation 'should remove the concept of illegitimacy from the law and equalise the rights of children born outside marriage with those of children born within marriage'.[15] The Status of Children Act, 1987, provides that the marital status of a child's parents is to have no effect on the child's relationship to its mother and father. The act allows the father of a child born outside of marriage to become the child's guardian and gives children born outside of marriage the same maintenance, succession and other property rights as children born inside marriage.

The Criminal Law (Sexual Offences) Act, 1993
In effect, the Criminal Law (Sexual Offences) Act, 1993, decriminalised homosexual acts. While homosexuality per se was not illegal prior to 1993, some nineteenth century laws rendered homosexual acts illegal. The legislation was the outcome of a campaign for reform that commenced in the early 1970s, and in which Senator David Norris of Trinity College played a prominent role. He was unsuccessful in a case taken to the Supreme Court in 1983 but successful in a case taken to the European Court of Human Rights in 1988. The court ruled that criminalisation of homosexuality in Ireland violated Article 8 of the

European Convention on Human Rights, which guarantees the right to privacy in personal affairs.

The Civil Partnership Act, 2010

An issue that had been a matter of increasing concern in recent years involved the legal rights of gay and lesbian couples, as well as cohabiting couples, by comparison with married couples. Following a period of campaign for change, the Civil Partnership and Certain Rights and Obligations of Cohabitants Act, 2010, provided rights not alone for gay and lesbian couples but also for couples in long-term, cohabiting relationships who have not entered into a civil partnership or marriage. Under the act, gay and lesbian couples benefit from the same rights as married couples in the areas of property, social welfare, succession, maintenance, pensions and tax. In an unusual display of solidarity, the legislation was supported by all the political parties and was passed without a vote in Dáil Éireann, where the Minister for Justice and Law Reform, Dermot Ahern, TD, referred to it as 'one of the most important items of civil rights legislation that has come before the house in some time'.[16]

Equality in a changing environment

Equality issues have broadened considerably from the focus on gender and marital status of the 1970s.

Among the factors that gave added impetus to the broadening of the equality agenda during the 1990s was the changing nature of the Irish population, which began to reflect far greater diversity than ever before. Irish society began to change from a relatively homogeneous culture to a multiracial and multicultural society. With significant improvement in the economy from the mid 1990s onwards, labour shortages emerged that necessitated the active recruitment of foreign nationals. During the period of the Celtic Tiger, annual net immigration increased, reaching a peak of almost 72,000 in 2006. In addition, the number of applications from asylum seekers/refugees increased dramatically from the early 1990s – from 39 in 1992 to a peak of 11,634 in 2002; the numbers declined in the following years and fell to 2,689 by 2009.[17] Not all applications for refugee status were granted. The net inflow of foreign nationals made an impact in cities and towns throughout the country. The increasing diversity of the population was highlighted by the 2006 census, which indicated that 420,000 persons, or almost 10 per cent of the total population, were non-Irish nationals representing 188 countries. These developments gave rise to a more culturally diverse population, and meant that different cultural norms and traditions have had to be accommodated.

Apart from the legislation to underpin equality, there was also a perceptible change in terminology and labelling to reflect a more inclusive, less stigmatising society. Examples include 'intellectual disability' (rather than 'mental handicap') and 'older persons' (rather than 'the aged' or 'the elderly').

As if to emphasise the evolving nature of the equality agenda, a report of the NESF in 2002 recommended, among other things, that the existing nine grounds on which discrimination is outlawed should be extended to cover socio-economic status, trade union membership, criminal conviction and political opinion.[18]

As part of the government's decentralisation programme, announced in Budget 2004, key sections of the Equality Authority were to be transferred to Roscrea, County Tipperary. In Budget 2008 the Minister for Finance, Brian Cowen, TD, announced an efficiency review in which each department and the state bodies under its aegis would be required to examine all administrative spending, with a special emphasis on possible inefficiencies due to the multiplicity of boards and agencies. During 2008, proposals to merge a number of the forty bodies under the aegis of the Department of Justice, Equality and Law Reform into a single agency were considered, involving specifically the Equality Authority, the Equality Tribunal, the National Disability Authority, the IHRC and the Office of the Data Protection Commissioner. While these proposals were not proceeded with, uncertainty as to the future and independence of the equality and rights agencies had been raised. In Budget 2009 the Minister for Finance, Brian Lenihan, TD, announced proposals to reduce the number of state-sponsored bodies by forty-one and to streamline other functions. Plans for the Equality Authority and the IHRC to integrate their administrative services formed part of this process.

Budget 2009 also provided for reductions in the budgets of government departments and their associated state bodies. The proposed reduction in the budget of the Equality Authority was 43 per cent, very high by comparison with other associated agencies of the Department of Justice, Equality and Law Reform; the proposed reduction for the IHRC was 24 per cent, with a 2 per cent reduction proposed for the National Disability Authority and 1 per cent reduction for the Legal Aid Board.

It was in this context that Niall Crowley, Chief Executive Officer of the Equality Authority, tendered his resignation in December 2008. In his view, the organisation had been made unviable by the extent of the cuts to its budget and also by the government's insistence on the decentralisation of the remaining staff to Roscrea. His resignation was followed by that of six members of the board of the authority. He subsequently wrote an informative history of the authority, detailing the events that led to his resignation and what he refers to as 'the neutering of the Equality Authority'.[19]

Concern over government proposals for restructuring equality and rights agencies that could affect their independence and work led to the formation of the Equality and Rights Alliance in 2008. It is a coalition of over 140 civil society groups and activists (voluntary organisations, trade unions, academics and individual activists) working together to protect and strengthen the statutory equality and human rights infrastructure.

Notes

1. Commission on the Status of Women, *Report to the Minister for Finance* (Stationery Office, Dublin, 1972), p. 7.

2. For background, see Office of the Minister of State for Women's Affairs, *Irishwomen Into Focus* (Department of the Taoiseach, Dublin, 1987), pp. 4–13; A. Stopper, *Monday at Gaj's: The Story of the Irish Women's Liberation Movement* (The Liffey Press, Dublin, 2006); N. Fennell, *Political Woman: A Memoir* (Currach Press, Dublin, 2009).

3. See B. Laffan and L. O'Mahony, *Ireland and the European Union* (Palgrave Macmillan, Basingstoke, 2008), pp. 39–40.

4. Commission on the Status of Women, op. cit., p. 225.

5. Women's Representative Committee, *Final Report of the Women's Representative Committee* (Stationery Office, Dublin, 1978).

6. The All-Party Oireachtas Committee on the Constitution, *The Constitution Review Group: Recommendations/Conclusions* (Stationery Office, Dublin, 1996), pp. 74–5.

7. 'Introducing divorce', *The Irish Times*, 26 September 1996.

8. Joint Committee on Justice, Equality, Defence and Women's Rights, *Second Report, Women's Participation in Politics* (Houses of the Oireachtas, Dublin, 2009).

9. *Irish Law Times*, Vol. 15, No. 6 (June 1997).

10. The Equality Authority, *Annual Report 2001* (The Equality Authority, Dublin, 2002), p. 40.

11. The Equality Authority, *Annual Report 2009* (The Equality Authority, Dublin, 2010), pp. 13–14.

12. The Equality Authority, *Implementing Equality for Older People* (The Equality Authority, Dublin, 2002).

13. The Equality Tribunal, *Annual Report 2009* (The Equality Tribunal, Dublin, 2010), p. 4.

14. Irish Human Rights Commission, *Submission to the UN CERD Committee on the Examination of Ireland's Combined Third and Fourth Periodic Reports* (Irish Human Rights Commission, Dublin, 2010).

15. The Law Reform Commission, *Report on Illegitimacy* (The Law Reform Commission, Dublin, 1982), p. 87.

16. Dáil Éireann, 'Civil Partnership Bill 2010: Fifth Stage', 1 July 2010, *Dáil Debates*, Vol. 714, No. 2.

17. Office of the Refugee Applications Commissioner, *Annual Report 2009* (Office of the Refugee Applications Commissioner, Dublin, 2010), p. 56.

18. National Economic and Social Forum, *Report No. 23, A Strategic Policy Framework for Equality Issues* (Stationery Office, Dublin, 2002).

19. N. Crowley, *Empty Promises: Bringing the Equality Authority to Heel* (A&A Farmer, Dublin, 2010), p. ix.

Select Bibliography

General

Burke, H., *The People Under the Poor Law in 19th Century Ireland* (The Women's Education Bureau, Dublin, 1987).

Considine, M. and F. Dukelow, *Irish Social Policy: A Critical Introduction* (Gill & Macmillan, Dublin, 2009).

Department of the Taoiseach, *Towards 2016: Ten-Year Framework Social Partnership Agreement 2006–2015* (Stationery Office, Dublin, 2006).

Fahey, T. and C.A. Field, *Families in Ireland: An Analysis of Patterns and Trends* (Department of Social and Family Affairs, Dublin, 2008).

Fahey, T. and J. Fitzgerald, *Social Welfare Implications of Demographic Trends* (Combat Poverty Agency, Dublin, 1997).

Government of Ireland, *Report of the Special Group on Public Service Numbers and Expenditure Programmes* (Stationery Office, Dublin, 2009).

Government of Ireland, *The National Recovery Plan 2011–2014* (Stationery Office, Dublin, 2010).

Healy, S., B. Reynolds and M. Collins, *Social Policy in Ireland; Principles, Practice and Problems*, 2nd edn (The Liffey Press, Dublin, 2006).

Kaim-Caudle, P., *Social Policy in the Irish Republic* (Routledge & Kegan Paul, London, 1967).

Kearney, C.P., *Selectivity Issues in Irish Social Services* (Family Study Centre, University College Dublin, Dublin, 1991).

Kennedy, F., *Public Social Expenditure in Ireland* (Economic and Social Research Institute, Dublin, 1975).

Kennedy, F., *Cottage to Creche, Family Change in Ireland* (Institute of Public Administration, Dublin, 2001).

Kiely, G., A. O'Donnell, P. Kennedy and S. Quin, *Irish Social Policy in Context* (University College Dublin Press, Dublin, 1999).

National Economic and Social Council, *Report No. 8, An Approach to Social Policy* (Stationery Office, Dublin, 1975).

National Economic and Social Council, *Report No. 61, Irish Social Policies: Priorities for Future Development* (Stationery Office, Dublin, 1981).

National Economic and Social Council, *Report No. 113, The Developmental Welfare State* (Stationery Office, Dublin, 2005).

Quin. S., P. Kennedy, A. O'Donnell and G. Kiely, *Contemporary Irish Social Policy*, 2nd edn (University College Dublin Press, Dublin, 2005).

Whyte, J.H., *Church and State in Modern Ireland* (Gill & Macmillan, Dublin, 1971).

Income maintenance

Callan, T., B. Nolan and B. Whelan, *Poverty, Income and Welfare in Ireland* (Economic and Social Research Institute, Dublin, 1989).

Callan, T., B. Nolan and C. Whelan, *A Review of the Commission on Social Welfare's Minimum Adequate Income* (Economic and Social Research Institute, Dublin, 1996).

Carey, S., *Social Security in Ireland 1939–1952: The Limits to Solidarity* (Irish Academic Press, Dublin, 2007).

Clark, C.M.A. and J. Healy, *Pathways to a Basic Income* (Justice Commission, Conference of Religious in Ireland, Dublin, 1997).

Commission on Social Welfare, *Report of the Commission on Social Welfare* (Stationery Office, Dublin, 1986).

Cousins, M., *The Birth of Social Welfare in Ireland, 1922–1952* (Four Courts Press, Dublin, 2003).

Department of the Taoiseach, *Basic Income: A Green Paper* (Stationery Office, Dublin, 2002).

Expert Working Group on the Integration of the Tax and Social Welfare Systems, *Report of the Expert Working Group on the Integration of the Tax and Social Welfare Systems* (Stationery Office, Dublin, 1996).

Farley, D., *Social Insurance and Social Assistance in Ireland* (Institute of Public Administration, Dublin, 1964).

Government of Ireland, *Final Report of the Social Welfare Benchmarking and Indexation Group* (Stationery Office, Dublin, 2001).

McCashin, A., *Social Security in Ireland* (Gill & Macmillan, Dublin, 2004).

O'Cinneide, S., *A Law for the Poor* (Institute of Public Administration, Dublin, 1970).

Review Group on the Treatment of Households in the Social Welfare Code, *Report of the Review Group on the Treatment of Households in the Social Welfare Code* (Stationery Office, Dublin, 1991).

Reynolds, B. and S.J. Healy (eds), *Poverty and Family Income Policy* (Conference of Major Religious Superiors, Dublin, 1988).

Housing

Baker, T.J. and L.M. O'Brien, *The Irish Housing System: A Critical Overview* (Economic and Social Research Institute, Dublin, 1979).

Blackwell, J. (ed.), *Towards an Efficient and Equitable Housing Policy* (Institute of Public Administration, Dublin, 1989).

Blackwell, J. and S. Kennedy (eds), *Focus on Homelessness* (Columba Press, Dublin, 1988).

Commission on the Private Rented Residential Sector, *Report of the Commission on the Private Rented Residential Sector* (Stationery Office, Dublin, 2000).

Department of the Environment and Local Government, *Homelessness – An Integrated Strategy* (Department of the Environment and Local Government, Dublin, 2000).

Department of the Environment, Heritage and Local Government, *A Plan for Social Housing* (Department of the Environment, Heritage and Local Government, Dublin, 1991).

Department of the Environment, Heritage and Local Government, *Social Housing – The Way Ahead* (Department of the Environment, Heritage and Local Government, Dublin, 1995).

Department of the Environment, Heritage and Local Government, *The Way Home: A Strategy to Address Adult Homelessness in Ireland 2008–2013* (Department of the Environment, Heritage and Local Government, Dublin, 2008).

Department of the Environment, Heritage and Local Government, *Homeless Strategy: National Implementation Plan* (Department of the Environment, Heritage and Local Government, Dublin, 2009).

Fahey, T., 'Social housing in Ireland: The need for an expanded role?', *Irish Banking Review*, Autumn (1999).

Fahey, T., 'Housing and local government', in Daly, M.E. (ed.), *County and Town: One Hundred Years of Local Government in Ireland* (Institute of Public Administration, Dublin, 2001).

Government of Ireland, *Homeless Preventative Strategy: A Strategy to Prevent Homelessness Among: Patients Leaving Hospital and Mental Health Care, Adult Prisoners and Young Offenders Leaving Custody, Young People Leaving Care* (Stationery Office, Dublin, 2002).

Government of Ireland, *Review of the Implementation of the Government's Integrated and Preventative Homeless Strategies* (Stationery Office, Dublin, 2006).

Homeless Agency, *Shaping the Future: An Action Plan on Homelessness in Dublin 2001–2003* (Homeless Agency, Dublin, 2001).

Homeless Agency, *A Key to the Door: The Homeless Agency Partnership Action Plan on Homelessness in Dublin 2007–2010* (Homeless Agency, Dublin, 2007).

National Economic and Social Council, *Report No. 23, Report on Housing Subsidies* (Stationery Office, Dublin, 1977).

National Economic and Social Council, *Report No. 87, A Review of Housing Policy* (Stationery Office, Dublin, 1989).

National Economic and Social Council, *Report No. 112, Housing in Ireland: Performance and Policy* (Stationery Office, Dublin, 2004).

National Economic and Social Forum, *Report No. 18, Social and Affordable Housing and Accommodation: Building the Future* (Stationery Office, Dublin, 2000).

Norris, M. and D. Redmond (eds), *Housing Contemporary Ireland: Housing, Society and Shelter* (Institute of Public Administration, Dublin, 2005).

O'Brien, L. and B. Dillon, *Private Rented: The Forgotten Sector* (Threshold, Dublin, 1982).

Education

Action Group on Access to Third Level Education, *Report of the Action Group on Access to Third Level Education* (Stationery Office, Dublin, 2001).

Bassett, M., B. Brady, T. Fleming and T. Englis, *For Adults Only: A Case for Adult Education in Ireland* (Aontas, Dublin, 1989).

Clancy, P., *College Entry in Focus: A Fourth National Survey of Access to Higher Education* (Higher Education Authority, Dublin, 2001).

Commission on Adult Education, *Lifelong Learning: Report of the Commission on Adult Education* (Stationery Office, Dublin, 1984).

Commission on Higher Education, *Commission on Higher Education, 1960–67* (Stationery Office, Dublin, 1967).

Conference of Religious of Ireland, *Religious Congregations in Irish Education – A Role for the Future?* (Education Commission, Conference of Religious of Ireland, Dublin, 1997).

Coolahan, J., *Irish Education: History and Structure* (Institute of Public Administration, Dublin, 1981).

Coolahan, J. (ed.), *Report on the National Education Convention* (Stationery Office, Dublin, 1994).

Department of Education and Science, *Delivering Equality of Opportunity in Schools: An Action Plan for Educational Inclusion* (Department of Education and Science, Dublin, 2005).

Department of Education and Skills, *National Strategy for Higher Education to 2030* (Stationery Office, Dublin, 2011).

Educational Disadvantage Committee, *Moving Beyond Educational Disadvantage, Report of the Educational Disadvantage Committee 2002–2005* (Department of Education and Science, Dublin, 2005).

Government of Ireland, *Programme for Action in Education 1984–1987* (Stationery Office, Dublin, 1984).

Government of Ireland, *Green Paper: Partners in Education* (Stationery Office, Dublin, 1985).

Government of Ireland, *Green Paper on Education: Education for a Changing World* (Stationery Office, Dublin, 1992).

Government of Ireland, *White Paper on Education: Charting our Education Future* (Stationery Office, Dublin, 1995).

Government of Ireland, *Learning for Life, White Paper on Adult Education* (Stationery Office, Dublin, 2000).

Government of Ireland/OECD, *Investment in Education* (Stationery Office, Dublin, 1965).

Higher Education Authority (National Access Office), *Achieving Equity of Access to Higher Education, Action Plan 2005–2007* (Higher Education Authority, Dublin, 2004).

Higher Education Authority (National Access Office), *National Plan for Equity of Access to Higher Education 2008–2013* (Higher Education Authority, Dublin, 2008).

Irish Catholic Bishops' Conference, *Catholic Primary Schools: A Policy for Provision into the Future* (Veritas, Dublin, 2007).

Mulcahy, D. and D. O'Sullivan (eds), *Irish Educational Policy: Process and Substance* (Institute of Public Administration, Dublin, 1977).

O'Connor, S., *A Troubled Sky: Reflections on the Irish Educational Scene, 1957–1968* (Education Research Centre, St. Patrick's College, Dublin, 1986).

Primary Education Review Body, *Report of the Primary Education Review Body* (Stationery Office, Dublin, 1990).

Tussing, A.D., *Irish Educational Expenditure: Past, Present and Future* (Economic and Social Research Institute, Dublin, 1978).

Walsh, J., *A New Partnership in Education: From Consultation to Legislation in the Nineties* (Institute of Public Administration, Dublin, 1999).

Walsh, J., *The Politics of Expansion: The Transformation of Educational Policy in the Republic of Ireland 1957–72* (Manchester University Press, Manchester, 2009).

White, T., *Investing in People: Higher Education in Ireland from 1960 to 2000* (Institute of Public Administration, Dublin, 2001).

Health services

Barrington, R., *Health, Medicine and Politics in Ireland, 1900–1970* (Institute of Public Administration, Dublin, 1987).

Burke, S., *Irish Apartheid: Healthcare Inequality in Ireland* (New Island, Dublin, 2009).

Consultative Council on the General Hospital Service, *Outline of the Future Hospital System, Report of the Consultative Council on the General Hospital Service* (Stationery Office, Dublin, 1968).

Department of Health, *Health: The Wider Dimensions* (Department of Health, Dublin, 1986).

Department of Health, *Green Paper on Mental Health* (Stationery Office, Dublin, 1992).

Department of Health, *Shaping a Healthier Future* (Stationery Office, Dublin, 1994).

Department of Health and Children, *Health Strategy: Quality and Fairness, A Health System for You* (Department of Health and Children, Dublin, 2001).

Department of Health and Children, *Primary Care: A New Direction* (Stationery Office, Dublin, 2001).

Department of Health and Children, *Audit of Structures and Functions in the Health System* (Stationery Office, Dublin, 2003).

Department of Health and Children, *The Health Service Reform Programme* (Department of Health and Children, Dublin, 2003).

Department of Health and Children, *Report of the Expert Group on Resource Allocation and Financing in the Health Sector* (Department of Health and Children, Dublin, 2010).

Expert Group on Mental Health Policy, *A Vision for Change: Report of the Expert Group on Mental Health Policy* (Stationery Office, Dublin, 2006).

Fealy, G.M. (ed.), *Care to Remember: Nursing and Midwifery in Ireland* (Mercier Press, Cork, 2005).

Fine Gael, *FairCare: Fine Gael Proposals to Reform the Health Service and Introduce Universal Health Insurance* (Fine Gael, Dublin, 2009).

Government of Ireland, *The Health Services and Their Further Development* (Stationery Office, Dublin, 1966).

Government of Ireland, *The Psychiatric Service: Planning for the Future* (Stationery Office, Dublin, 1984).

Government of Ireland, *Report of the Commission on Health Funding* (Stationery Office, Dublin, 1989).

Government of Ireland, *Report of the Commission on Financial Management and Control Systems in the Health Service* (Stationery Office, Dublin, 2003).

Health Service Executive, *Health Status of the Population of Ireland 2008* (Health Service Executive, Dublin, 2009).

Hensey, B., *The Health Services of Ireland*, 4th edn (Institute of Public Administration, Dublin, 1988).

Labour Party, *Curing Our Ills: Irish Healthcare 2000 Delivering Excellence for All. Labour Party Proposals for Hospital and GP Care in a New Century* (Labour Party, Dublin, 2000).

McAuliffe, E. and L. Joyce, *A Healthier Future? Managing Healthcare in Ireland* (Institute of Public Administration, Dublin, 1998).

McCluskey, D. (ed.), *Health Policy and Practice in Ireland* (University College Dublin Press, Dublin, 2006).

National Economic and Social Council, *Community Care Services: an Overview* (Stationery Office, Dublin, 1987).

O'Morain, P., *The Health of the Nation: The Irish Healthcare System 1957–2007* (Gill & Macmillan, Dublin, 2007).

O'Sullivan, T. and M. Butler, *Current Issues in Irish Health Management: A Comparative Review* (Institute of Public Administration, Dublin, 2002).

Robins, J. (ed.), *Reflections On Health; Commemorating Fifty Years of the Department of Health 1947–1997* (Department of Health, Dublin, 1997).

Thomas, S., C. Normand and S. Smith, *Social Health Insurance: Options for Ireland* (The Adelaide Hospital Society, Dublin, 2006).

Tussing, A.D. and M. Wren, *How Ireland Cares: The Case for Health Care Reform* (New Island, Dublin, 2006).

Working Party on the General Medical Service, *Report of the Working Party on the General Medical Service* (Stationery Office, Dublin, 1984).

Wren, M., *Unhealthy State: Anatomy of a Sick Society* (New Island, Dublin, 2003).

Welfare of certain groups

Central Statistics Office, *Ageing in Ireland 2007* (Stationery Office, Dublin, 2007).

Commission on Itinerancy, *Report of the Commission on Itinerancy* (Stationery Office, Dublin, 1963).

Commission on the Status of People with Disabilities, *A Strategy for Equality: Report of the Commission on the Status of People with Disabilities* (Stationery Office, Dublin, 1996).

Committee to Monitor and Co-ordinate the Implementation of the Recommendations of the Task Force on the Travelling Community, *First Progress Report of the Committee to Monitor and Co-ordinate the Implementation of the Recommendations of the Task Force on the Travelling Community* (Stationery Office, Dublin, 2000).

Department of Health, *Care of the Aged* (Stationery Office, Dublin, 1968).

Department of Health, *Report on the Industrial and Reformatory School System* (Stationery Office, Dublin, 1970).

Department of Health and Children, *Children First: National Guidelines for the Protection and Welfare of Children* (Stationery Office, Dublin, 1999).

Department of Health and Children, *Traveller Health: A National Strategy 2002–2005* (Department of Health and Children, Dublin, 2002).

Department of Health and Children, *All-Ireland Traveller Health Study* (Department of Health and Children, Dublin, 2010).

Department of Social and Family Affairs, *National Pensions Framework* (Stationery Office, Dublin, 2010).

Flannery, T. (ed.), *Responding to the Ryan Report* (Columba Press, Dublin, 2009).

Gilligan, R., *Irish Child Care Services: Policy, Practice and Provision* (Institute of Public Administration, Dublin, 1991).

Government of Ireland, *Towards a Full Life: Green Paper on Services for Disabled People* (Stationery Office, Dublin, 1984).

Government of Ireland, *National Childcare Strategy: Report of the Partnership 2000 Expert Working Group on Childcare* (Stationery Office, Dublin, 1999).

Government of Ireland, *Towards Equal Citizenship, Progress Report on the Implementation of the Recommendations of the Commission on the Status of People with Disabilities* (Stationery Office, Dublin, 1999).

Government of Ireland, *The National Children's Strategy: Our Children – Their Lives* (Stationery Office, Dublin, 2000).

Government of Ireland, *Commission to Inquire into Child Abuse Report, Vols I–V* (Stationery Office, Dublin, 2009).

Kearney, N. and C. Skehill (eds), *Social Work in Ireland: Historical Perspectives* (Institute of Public Administration, Dublin, 2005).

National Council on Ageing and Older People, *The Years Ahead Report: A Review of the Implementation of its Recommendations* (National Council on Ageing and Older People, Dublin, 1997).

National Economic and Social Council, *Report No. 50, Major Issues in Planning Services for Mentally and Physically Handicapped Persons* (Stationery Office, Dublin, 1980).

National Economic and Social Forum, *Report No. 38, Implementation of the Home Care Package Scheme* (Stationery Office, Dublin, 2009).

Raftery, M. and E. O'Sullivan, *Suffer the Little Children: The Inside Story of Ireland's Industrial Schools* (New Island Books, Dublin, 1999).

Review Group on Health and Personal Social Services for People with Physical and Sensory Disabilities, *Towards an Independent Future, Report of the Review Group on Health and Personal Social Services for People with Physical and Sensory Disabilities* (Stationery Office, Dublin, 1996).

Review Group on Mental Handicap Services, *Needs and Abilities, A Policy for the Intellectually Disabled: Report of the Review Group on Mental Handicap Services* (Stationery Office, Dublin, 1990).

Rottman, D.B., A. Tussing and M. Wiley, *The Population Structure and Living Circumstances of Irish Travellers: Results from the 1981 Census of Traveller Families* (Economic and Social Research Institute, Dublin, 1986).

Task Force on the Travelling Community, *Report of the Task Force on the Travelling Community* (Stationery Office, Dublin, 1995).

Travelling People Review Body, *Report of the Travelling People Review Body* (Stationery Office, Dublin, 1983).

Working Party on Services for the Elderly, *The Years Ahead – A Policy for the Elderly* (Stationery Office, Dublin, 1988).

Voluntary organisations

Faughnan, P., *Partners in Progress: Voluntary Organisations in the Social Service Field* (Social Science Research Centre, University College Dublin, Dublin, 1990).

Government of Ireland, *Supporting Voluntary Activity: A Green Paper on the Community and Voluntary Sector and its Relationship with the State* (Stationery Office, Dublin, 1997).

Government of Ireland, *Supporting Voluntary Activity: A White Paper on a Framework for Supporting Voluntary Activity and for Delivering the Relationship between the State and the Community and Voluntary Sector* (Stationery Office, Dublin, 2000).

National Social Service Board, *The Development of Voluntary Social Services in Ireland: A Discussion Document* (National Social Service Board, Dublin, 1982).

O'Sullivan, E., 'Voluntary agencies in Ireland – What future role?', *Administration*, Vol. 47, No. 4 (2000).

O'Sullivan, T., 'The voluntary–statutory relationship in the health services', *Administration*, Vol. 42, No. 1 (1994).

Taskforce on Active Citizenship, *Report of the Taskforce on Active Citizenship* (Department of the Taoiseach, Dublin, 2007).

Poverty and exclusion

Department of Social and Family Affairs, *National Action Plan for Social Inclusion 2007–2016* (Stationery Office, Dublin, 2007).

Department of Social, Community and Family Affairs, *Building an Inclusive Society: Review of the National Anti-Poverty Strategy under the Programme for Prosperity and Fairness* (Department of Social, Community and Family Affairs, Dublin, 2002).

Government of Ireland, *Sharing in Progress: National Anti-Poverty Strategy* (Stationery Office, Dublin, 1997).

O'Cinneide, S., 'Poverty and policy: north and south', *Administration*, Vol. 33, No. 3 (1985).

O'Flynn, J. (ed.), *Poverty, Policy and Practice: Combat Poverty 1986–2009* (Institute of Public Administration and Combat Poverty Agency, Dublin, 2009).

Equality issues

Barry, U. (ed.), *Where are We Now? New Feminist Perspectives on Women in Contemporary Ireland* (Tasc at New Island, Dublin, 2008).

Commission on the Status of Women, *Report to the Minister for Finance* (Stationery Office, Dublin, 1972).

Crowley, N., *Empty Promises: Bringing the Equality Authority to Heel* (A&A Farmer, Dublin, 2010).

Department of Justice, Equality and Law Reform, *National Women's Strategy 2007–2016* (Stationery Office, Dublin, 2007).

Finnegan, R.B. and J.L. Wiles, *Women and Public Policy in Ireland: A Documentary History 1922–1997* (Irish Academic Press, Dublin, 2005).

National Economic and Social Forum, *Report No. 23, A Strategic Policy Framework for Equality Issues* (Stationery Office, Dublin, 2002).

Second Commission on the Status of Women, *Report to Government* (Stationery Office, Dublin, 1993).

Some useful websites

Catholic Schools Partnership: www.catholicbishops.ie
Central Statistics Office: www.cso.ie
Children's Rights Alliance: www.childrensrights.ie
Citizens Information Board: www.citizensinformationboard.ie
Department of Education and Skills: www.education.ie
Department of Environment, Community and Local Government: www.environ.ie
Department of Finance: www.finance.gov.ie
Department of Health: www.dohc.ie
Department of Justice, Equality and Defence: www.justice.ie
Department of Social Protection: www.welfare.ie
Department of the Taoiseach: www.taoiseach.gov.ie
Disability Federation of Ireland: www.disability-federation.ie
Economic and Social Research Institute: www.esri.ie
Educate Together: www.educatetogether.ie
Equality Authority: www.equality.ie
Health Information and Quality Authority: www.hiqa.ie
Health Insurance Authority: www.hia.ie

Health Service Executive: www.hse.ie
Higher Education Authority: www.hea.ie
Homeless Agency: www.homelessagency.ie
Housing and Sustainable Communities Agency: www.housing.ie
Inclusion Ireland – National Association for People with an Intellectual
    Disability: www.inclusionireland.ie
Irish Human Rights Commission: www.ihrc.ie
Mental Health Commission: www.mhcirl.ie
National Council for Special Education: www.ncse.ie
National Disability Authority: www.nda.ie
National Economic and Social Council: www.nesc.ie
National Educational Welfare Board: www.newb.ie
National Parents Council – Post-Primary: www.npcpp.ie
National Parents Council – Primary: www.npc.ie
National Treatment Purchase Fund: www.ntpf.ie
National Women's Council of Ireland: www.nwci.ie
Office for Social Inclusion: www.socialinclusion.ie
Office of the Comptroller and Auditor General: www.audgen.gov.ie
Ombudsman for Children's Office: www.oco.ie
Private Residential Tenancies Board: www.prtb.ie
Residential Institutions Redress Board: www.rirb.ie
Social Justice Ireland: www.socialjustice.ie
Social Welfare Appeals Office: www.socialwelfareappeals.ie

Index